The control of competition is designed, at best, to reconcile socio-economic stability with innovation, and at worst, to keep competitors out of the market. In this respect, the nineteenth century was no more liberal than the eighteenth century. Even during the presumed liberal nineteenth century, legal regulation played a major role in the economy. The industrial revolution was based on market institutions and organisations formed during the second half of the seventeenth century. If indeed there is a break in the history of capitalism, it should be situated at the turn of the nineteenth and twentieth centuries, with the eruption of mass production, consumption and the welfare state, which introduced new forms of regulation. This book provides a new intellectual, economic and legal history of capitalism from the eighteenth century to the early twentieth century. It analyses the interaction between economic practices and legal constructions in France and compares the French case with other Western countries during this period, such as the United Kingdom, the United States, Germany and Italy.

Alessandro Stanziani is a professor at the Ecole des Hautes Etudes en Sciences Sociales (EHESS) and Senior Researcher at the Centre National des Recherches Scientifiques (CNRS) in Paris. He earned a PhD in economics from the University of Naples and a PhD in history from the EHESS, Paris. He has received numerous grants for his research, including one from the CNRS for a project on bonded labour in the Indian Ocean and one from the British Academy and French Ministry of Research program on food policies in France and Britain in the eighteenth to twentieth centuries (with Peter Atkins). Stanziani has written approximately eighty articles and book chapters in English, French, German and Russian. He is the author of *L'économie en révolution. Le cas russe, 1870–1930* and *Histoire de la qualité alimentaire, 18e–20e siècles*. He is the editor of *La travail contraint en Asie et en Europe, XVIIe–XXe siècles* and *La qualité des produits en France XVIIIe–XXe siècles* and co-editor of *Nomenclatures et classifications. Enjeux économiques et dynamiques historiques* (with Martin Bruegel and Jérôme Bourdieu).

RULES OF EXCHANGE

French Capitalism in Comparative Perspective, Eighteenth to Early Twentieth Centuries

ALESSANDRO STANZIANI

Ecole des Hautes Etudes en Sciences Sociales, Paris,
and
Centre National des Recherches Scientifiques, Paris

CAMBRIDGE UNIVERSITY PRESS
Cambridge, New York, Melbourne, Madrid, Cape Town,
Singapore, São Paulo, Delhi, Mexico City

Cambridge University Press
32 Avenue of the Americas, New York, NY 10013-2473, USA

www.cambridge.org
Information on this title: www.cambridge.org/9781107003866

First published 2012

Printed in the United States of America

A catalog record for this publication is available from the British Library.

Library of Congress Cataloging in Publication data
Stanziani, Alessandro.
Rules of exchange : French capitalism in comparative perspective, eighteenth
to early twentieth centuries / Alessandro Stanziani.
p. cm.
Includes bibliographical references and index.
ISBN 978-1-107-00386-6 (hardback)
1. Capitalism – France. 2. France – Economic conditions. 3. Capital – France.
4. Capital – Law and legislation – France. I. Title.
HB501.S8923 2010
330.12′20944–dc22 2010031515

ISBN 978-1-107-00386-6 Hardback

CONTENTS

CONTENTS

TABLES

ACKNOWLEDGEMENTS

This book would have not been possible without the help of friends, colleagues and institutions. The French Ministry of Research and the CNRS provided resources (ANR) for archival research and translation of some chapters.

Over the past years, many friends have made valuable comments on earlier versions of this book or parts of it; among them are Maurice Aymard (EHESS), Gilles-Postel Vinay (EHESS), Philippe Minard (EHESS), Jean-Pierre Hirsch (Université Lille III), Evelyne Serverin (CNRS) and Patrick Verley (University of Geneva). I also express my gratitude to Peter Scholliers (University of Bruxelles), Jean-Laurent Rosenthal (Caltech, California), Paul Duguid (University of California, Berkeley), Ron Harris (University of Tel Aviv), Simon Deakin (University of Cambridge), Philip Scranton (Rutgers University), Franco Amatori (Università Bocconi, Milan) and Paul-André Rosental (Institut d'études politiques, Paris). Finally, I thank Susan Taponier who has translated the initial version of several of the following chapters.

INTRODUCTION

The ideal of competition, as it has been proposed, imposed or rejected, debated and analysed, at least since the end of the eighteenth century in France, Great Britain, Italy, Germany, Japan, China and elsewhere, is an intellectual invention that bears little resemblance to the way economic systems actually work. In the course of the last three centuries, this ideal has engendered the main oppositions in economic policies: the opposition between liberalism and interventionism in the eighteenth century and a good part of the nineteenth century; between liberalism and Marxism, planned versus market economies, Keynesianism versus monetarism in the twentieth century; and today, between free competition and the welfare state. At present, the debate over competition is affecting the construction of Europe, development policies, "North–South" relations and tensions between growth and inequalities.

Our aim is twofold: firstly, we want to go back and identify the sources and explain the success of this intellectual construct, that is, the principle of competition; secondly, we would like to demonstrate how capitalism really works. This will involve writing a history that is both intellectual and factual; we will show that, in the name of competition, markets actually express an ideal of non-competition. In reality, the control of competition and the attempt to invent a competitive market are designed, at best, to reconcile socioeconomic stability with innovation, and at worst, to keep some of the competitors out of the market. From there, we will go on to emphasise that the impulse to regulate the market was not only characteristic of the guild-controlled eighteenth century or the regulatory, state-controlled twentieth century, but also expressed itself forcefully in the nineteenth century, during the so-called liberal period and in the "neo-liberal" twenty-first century. If these periods are usually in opposition, it is because intervention and regulation have been reduced to macroeconomic and administrative policies (taxation, interest rates). On the contrary, the greatest amount of economic regulation and its most ongoing form did not originate in the market itself or in public administrative action, but rather in contract law and regulation of micro-economic relationships. This book argues that microlegal regulation ensured the main part of market operations and thereby influenced social hierarchies. In other words, the nineteenth century was not more "liberal" than the eighteenth or twentieth century; the entire period should be studied as a whole from a single perspective that transcends the traditional cleavages of historiography and of political and economic thought. In this regard, no real break occurred with the industrial revolution which was based on market institutions and organisations formed between the second half of the seventeenth century and the eighteenth century. Contrary to widely accepted arguments, if indeed there was a break in the history of capitalism, it should be situated at the turn of the nineteenth and twentieth centuries, with the radical transformation of the economy and its institutions (mass production and consumption, the welfare state, collective bargaining).

We intend to call the accepted history of capitalism into question not only from the standpoint of chronology but also in terms of its geographical scope; we will show that, as regards market regulation, there is little reason to juxtapose so-called civil law countries (France in particular) to Anglo-Saxon common law countries, distinguishing the former by significant state intervention in the economy from the latter's self-regulating market. On the contrary, case law has played a decisive role in the development of legal rules and economic behaviour in France, whereas in Anglo-Saxon countries, legislation, positive law and the State intervened quite systematically in regulating the economy.

Markets have thus been regulated and institutionally situated everywhere; there are no free markets to compare to regulated markets, but merely forms of regulation that are sometimes similar and sometimes different. The history of markets is a global history in the sense that analogous changes have taken place in the various countries more or less at the same time. On the other hand, the solutions adopted have always been local. This is why we speak of global history at local time.

THE AIM: CAPITALIST ECONOMY AND LAW FROM A HISTORICAL PERSPECTIVE

Market dynamics and the industrial revolution relied on rules, markets and social actors essentially rooted in the late seventeenth and eighteenth centuries. This is why, unlike Polanyi, we will not speak of a "great transformation" to show a break in the eighteenth and early nineteenth centuries that swept away the old pre-capitalist world through enclosures and the poor law and replaced it with a self-regulating economy which, in turn, is said to have been replaced by a new form of interventionism in the twentieth century. This chronology is false not only because new economic and legal rules were introduced over the long term, but also because the nineteenth-century market was anything but self-regulated.

On the contrary, according to our approach, there is no reason to contrast the liberal nineteenth century to the eighteenth and twentieth centuries described as interventionist, each in its own way. What differentiated these periods was not liberalism versus regulation, but different forms of regulation. For example, in the nineteenth century, the consumer did not exist from a legal standpoint; the law referred only to the purchaser, in keeping with the idea that the final consumer, like any professional buying a product, should be protected only by ordinary contractual rules. Thus, it was not until the very end of the nineteenth century that case law decisions began talking about the consumer rather than the purchaser; these decisions usually pointed to the unequal positions of the parties when they entered into the contract, particularly regarding their knowledge of product characteristics, to explain the deception to which the end consumer claimed to have been subject. Hence, special protection was seen to be necessary and it took the form of regulating food-related fraud and falsification. This legal innovation would have a major impact on political and economic hierarchies during the twentieth century and up to today.

Similarly, nineteenth-century firms had little in common with the way the era is portrayed by historians and economists. The relationship between firm, company and family remained at the heart of capitalist organisation not only in France, but also in Great Britain and even in Germany; companies in the strict sense grew out of this tradition rather than out of anonymous capital markets. Family law, credit law and the rules governing the land market remained closely intertwined and were not separated until after the First World War. Again, this major change belongs to the turn of the nineteenth–twentieth centuries not to the first industrial revolution; we need to escape backward historical interpretations.

Of course, trade institutions, market control and the rules of competition came into being before the nineteenth century. Yet doing history involves more than simply asserting "everything was already there"; a chronological division is justified by the question raised and the theories formulated. In the present case, we do not intend to call into question the long development of capitalism so dear to Braudel; on the contrary, by situating the "break" well downstream in time (late nineteenth–early twentieth century), I intend to argue that the script was not entirely written in the eighteenth century and, although the first industrial revolution owed a great deal to the slow development of capitalism and its institutions, beginning at least in the twelfth century, at the same time that world was radically transformed only in the twentieth century. In short, we agree that the industrial revolution should be included in the long-term development of capitalism, provided the break is situated not in the eighteenth century, but much later, at the beginning of the twentieth century. This issue finds its justification in the fact that we integrate Braudel's approach (long-term evolution) with institutionalist history.

This chronology is therefore much closer to that advanced by Douglass North, Alfred Chandler and Arno Meyer.[1] However, we provide different content for this breakthrough and its main features and origins. Not only Chandler's (and Williamson's) business organisation, but above all the rules of the game and the law matter in our scheme. But, unlike North, we maintain that legal rules cannot be reduced to

[1] Douglass North, *Structure and Change in Economic History*. New York and London, Norton, 1981; Alfred Chandler, *The Visible Hand*. Cambridge, Mass., Harvard University Press, 1977; Arno Meyer, *The Persistence of the Old Regime: Europe to the Great War*. New York, Pantheon, 1981.

4

property rules and, above all, the introduction, affirmation and decline of legal institutions and institutions in general do not necessarily respond to efficiency. The economic rationale seeking efficiency's optimisation was far from being the prime or unique mover in the history of markets.

To confirm these statements, the chronology we are proposing for France will be shown to be a widespread phenomenon; in Great Britain, Italy, Germany and the United States, the industrial revolution and growth in the eighteenth and nineteenth centuries took place through markets and institutions rooted in family-type economies, hostile to limited liability companies, speculation and sudden innovation, in which the consumer was barely taken into account by the law.

Together with trade and consumption, the control of capital constituted one of the pillars of the organisation of competition. There were significant continuities in this area in France (between the eighteenth and early twentieth centuries) and between France and the other countries. Everywhere, capital markets were highly controlled until around the last quarter of the nineteenth century, and even then it would be more accurate to speak of new forms of regulation than of liberalisation. Forward transactions, which had long been prohibited, were now accepted and with them, the produce exchanges. However, new rules intervened (anti-trust and anti-speculation norms). In this context, immaterial capital (shares, future products) or intangible capital (reputation–goodwill) emerged alongside more traditional forms of material capital (land) as an object of economic investment and source of social legitimacy and was recognised in France as well as the United States, Great Britain and Germany. A common wave lifted up the entire capitalist world. In the eighteenth and nineteenth centuries it brought about growth through small firms and innovations that ultimately required little capital. Purchasers (not consumers), servants and apprentices (rather than "salariés") held centre stage. The second industrial revolution shattered this world, leading to new participants in the economy: wage earners, consumers, limited liability companies and competition law. The rise of the welfare state and the stock exchange, large firms and standardised products took hold in every country undergoing industrialisation. Everywhere, contract law ran up against wide-ranging restrictions in the name of social balance.

The regulation of consumption, work, companies and stock market transactions fulfilled these same requirements. Henceforth, the law intervened not to confirm but rather to correct social inequalities.

Yet, within these common occurrences, differences appeared among countries. In particular, the legal status of the actors remained far more important in continental Europe than in common law countries, as the legal definitions of the tradesman and the consumer demonstrate. Current differences between business law and consumer law in European countries and at the international level testify to the tenacity of these diverging orientations. Thus, in France, the control of forward transactions was situated at the intersection of the old norms regarding monopoly and the new concerns of wage earners and farmers faced with "globalisation". In the United States and Germany, on the contrary, new controls on forward transactions were defined in relation to farmers on the one hand and industry concentration on the other. These differences had equally far-reaching consequences. In France, the recognition of know-how and reputation as forms of capital helped small shops, whereas elsewhere, these items were immediately included in the valuation of all forms of enterprise. In common law countries, the reputation of the actor and of the products and services he offered came together in the trademark, the trade name and goodwill. In France, on the contrary, this convergence proved to be more problematic, and the solution was found in rooting reputation more strongly in a territory (*Appelation d'Origine Contrôlée*).

Finally, these differences also reflected those between fair competition, free trade and the overall control of competition. In France, the notion of fair competition gradually emerged in case law during the second half of the nineteenth century, whereas no antitrust laws had been adopted, and industry concentration was regulated by long-standing norms pertaining to goodwill.

In the United States, while antitrust norms developed rather early on, the notion of unfair competition was less common than in Germany or France, because it tended to be reduced (by the judges as well as by the economic actors) to patent law. In the United States, these features in turn supported the development and strength of major family-based company capitalism, just as the secondary place assigned to fair competition was to enable the rise of advertising (including comparative advertising). In other words, if the United States enjoyed a successful second industrial revolution, it was because forward transactions were quickly regulated, fairness was identified with patent ownership, and advertising and alliances between groups were allowed, whereas sector control (monopoly) was prohibited.

Conversely, if France's performance over the very long term (from the eighteenth century to today) ultimately proved to be more stable than that of its Anglo-Saxon rivals, it is because it afforded no protection to the consumer during the nineteenth century, fairness prevailed over vertical integration as the ideal for competition, and finally, the private order of the market was never altogether disconnected from the public order.

SCALES OF COMPETITION

Is it relevant to compare forms of capitalism on a national basis? Naturally, approaching this topic through law gives decisive weight to national factors, as one can speak of English law, French commercial law, and so on. Legal institutions are also defined on a national scale. The rules of law as asserted beginning in the eighteenth century were given national legitimacy, if not necessarily content, which is indispensable to understanding capitalist industrialisation. Legal nationalism often went together with economic nationalism in the nineteenth century.[2] At the same time, this national dimension had to cope with fragmented legal decisions and trade customs on the one hand and capitalist dynamics on the other, which in the end were more regional and international than national.[3] Outside state policy, the nation is not a unit that travels very well.[4]

---

[2] Willibald Steinmetz, *Private Law and Social Inequality in the Industrial Age: Comparing Legal Cultures in Britain, France, Germany and the United States.* Oxford, Oxford University Press, 2000; Michael John, *Politics and the Law in Late Nineteenth Century Germany: The Origin of the Civil Code.* Oxford, Oxford University Press, 1989; Jean Carbonnier, "Le code civil." In Pierre Nora, *Les lieux de mémoire*, II, *La nation.* Paris, Gallimard (1986): 293–315.

[3] Sidney Pollard, *Peaceful Conquest: The Industrialization of Europe, 1760–1970.* Oxford, Oxford University Press, 1981; Jeffrey Williamson, "Globalization, Convergence and History." *Journal of Economic History*, 80 (1990): 651–68; Kenneth Pomeranz, *The Great Divergence.* Princeton, NJ, Princeton University Press, 2000.

[4] Pomeranz, *The Great Divergence*, 7.

The scale of analysis does not privilege the (external) observer; involved actors and institutions also think and act according to their historical perceptions of local, international, global and regional markets. Spatial variables are operational tools, not merely conceptual categories. Territorial roots, the relationships between actors and companies, trust and local customs, and "specific regional features" in general, do not exist outside institutional control; these elements are subject to tensions and agreements that are in no way spontaneous. The possibility of gaining recognition for local trade customs or product value through regional appellations is an example of this process. One of the mainsprings of capitalist economies lay in these tensions between national institutions, global dynamics and local recognition of products, services and actors.

At the same time, the tensions between the local dimension and national stakes fit into a resolutely international framework. The history of trade customs and *lex mercatoria* shows that over the very long term, trade customs were not opposed to state rules, but instead were perfectly in keeping with them, and in fact complementary.

This is all the more true in that, since the twelfth century, but particularly beginning at the end of the eighteenth century, trade involved not only objects and human beings but also knowledge, techniques, theories and norms. For example, France exported the civil code as well as silk; similarly, towards the end of the nineteenth century, American antitrust law was debated in France where different solutions were adopted, which in turn influenced the dynamics of the American economy and law.

Circulation of models and ideas cannot be excluded from the analysis, but it is not everything. Historical paths and bifurcations in markets and societies are the ultimate goal of our study.

THE SCOPE OF THE BOOK

This book is mostly about market in its triple meaning: as a physical place, as transaction and as regulatory principle. Braudel has already mentioned these levels; I wish to add an institutional dimension. Of course, we are not going to study all the rules and all the markets. We will confine ourselves to studying product markets discussing certain aspects of credit, but we will leave aside labour and the land market. These aspects are no doubt related (the exchange of goods is linked to the sale of labour) and, even from the standpoint of the history of regulations, for a long time the control of competition came under the control of labour and was not separated from it until the end of the nineteenth century (coalition offences were long reserved for the labour market before becoming a core item in anti-trust legislation). At the same time, labour competition would require a book of its own.

Similarly, it would seem necessary from the start to include the land market in any study of competition. Indeed, this market has been perhaps one of the most regulated over the long term (we need only to think of the control of land and real estate transactions). It is precisely the strong, ongoing regulation of the land market that has prompted us to put it aside; if we succeed in establishing that other markets were regulated everywhere by showing the control of commercial transactions in movable property, products and goods, the argument will hold all the more for the real estate market.

We will not study the financial market itself. We will rather examine its historical and economic emergence as a market distinct from labour and produce markets. This separation was far from spontaneous and requires an explanation. To this end, we will focus on certain types of credit, particularly commercial credit, shop financing, forward transactions and the commodity exchange. These will help us understand how the borderline between products and goods on the one hand and credit and money on the other was historically defined, negotiated and shifted. Commercial credit, commodities markets and shops have played an important role not only in commercial and industrial capitalism, but also in advanced, post-industrial and financial capitalism. This is in no way to deny the importance of finance and the stock exchange in themselves; on the contrary, we are eager to show that the ways in which the various forms of capitalism have historically regulated stock exchange and financial dealings are indebted to commodities markets, produce exchanges and speculation, the intangible capital of companies and their forms of financing.

Finally, a remark concerning the geographical area we will be covering. We will emphasise the case of France and then compare it with certain Western countries. The case of France is not of interest because it was the country of "Colbertism" as opposed to liberal England; on the contrary, France is a perfect example of the ability to adapt pre-industrial rules to a dynamic context through legal codes, the adoption of trade customs and all the rules in support of family firms, intangible capital, and the reputations of actors and products. The comparison with other European countries and the Anglo-Saxon countries is justified by the question we are studying, namely the "specificities" of civil law countries in relation to common law countries in the construction of capitalism.

No doubt, these reflections could be enlarged to a much wider context including Russia, the Asian countries and Latin America. However, a real global analysis of trade and capitalism and a departure from Eurocentric approaches require a previous analysis of what the West and its economies really were. This book aims to answer this question.

The first two chapters will study representations and perceptions of market in a broad sense. After a look at the main economic history approaches to the topic of competition from the eighteenth century to today, we will study general legal-economic institutions. I will discuss the relationship between civil law and commercial law, law and customs, norms and case law. In particular, we will see how customs were incorporated into so-called formal law and the crucial role played by interpretation and jurisprudence in French law.

We will then go on to study the market and competition by differentiating three main levels: the market as a place of exchange (covered markets, shops, produce exchanges); the market as transactions and contracts; and finally, the market as a regulatory mechanism (control of competition). Although covered markets, shops and produce exchanges have often been seen as the expression of the competitive market, they were in fact regulated by a range of rules concerning access to places and the classification of the actors and traded goods.

I will then analyse the market as synonymous with exchange; within this scope, I will examine the rules for accepting products in the market, the criteria of product quality at the time of trade, as well as fraud and falsification. From there, I will examine the process of product standardisation. Contrary to commonly accepted theories, I shall show that standardisation and the definition of product characteristics in general are not due solely to production but are also indebted to exchange. Standardisation is never complete and affects only certain aspects of production and of the product; this level of indeterminacy does not hinder exchange but instead makes it possible.

The final part of the book will be devoted to the control of competition in all its forms (monopolies on foodstuffs, commodities markets, trusts and cartels, unfair competition).

METHODOLOGY: RULES, INSTITUTIONS AND MARKETS IN HISTORY

Whereas "traditional" liberal thought maintains that markets can operate alone without any interference, and Marx and his followers held that law merely confirms and strengthens the class structure already in place, neo-institutionalist thinkers have been endeavouring to prove that law and institutions intervene to ensure efficient market operation. Numerous authors (Douglass North among them) have thus shown that the rise of capitalism owed a great deal to the introduction of rules protecting private property.

My approach is at variance with all three orientations. In contrast to "neoclassical" thought, I do not think law is restricted to dictating the rules of the game while remaining, as such, outside economic action itself. On the contrary, I will show that the connection between rules and the way they were formulated, together with procedures, had a considerable impact on economic relationships, the legal and economic chances of the actors, and thereby economic and social hierarchies.

My approach also differs from three (Keynesians and post-Keynesians, socialists, etc.) who stress that even in ultra-liberal capitalism and contrary to official declarations (e.g., Reagan's America), the state intervenes in the economy through its monetary and fiscal policies, its support for companies, and the like. This argument is no doubt well founded in that, in both the history and present-day workings of

capitalism, fiscal and monetary policies largely contribute to determining social and economic dynamics. I only argue that macro-
economic public policies do not tell the whole story of the relations
between the state and the economy under capitalism. The state
intervenes by adopting and enforcing rules of law, not only through
macro-economic policies. Rules of law control the action of the
state and public authorities (administrative law), as well as relationships between private individuals (contract law, commercial law, etc.).
They help to create and maintain hierarchies and even exclusions.
It is precisely because micro-rules and macro-regulation count that
macro-public policies alone cannot provide a given social hierarchy
and economic dynamics.

This is also why it is important to distinguish our approach from
mainstream law and economics. In my view, the institutions that regulate the operations of capitalism arose and evolved more as a result
of procedural constraints and political issues than out of concern for
economic efficiency. The pressure of lobbies, the institutions already
in place and the values – not only economic but also ethical – of a
given society influenced the emergence and development of market
institutions.[5]

I support another approach, according to which bifurcations in history matter, economic and legal systems do not evolve in response
to the sole criteria of economic efficiency (lobbies, legal procedures
and ethics are important) and in general, functionalist explanations of
economic and historical development should be set aside. Law offers
neither infinite solutions (the position of those who insist on the
importance of informal rules) nor a single, predetermined outcome
(the Marxist thesis), but rather a limited set of possibilities. These possibilities stem from several factors: the formulation of rules and hence,
the pressure groups that back them; the country's legal traditions; and
the intellectual and social framework in which rules are used and interpreted. My four main issues – civil law was not "economically" inefficient in comparison with common law; the first industrial revolution

---

[5] Brilliant examples of this approach are: Ron Harris, *Industrializing English Law:
Entrepreneurship and Business Organization, 1720–1844*. Cambridge, Cambridge University
Press, 2000; Simon Deakin, Frank Wilkinson, *The Law of the Labour Market*. Oxford,
Oxford University Press, 2005.

and the great transformation did not break pre-industrial economic institutions, rather, the new institutions were mostly based upon them; private property was not the ground for a solid economic growth; stability and innovation were the two "legs" of capitalist dynamics – are directly linked to this approach.

The connection I am proposing between rules and markets has its precursors. In the eighteenth century, the best representative of this approach was unquestionably Adam Smith. This reference may seem surprising at first glance: How can we possibly point to the theoretician of the invisible hand and the self-regulating market as heralding an approach that relies on precisely the institutional and legal construction of markets?

In reality, as I will show in detail in Chapter 1, the Scottish author has little to do with the invisible hand and the free market; he was, above all, an expert in jurisprudence who studied economics and its history in relation to the implementation of law and the presence of ethical principles. The myth of Adam Smith as the theoretician of the free, self-regulating market is an invention of the nineteenth century, which has persisted to this day.

In the nineteenth century, the inevitable reference is Max Weber's "law in action". According to Weber, law can be better understood by the way the actors appropriate it than by its theory or the rules of positive law alone. Much of the sociology of law, particularly in France, Germany, Italy and the Anglo-Saxon countries which follow law in action, claims this Weberian legacy. [6]

However, independent of Weber, the theory of "law in action" has been considerably developed in the United States from the early twentieth century until today.[7] The historical workings of capitalism

---

[6] Neil Fligstein, *The Architecture of Markets*. Princeton, NJ, Princeton University Press, 2001; Brian Uzzi, "The Sources and Consequences of Embeddedness for the Economic Performance of Organisations: The Network Effect." *American Sociological Review*, 61, 4 (1996): 674–98; William Powell, Paul Di Maggio, *The New Institutionalism in Organizational Analysis*. Chicago, University of Chicago Press, 1991.

[7] Roscoe Pound was first to develop this point in Roscoe Pound, "Law in Books and Law in Action." *American Law Review*, 44 (1910): 12–36. The so-called pragmatic school further developed this approach: John Commons, *Legal Foundations of Capitalism*. London, Macmillan, 1924, new edition, New Brunswick and London, Transaction Publishers, 1995; Karl Llewellyn, "What Price Contract? An Essay in Perspective." *Yale Law Journal*, 40, 5 (1931): 704–51. The major development of "law in action" to explain historical

and of the main markets (labour, products, capital) have been framed by strong institutional and legal dimensions.

In continental Europe, the interrelationship between the history of law and the history of economics has been demonstrated, above all, by legal experts who focused more on positive law and case law decisions than on legal practices.[8] However, we cannot limit ourselves to the study of major case law; we have to get our hands dirty and dig into legal archives. The problem is that, aside from some remarkable exceptions,[9] economic and social historians have shown little interest in legal categories, and when they have done so, they tended to study positive law rather than case law. What is missing, therefore, is a study of the relationship between rules and markets in a civil law country at the time of the industrial revolution, drawing on legal as well as economic archives and sources. This book aims to fill this gap while taking into account the methodological and empirical contributions already made by the works mentioned earlier.

dynamics was linked to the "Wisconsin school": J. Willard Hurst, *Law and the Condition of Freedom in the Nineteenth Century United States*. Madison, University of Wisconsin Press 1956; J. Willard Hurst, *Law and Economic Growth: The Legal History of Lumber Industry in Wisconsin, 1836–1915*. Cambridge, Mass., Harvard University Press, 1964. Hurst's approach is further developed in: Lawrence Friedman, *A History of American Law*. New York, Simon and Schuster, 1973; Morton Horwitz, *The Transformation of American Law, 1780–1860*. Cambridge, Mass., Harvard University Press, 1977; Robert Steinfeld, *The Invention of Free Labour*. Chapel Hill and London, University of North Carolina Press, 1991; William Novak, *The Peoples Welfare: Law and Regulation in Nineteenth Century America*. Chapel Hill and London, University of North Carolina Press, 1996.

[8] Among others, in France: Georges Ripert, *Aspects juridiques du capitalisme moderne*. Paris, LGDJ, 1951; Jean Hilaire, *Introduction historique au droit commercial*. Paris, LGDJ, 1986; Alessandro Stanziani (ed.), *Dictionnaire historique de l'économie-droit*. Paris, LGDJ, 2007. In Italy: Guido Alpa, *La cultura delle regole*. Bari, Laterza, 2000; Francesco Galgano, *Lex mercatoria*. Bologna, Il Mulino, 1991; Natalino Irti, *L'ordine giuridico del mercato*. Bari, Laterza, 1998.

[9] Jean-Pierre Hirsch, *Les deux rêves du commerce*. Paris, EHESS, 1991; Renata Ago, *L'economia barocca*. Roma, Donzelli, 1998.

PART I

BUILDING IDEAL MARKETS: ECONOMIC AND LEGAL CULTURE

The history of markets and market systems is both intellectual and factual. Economic and legal cultures are hardly separable from practises. On this ground, the relevant point is not to stress the "abstraction" of economic models and legal rules and their gap from "reality" (the latter being uncertainly and a priori defined), but rather to understand the origins of different market representations and their impact on economic behaviours. In particular, I will stress that most current interpretations of major economists and legal scholars of the eighteenth and nineteenth centuries are biased insofar as they look at them through a twentieth-century lens. I will then rediscover Smith, Bentham and Walras (among others) and on this ground I will correctly identify their theories and representations and their link with culture, politics and market realities of that time.

This same approach is at the root of the second chapter which studies the political and general institutional framework of market rules, that is, the relationships between positive law and jurisprudence and those between trade customs, commercial codes and civil codes.

I

ECONOMIC THOUGHT AND COMPETITION

Where does the currently accepted idea that rules are opposed to the market come from?

It is a commonplace to trace the idea of the market regulated by an invisible hand to Adam Smith. Another commonplace is that the specific traits of the French market can be attributed to guild constraints and the attitude of the economists of the period who, with the exception of the liberal Physiocrats, were in favour of such interventions. These commonly held ideas are simply false. As we shall see, economic thought during the Ancien Régime associated social order with market order according to an approach strongly influenced by ethical values. Smith was also close to this thinking; he spoke of providence rather than a free market. Adam Smith as we know him today is an invention of his nineteenth-century interpreters. Moreover the ideal of a free market cannot be attributed to Walras, the other great icon of liberal thought, because, as we tend to forget today, Walras was a socialist and frequently shared Marxist attitudes. The portrayal of Walras as a liberal is an invention of the twentieth century. So then where did our thinking about rules and markets originate?

THE LEGACY OF THE ANCIEN RÉGIME: MARKET LAW FROM JUST PRICES TO COMPETITION

"A great painter sells his works himself because he alone can produce them. He raises his wages as high as possible: he is guided by no other rule than the fortune of art lovers who are curious about his paintings... He will charge a hundred *louis* for a portrait, or even

17

more if he is asked to do more for that price than he is able to do ...
The price may seem exorbitant. But it is not; it is the true price. It is
regulated by an agreement freely made between the painter and the
person who asks to be painted, and no one loses out."

On the contrary, "[i]f you were the only grain merchant in town,
and you made me pay a hundred francs per *septier*, you could not say
that you have sold it to me under a free agreement between us: it
would be obvious that I was forced by need and that you have cruelly
taken advantage of my situation."[1]

These passages from the Abbé de Condillac could easily summarise
the principal orientations of eighteenth-century economic thought
regarding competition and markets. The way eighteenth-century
economists discussed competition has been subjected ever since to
totally contradictory interpretations that try to radicalise the debates
of the period and reinterpret them in the light of modern debates
(the discussion of liberalism, state planning, the welfare state, etc.). In
reality, as recent interpretations have underscored,[2] these oppositions
need to be qualified. Thus, debates about competition and monopoly in the eighteenth century pertained not only to the control of
economic activity but also to the whole organisation of society; they
referred to the philosophical order. The discussions were concerned
with knowing whether human beings are basically selfish or if, on
the contrary, they exhibit spontaneous tendencies to cooperate. It
is nevertheless important to note that the first hypothesis does not
necessarily lead to conceiving forms of market regulation. Indeed,
one might imagine that selfishness and individualism will produce
the best possible solution (through competition) or, on the other
hand, that they engender situations of inequality and abuse. In the
first case, there is little room for the law and for regulation of the
economy (except ensuring compliance with the rules of the game),
whereas in the second case, these are required for the market to

---

[1] Étienne Bonnot de Condillac, *Le commerce et le gouvernement considérés relativement l'un à l'autre*. Text of 1776, reprint, Frantext, 1995: 174–6.

[2] Jean-Claude Perrot, *Pour une histoire intellectuelle de l'économie politique*. Paris, EHESS, 1992; Jean-Yves Grenier, *L'économie d'Ancien Régime*. Paris, Albin Michel, 1996; Alain Bérraud, Gilbert Faccarello, *Nouvelle histoire de la pensée économique*. Paris, La découverte, 3 vols. 1992.

work properly. From the eighteenth century until today, these three approaches (a spontaneous tendency to cooperate, selfishness as the basis for effective competition, selfishness and competition causing distortions and inequalities) have dominated discussions of the relationship between rules and markets.

In the eighteenth century, economic thought envisioned competition and monopolies in relation to the following issues: the sale of wheat, guilds and labour, foreign trade and finally monetary and financial mechanisms. Indeed, "liberals" took a similar position in the areas I have mentioned. They emphasised that the monopoly on the wheat trade did not protect the most disadvantaged but rather created annuities favourable to a few merchants, who were responsible for the rise in prices and decline in quality that ultimately affected the most disadvantaged. That is, unless the state ensured a "political price", and in that case, the most productive groups had to pay for the others.

The proponents of regulation replied that a free grain market would lead to concentration, and hence to the elimination of small producers and traders and to a situation of oligopoly, along with higher prices and lower quality. For example, Necker defined freedom as "the permission given to owners to deploy their full power".[3]

In this context, natural monopolies were opposed to legal monopolies. Interventionists were of the opinion that the market created monopolies; consequently, it was better to establish legal monopolies, which would ensure justice and fairness rather than the profit of a minority at the expense of the well-being of the masses. Conversely, liberals held that legal monopolies resulted in corruption, abuse and negative effects for workers as well as for owners and the people.

These discussions of monopolies and the operation of the market focused on the notion of speculation, which each group understood to mean quite different things. The partisans of regulation associated speculation with monopolies on commodities and therefore wanted it condemned and stopped. Conversely, for liberals, the word speculation gradually acquired a new meaning: the desire for profit,

---

[3] Jacques Necker, *Sur la législation et le commerce des grains*. Paris, Pissot, 1775, vol. 2: 101.

the basis for competition and therefore the engine of the economy. Speculation was not only legitimate but even necessary to ensure the country's prosperity.

The opposition between rules and markets was formulated in this conceptual framework. Liberals considered rules and forms of government intervention to be synonymous with distortions and abuse and thus harmful to the proper working of markets and the prosperity of the kingdom (with the exception of the norms that ensured simple market play). Conversely, for interventionists, rules, especially regulations, served precisely to avoid the abuses and distortions of the free market.

At the same time, it would be a mistake to place too much emphasis on the tensions between liberals and interventionists. The opposition was no doubt considerable, but it has been overly accentuated by subsequent interpretations. In general, except in certain later arguments belonging to a strictly political debate, eighteenth-century economic thought never put forward extreme positions aimed either at denying any benefits from competition or presuming that the latter alone could solve all the political, social and economic problems linked to market operation. The economy remained political, and as such it could not be reduced merely to concerns about efficiency, as is the case in economic analysis today. Moreover, interventionists and liberals identified the "market" not only with a physical place (covered markets) or a particular sector (the meat market), but also with the mechanism of competition. It was precisely the workings of competition that was under discussion. In this context, the notion of "just price" was crucial.[4] In recent interpretations, the notion of just price is viewed in two different ways; some see it as an anticipation of utilitarian theory: the just price is the market price and it is based on the utility of the goods.[5] According to this interpretation, there is little

---

[4] Jean Domat, *Les lois civiles dans leur ordre naturel; le droit public and legum delectus*. Paris, Le clerc, 1777: 60. Also: Jeanne-Marie Tuffery, *Ebauche d'un droit de la consommation. La protection du chaland sur les marchés toulousains au XVIIe et au XVIIIe siècles*. Paris, LGDJ, 1998; Steve Kaplan, *Le meilleur pain du monde*. Paris, Fayard, 1996; Raynald Abad, *Le grand marché*. Paris, Fayard, 2004; Jean-Yves Grenier, "Une économie de l'identification. Le juste prix et l'ordre des marchandises dans l'Ancien Régime." In Alessandro Stanziani (ed.), *La qualité des produits en France, XVIIIe–XXe siècles*. Paris, Belin, 2003: 25–54.
[5] Roger De Roover, "The Concept of Just Price: Theory and Economic Policy." *Journal of Economic History*, 18, 4 (1958): 418–34.

difference between pre-industrial thinking and later approaches – utility is the foundation of economic activity.

Others, at least until the eighteenth century, have stressed that the notion of just price cannot be reduced to that of market price. Just price referred instead to moral economics. It meant ensuring that the population received enough bread and meat of good quality at an affordable price.[6] Just prices reflected a qualitative hierarchy of goods, which in turn reflected a definite social hierarchy.[7]

The complexity of the notion of just price, which deals with contracts and their inclusion in law and public order, helps to explain the multiplicity of the interpretations we have mentioned. In reality, until the eighteenth century, a great majority of authors maintained that the notion of just price expressed the fact that law, morality and economics were part of one and the same comprehensive reflection. The control of the market fell within the sphere of public order precisely because individual interests had meaning only within the scope of the general interest and the latter arose from the convergence of economics and morality, profit and justice. Hence the aim of market regulation policies: to ensure just prices, sufficient quantities and good quality.[8]

We are thus in neither a utilitarian system that "anticipated" in some way the capitalist ethic, nor in a world in which ethics and social solidarity were imposed. On the contrary, individual interests and the contract were definitely taken into account and protected, although integrated into a more general moral order.

To sum up, in the eighteenth century, economics, law and ethics were still closely tied together. Intervention was not always opposed to freedom. However, within this framework, new trends began to take shape and in some more extreme interpretations, these ties were severed: The free, self-regulating market was opposed to regulation. Contrary to all received ideas, this took place in the late eighteenth and early nineteenth centuries, and it was accomplished not by Adam Smith but by Jeremy Bentham.

---

[6] Monica Martinat, *Le « juste » marché. Le système annonaire romain au XVIe et XVIIe siècles.* Rome, Ecole française, 2005.

[7] Grenier, "Une économie".

[8] Kaplan, *Le meilleur.*

ADAM SMITH VERSUS JEREMY BENTHAM:
FROM PROVIDENCE TO UTILITY AS THE
MARKET REGULATOR

Adam Smith is currently associated with the notion of laissez-faire, the self-regulation of the market by the invisible hand and the division of labour. This is in large part a myth invented in the nineteenth century. In his courses at the University of Glasgow, Smith did not discuss the *Wealth of Nations* or devote any time to competition as such. On the contrary, Smith's courses, as well as his writings, fit into the broader scope of jurisprudence. Smith wrote in the eighteenth century; it would be trite to observe that his thought belongs entirely to that century by linking economics to morality and law if it had not been distorted from the nineteenth century until today into something else. It would in fact be difficult to associate Smith with liberals who preached non-intervention by the state and its role as mere policeman. In Smith's view, the task of the state is to defend property, but at the same time its action is, first and foremost, a response to the inequalities present in society. Smith's critique was levelled more against the so-called mercantilist forms of intervention (protectionism, building up reserves of precious metals, etc.) than against the State in general. The invisible hand, so often associated with Smith, actually played only a marginal role in his work and was usually not connected to the action of the market and competition. In reality, Smith mentioned it in order to introduce Providence and the "illusions" that lead men to accumulate wealth in vain, whereas "an invisible hand" would eventually force them to share it.[9] Finally, the invisible hand transforms selfish action but it has little to do with the rational calculus of action useful for society as a whole. Although a certain evolution is perceptible in Smith's thought, economics and morality coexist in all his work. This link was gradually lost in nearly all later interpretations of Smith (both liberal and socialist, with the sole exception of Sismondi) that have continued almost to today[10] to associate this author with the ideal of a deregulated free market.

---

[9] Adam Smith, *The Theory of Moral Sentiments*. Glasgow, Bell, 1759: 49, 207, 211.

[10] Recent analyses of Smith supporting this interpretation: Emma Rotschild, *Economic Sentiments: Adam Smith, Condorcet and the Enlightenment*. Cambridge, Mass., Harvard

Another important aspect of Smith's thought and of English thought in general during the second half of the eighteenth century disappeared in the course of the nineteenth century: the role of law in economic activity. Smith developed an analysis of jurisprudence based on the assumption that in a mercantile society, the State is supposed to oversee the protection of property and transactions. Temporary privileges and concessions enter into this logic along with the legal model for all public services (the user pays). His *Lectures on jurisprudence* (1762–1763)[11] shows that he associates the protection of property more with judicial law than with legislation. Here he makes a clear distinction between the rights of the individual as an individual, as a member of a family and as a citizen. Whereas the first task of the State is to protect private property, the second, which can only follow from the first, is to ensure prosperity. In this context, he notes the considerable number of police regulations in France, which he contrasts with their virtual disappearance in Great Britain. He explains this difference by the persistence of feudal elements in France, which prompted nobles to monitor their serfs and the serfs to cheat. He concludes that the establishment of trade and manufacturing, which brought about the independence of the serfs, is the best form of police to prevent crime. It was in a sense a demand for the autonomy of commercial law in relation to administrative and police law.[12] Here Smith's position dovetails with those of the French "liberals" of the eighteenth century .

University Press, 2001; Spencer Pack, *Capitalism as a Moral System: Adam Smith's Critique of Free Market Economy*. Aldershot, Edward Elgar, 1991; Patricia Werhane, *Adam Smith and His Legacy for Modern Capitalism*. Oxford, Oxford University Press, 1991; Keith Tribe, "Adam Smith: Critical Theorist?" *Journal of Economic Literature*, 37, 2 (1999): 609–32; Gary Anderson, "The Butcher, the Baker and the Policy-Maker: Adam Smith on Public Choice, With a Reply to Stigler." *History of Political Economy*, 21 (1989): 641–60; Vivienne Brown, *Adam Smith's Discourse. Canonicity, Commerce and Conscience*. London, Routledge, 1994; Athol Fitzgibbons, *Adam Smith's System of Liberty, Wealth and Virtue: The Moral and Political Foundations of the Wealth of Nations*. Oxford, Oxford University Press, 1995; Robert Heilbroner, *The Essential Adam Smith*. Oxford, Oxford University Press, 1986; Spencer Pack, *Capitalism as a Moral System. Adam Smith's Critique of the Free Market Economy*. Aldershot, Edward Elgar, 1991; Quentin Skinner, *Liberty Before Liberalism*. Cambridge, Cambridge University Press, 1998.

11 Adam Smith, *Lectures on Jurisprudence*. In Ronald I. Meek, David Daiches Raphael, Peter G. Stein (eds.), *The Glasgow Edition of the Works and Correspondence of Adam Smith*. Vol. 5, Oxford, Clarendon Press, 1978.

12 Ibid.: 487.

when he underscores the fact that trade associations (guilds, *jurandes*) and mercantile policies of the Ancien Régime produced an artificial scarcity of goods.[13]

This premise leads him to an original interpretation of the relationship between law and economics: Judicial interpretation is a factor in economic stability. By this, Smith meant not only that the law takes customs into account but also — and above all — that jurisprudence makes use of common law and validates it.

To sum up, contrary to the dominant interpretations of the nineteenth century, Smith's thought took judiciary law and its interaction with the economy into consideration. Thus, he maintained that competition does not reflect a purely rational mechanism but rather interaction between economic elements, moral factors and legal aspects. But if it was not Adam Smith who preached the free market and the benefits of competition and emphasised the separation or even opposition between norms and the market, where did these ideas come from?

Today, the collapse of the ideological wall and the so-called socialist countries has radically altered the list of the greatest economic "classics" of all time. It is now difficult to find Marx or even Ricardo; in contrast, Jeremy Bentham is unquestionably among those enjoying success that could be described as long term because it was assured throughout the nineteenth and twentieth centuries, especially in the Anglo-Saxon countries. For more than two hundred years, Bentham's thought has been associated with utilitarian theory, liberalism and the liberal philosophy of law. At first glance, Bentham, more than others, links economics to law. Our position is that, contrary to appearances, Bentham, rather than Smith, is among those chiefly responsible for separating economics from law, at least from judiciary law; Bentham also contributed more than Smith to giving normative pretensions to the analysis of competition. Indeed, unlike Smith, he associated law more with legislation than with common law and custom and therefore tended to develop the link with economics through the philosophy of law rather than legal procedure. In

[13] Ibid.: 347.

other words, Bentham was less concerned with how the actors contribute to the creation and use of norms than with the fundamental principles of law and their consistency. This is why his approach is accompanied by an attempt to systematise the law. Bentham shared this goal with many of his contemporaries in England and on the European continent. It consisted of replacing law reports and case law decisions with codes that sought to be as complete as possible and based on legal reasoning.[14]

At the same time, in his schema, the sovereignty and stability of rules were associated with utility and scarcity: Every measure should be studied in the light of this principle. In other words, the logic of law is not internal to this discipline and rooted in procedure; rather, it must meet the universal principle of utilitarianism. The imperfections of competition can then be resolved through rules, but the construction and use of the latter is done through a utilitarian calculus.[15]

However, Bentham also sought to distinguish himself from all his predecessors who had tied the principles of ethics, law and economics to one of the two alternative hypotheses of sympathy or selfishness as the source of human action. In Bentham's view, these two principles cannot guide public action because, unlike the principle of utility, they do not establish a "scientific" foundation – namely a comparison between pleasure and pain – for political action.[16] From this point of view, in relation to Smith, Bentham radicalised the utilitarian principle and the idea of linking utility and individual well-being to collective utility.[17] Although he asserted that law and ethics are related, in reality

[14] Jeremy Bentham, *Legislator of the World: Writings on Codification, Law, and Education.* Edited by Philip Scholfield and Jonathan Harris. Oxford, Clarendon Press, 1998.

[15] Jeremy Bentham, *An Introduction to the Principles of Moral and Legislation.* In *The Works of Jeremy Bentham*, 11 vols., John Bowring, ed., Edinburgh, William Tait, 1838–1843, vol. 1, chapter II, section 8: 5.

[16] Herbert Lionel Hart, *Essays on Bentham: Jurisprudence and Political Theory.* New York, New York University Press, 1982.

[17] Elie Halévy, *La jeunesse de Bentham, 1776–1789.* Paris, Alcan, 1901, new edition, Paris, PUF, 1995; Elie Halévy, *L'évolution de la doctrine utilitaire de 1789 à 1815.* Paris, Alcan, 1901, new edition, Paris PUF, 1995; Annie Cot, "Jeremy Bentham et la révolution française." In Gilbert Faccarello, Philippe Steiner (eds.), *La pensée économique pendant la révolution française.* Grenoble, Presse universitaire de Grenoble, 1990: 477–85; Ross Harrison,

he unified them not on the basis of jurisprudence and Providence as Smith did, but according to the principle of maximum utility.[18] This led him to criticise Smith and his defence of a legal interest rate precisely in the name of the market's ability to cope with any speculative phenomena.[19]

Whereas Smith insisted on the link between economics and ethics, Bentham sought to justify both by the yardstick of utilitarian calculus; whereas the Scottish author made room for jurisprudential autonomy, Bentham emphasised legislative intervention. Thus, for Smith, competition refers to the balance between exchange value and use value through the principle of the division of labour and free trade under the simultaneous protection of Providence and jurisprudence. On the contrary, Bentham associated competition with a balance between pleasure and pain, which is guaranteed by a rational legal architecture. Smith's thought enjoyed immediate success from which it would later suffer. The nineteenth century was to transform his thought into something else, particularly by breaking the connection between economics and ethics by ruling out jurisprudence as an instrument of economic coordination.

Bentham's ideas, on the other hand, were less well received, at least initially. As time went by, his most important legacy was to consist precisely of having identified law with the rationality of codes and including the construction of codes among the general principles of maximum utility.[20] In the following pages, we are going to see that the notion of utility and the relationship between norms and the market in general were considered by the vast majority of nineteenth-century liberals and utilitarians synonyms for non-intervention of the state, just as Smith's Providence was to disappear in favour of free competition. This radical transformation of economic thought accompanied the rise of industrial capitalism.

Bentham. London, Routledge, 1983; Terence W. Hutchinson, "Bentham as an Economist." *The Economic Journal*, 66, 2 (1956): 288–308.

[18] Jeremy Bentham, *An Introduction to the Principles of Morals and Legislation*, chapter XIX, section 2 in *The Works of Jeremy Bentham*, vol. 1: 142.

[19] Jeremy Bentham, *Defence of Usury* (original: 1787) reprinted in *Jeremy Bentham's Economic Writings*. Edited by W. Stark, vol. 1, London, Allen and Unwin, 1952.

[20] University College London Bentham project, http://www.ucl.ac.uk/Bentham-Project/info/wstnthgt.htm.

ECONOMICS AND COMPETITION IN NINETEENTH-CENTURY ECONOMIC THOUGHT

In nineteenth-century France, the notions of competition and law were at once extremely general and extremely limited. If we take the table of contents of the *Journal des économistes* from 1841 to 1891, the word "law" is found in only two issues, 1867 and 1872, whereas the word "competition" appears only in 1845, 1855 and 1862 (all of them in three cases referring to international trade). This result can be explained by the fact that neither law nor competition as such was the subject of economists' work but, on the contrary, were explicitly or implicitly mobilised in virtually every area of economic thought. Whether it was a question of taxes, land registry, butchery regulations, foreign trade, company subsidies, the world of labour or the credit market, rules and competition constantly entered into debates, without any real effort to define them. It was no accident that in 1885, when the Academy of Moral and Political Sciences decided to institute a prize for the best work relating economics to law, it found no one able to establish such a connection and ended up awarding the prize to Alfred Jourdan who, according to the commissioners, erred by limiting law to a set of legal and moral rules while ignoring their application.[21]

We might well wonder what gave rise to this state of affairs: Did it express the fact that in the nineteenth century, the notions of competition and economic rules had become "common knowledge" for economists and therefore hardly needed to be made explicit? It is significant that law was identified with legislation and with fiscal or social policies, but very rarely with procedure and litigation. The bridge between economics and law, if indeed there was one, was made through legislation and tax policies or the philosophy of law. Why?

In France, this was partly due to the fact that economists thought they had found confirmation of their indifference to judiciary law in the attitude of legal experts who emphasised that the courts do not interpret but merely apply rules, and only major case law decisions

---

[21] Alfred Jourdan, *Des rapports entre le droit et l'économie politique ou philosophie comparée du droit et de l'économie politique.* Paris, Rousseau, 1885, préface.

and doctrinal commentaries hold any weight. What was the point in taking an interest in the many, varied applications of the law?

In reality, it was the search for universality, and hence the "scientific nature" of economics, on the one hand and the "rationality" of the law on the other that led them to dismiss from their analyses judiciary law, which they quickly associated with casuistry. Legal experts sought to uncover the rationality of institutional and normative architecture, whereas economists set out to find the rational behaviour of economic actors. These two aims, which differed in many ways, came together in their ambition to arrive at universality. Within this scope, "competition" was henceforth separated from Smith's providential order and from the connection between norms and the market through jurisprudence. Competition thus became synonymous with the natural order (or disorder, depending on the current) of the market. Thus, Jean-Baptiste Say, who did not subscribe to Ricardo's association of value with labour, nevertheless agreed with his particular interpretation of Smith, which underscored the division and specialisation of labour and the free circulation of goods rather than Providence and jurisprudence. Say's idea was simple: Competition ensures the convergence between the current price (the market price) and the natural price of goods, namely the price required to remunerate production factors. Starting from these premises, Say criticised the forms of state intervention in the economy. Like Ricardo (whom he translated) and Bentham (whom he was to influence), Say also stressed the priority of economic laws over judicial laws. He rebelled against "legal despotism" and reproached the Physiocrats for linking economic laws to political laws. He maintained there was a natural economic order which supports and confirms the fundamental unity of individual interests precisely through the market.[22] These assumptions also underpinned his critique of the legal limit of the interest rate, the *jurandes* and administrative regulations in general.

Public action was meaningful, he believed, only if it did not infringe upon private interests; this objective can be reached by keeping public intervention to a minimum and above all by making clear, stable laws

---

[22] Jean-Baptiste Say, *Cours complet d'économie politique pratique*. Bruxelles, Société typographique belge, 1845, introduction, and part III, chapter IV.

rooted in practices and customs. The clarity and stability of laws enable the actors to bring consistent economic action into being (to shape their anticipation, we would say today).[23] Say's interest in clear, stable norms led him to a careful study of property law and its various legal expressions (intellectual property rights, rights to goods, fraud and falsification, capital funds, etc.).

As several others have already noted, Say's approach to economics and law through the notion of competition responded partly to the legacy of eighteenth-century "liberal" thought, partly to Bentham's suggestions and partly to the debate that took place in France during the revolutionary era and the Empire over how the economy should be administered and the drafting of the Napoleonic codes. The identification of the sources of property rights (natural law or civil law), as well as the limit between private and public law in the market order were on the agenda. In this context, Say's orientations expressed an attempt to synthesise these aims. This attempt emphasised the market rather than laws and regulations, expressing the same concerns as the liberal and republican circles confronted first with the Empire and then with the Restoration.[24] Economics, together with legislation and morality, was the guide for both individual and public action.

It is precisely this complexity that accounts for the multiplicity and diversity of later authors who claimed to be followers of Say. During the first half of the nineteenth century, and even under the Second Empire and the Third Republic, the vast majority of French economists who saw themselves as heirs of liberal thought, and of Say in particular, did not hesitate to combine the spontaneous laws of

[23] Jean-Baptiste Say, *Cours complet d'économie politique*. Bruxelles, Société typographique belge, 1852: 513, 516, 149.

[24] On these aspects of Say, see among others: Robert Palmer, *J.-B. Say: An Economist in Troubled Times*. Princeton, NJ, Princeton University Press, 1997; Evelyn Forget, *The Social Economics of J.-B. Say: Markets and Virtue*. London, Routledge, 1999; Philippe Steiner, "L'économie politique pratique contre les systèmes: quelques remarques sur la méthode de J.-B. Say." *Revue d'économie politique*, 100, 5 (1990): 664–87; Philippe Steiner, "Jean-Baptiste Say: The Entrepreneur, the Free Trade Doctrine and the Theory of Income Distribution." In Gilbert Faccarello (ed.), *Studies in the History of French Political Economy*. London, Routledge, 1998: 196–228; Roger Whatmore, "The Political Economy of J.-B. Say's Republicanism." *History of Political Thought*, 19, 3 (1998): 439–56; Roger Whatmore, *Republicanism and the French Revolution: an Intellectual History of J.-B. Say's Political Economy*. New York, Oxford University Press, 2000.

the market with demands for state intervention in a given segment. Thus, during the 1850s, Michel Chevalier claimed to be a disciple of Cobden, Smith and Say; he favoured free trade while accepting support for companies and anti-coalition rules in the labour market.[25]

Similarly, under the Third Republic, Léon Say and Yves Guyot, among others, opposed state monopolies, and called for minimal administrative and fiscal intervention, which they described as arbitrary, but at the same time focused their attention on patent laws, competition and products.[26]

These elements did not necessarily lead these so-called liberal authors to rule out state intervention altogether. The connection between the ideas of a pure market and efficiency did not take hold in "liberal" economic thought until the mid-twentieth century, and cannot be detected as such in the nineteenth century. In other words, beyond significant differences among authors, countries and periods, nineteenth-century liberal economic thought had common features that made it far more complex than twentieth-century neoclassical and later "liberal" thought (especially the Austrian variant) which were to succeed in transforming these nineteenth-century currents into something else.

In reality, these reinterpretations of the thought (and hence, the reality) of the nineteenth century affected not only the authors mentioned here, but also and especially those who were to be transformed by the twentieth century into the two champions of liberalism and socialism in economics: Walras and Marx.

AT THE CROSSROADS OF UTILITARIANISM AND SOCIALISM: WALRAS AND MARX

It may appear arbitrary to associate Walras and Marx, because the former is usually presented as the champion of neoclassical and liberal thought and the latter as the champion of socialist economic thought. No doubt the theoretical foundations that inspired

---

[25] Michel Chevalier, *Cours d'économie politique*. First edition Paris, 1842–1850, 2ᵉ édition, Paris, 1855–1856.
[26] Yves Guyot, *Le commerce et le commerçant*. Paris, O. Doin and fils, 1909: 51.

these authors were profoundly different; English classical thought (although strongly influenced by German philosophical traditions) in the case of Marx and the utilitarian currents in the case of Walras had little to do with each other. We are not going to call these differences into question. They should nevertheless be included in broader methodological and intellectual approaches that will give us the basis for evaluating the conception of competition proposed by each of these authors.

Walras is undoubtedly a remarkable case of the successful construction of a myth a posteriori not only among the partisans of liberalism, but even among his detractors. Liberal economic thought in the twentieth century saw Walras as one of its founding fathers due to his use of both mathematics and utilitarianism. The merging of the economist with the mathematician or social engineer was an ambition of the twentieth century, whereas it was criticised at the time Walras was writing, even by "liberals". The instrumental use of Walras's thought in the twentieth century also explains why a fundamental aspect of his thought was brushed aside: Walras was a socialist who hoped to provide a scientific justification of his theses through marginal utility calculus. Liberals in the twentieth century were not solely responsible for the disappearance of this aspect; socialists contributed to it as well. They criticised Walras's recourse to utilitarianism and his use of mathematics. Indeed, the socialists thought that the scientific nature of economics should not overshadow its political character, which was incompatible with mathematics. In reality, it was precisely Walras' scientific ambition that irritated the "scientific" socialists because from this point of view, Walras was similar to Marx in proposing an analysis of capitalism that was more "scientific" than moral.[27] Like Marx, Walras also subordinated moral aspects to "pure" political economic analysis.

When we clear away all these successive interpretations, we find that Walras defended the free market but criticised its utilitarian interpretation, at least by Say and Bentham. Thus, he distinguished the

---

[27] On Walras and socialism, see Alain Reyberol, *La pensée économique de Walras*. Paris, Dunod, 1999; André Zylberberg, *L'économie mathématique en France, 1870–1914*. Paris, Economica, 1990.

principle of free competition from his conception of it; the latter defines what competition means, whereas the principle studies how it works. This is an important passage, because Walras realised that since the time of Smith, Cantillon and Turgot, the word "competition" had been used constantly without being defined. This observation, no doubt well founded, refers to Walras's attempt to show firstly, that pure theory was not incompatible with socialism and secondly, that the free market is not necessarily synonymous with utilitarianism.[28]

Like most of the authors of the time, Walras talked about the relationship between justice and economics against the backdrop of debates over private property and revenue distribution and taxation. In his approach, justice, income tax and property are indissolubly linked. In his *Introduction to the Study of the Social Question*, he criticised Louis Blanc for wrongly identifying competition with individualism. In line with the utilitarian principle, Walras thought it was necessary to reason not in terms of justice but rather of utility. In this context, "private interest naturally and of itself works towards the satisfaction of the general interest".[29]

Walras's use of utilitarianism and the emphasis he placed on individual interest no doubt widened the distance separating him from certain socialist circles (but not all of them)[30] and even more from Marx. At the same time, when Marx talks about the "laws of economics", he is not far from Ricardo or Walras; he shows the same ambition to transcend the contingent as well as legal rules. For both Marx and Walras, economic laws take precedence over judicial laws, and this hierarchy is necessary to arrive at a scientific "model" of capitalism.[31] The similarities end there, however, because Marx goes on to consider law an instrument in the hands of the ruling classes, whereas Walras finds it useful, provided it is limited to indicating the rules of the game.

We encounter the same similarities and differences with regard to law in the area of competition. For Marx, as for Ricardo, Say and

[28] Léon Walras, *L'économie politique et la justice. Œuvre économique complète*. Vol. V, Paris, Economica, 2001.
[29] Walras *Introduction à la question sociale* in *Œuvre economique complète*, vol. V.
[30] Reyberol, *La pensée*.
[31] Karl Marx, *Das Kapital* (Italian translation *Il capitale*). Roma, Editori riuniti, 1967, vol. 1: 200 and vol. 3: 405.

Walras, competition was above all a mechanism that allowed him to talk about something else, namely the "laws" of the capitalist economy, particularly the levelling of profit rates.[32] Of course, Marx was seeking proof of the fundamental imbalances of capitalism in the laws of competition, whereas Walras tried to bring out the stability and efficiency of this same mechanism. Yet this difference should not make us lose sight of the common ambition of these two authors, which was to provide a scientific representation of capitalism. Walras's general equilibrium and Marx's laws of reproduction both aimed at identifying the point of equilibrium of the capitalist economy as a whole. It is no accident that Enrico Barone, who was close to Pareto and Walras, developed the latter's model for the interventions of the "ministry of production".[33] Walras was initially studied within the scope of "the economics of well-being" introduced at the end of the nineteenth century, which attracted both reformist liberal economists and socialists. This approach aimed at examining the imperfections of the market and the most appropriate forms of intervention from the fiscal, monetary and social standpoints. In a sense, it was the theoretical basis for the welfare state, conceived and introduced well before Keynes, starting precisely from "liberal" thinking.

The same ministry of production model (hence, a synthesis of Walras and Pareto) was to become the theoretical basis for state planning calculations at the time of the First World War and later in twentieth-century socialist economics and thought. Wassilli Leont'ev, a Russian who emigrated first to Berlin and then to the United States, and won the Nobel Prize in economics for inventing the input-output tables linking all segments of production, officially declared he had been inspired by Walras. In fact, in his youth, Leont'ev was well trained in post-revolutionary Soviet universities and collaborated on the initial work of the Gosplan.[34] In other words, from the middle of the nineteenth century until the 1970s, it is possible to find an analytical and

---

[32] Marx, *Il capitale*, vol. 1: 355.

[33] Enrico Barone, "Il ministro della produzione nello stato collettivista." *Giornale degli economisti* (1908): 267–93 and 391–414. On Pareto Alain Bouvier (ed.), *Pareto aujourd'hui*. Paris, PUF, 1999; Corrado Malandrino, Roberto Marchionnatti (eds.), *Economia, politica, sociologia nell'opera di Vilfredo Pareto, 1897–1997*. Firenze, Olschky, 1999.

[34] On these aspects, Alessandro Stanziani, *L'économie en révolution*. Paris, Albin Michel, 1998.

methodological correspondence between general equilibrium and state planning. All the theoretical and political debates that took place during that century and even later have forgotten this common source of inspiration and goals.

COMPETITION OR THE LOST WORLD
OF ECONOMISTS

General traits of nineteenth-century economic thought should not make us lose sight of the nuances and important differences among the various authors and currents, between periods and ultimately between countries. Thus, in Great Britain, the association of laissez-faire with Smith or of laissez-faire with utilitarianism is an end-of-the-nineteenth-century invention. Neither Smith nor Bentham, nor, for the most part, the other authors of the nineteenth century, were radically hostile to state intervention in the economy. As I have pointed out in discussing these authors, they were against specific policies (e.g., protectionism, a special status for the Bank of England, etc.), but not against state intervention as such. Ricardo and Bentham went even further in the direction of laissez-faire; they were immediately criticised by public opinion, and political representatives accused them of ignoring the relationship between economics and morality and justice.[35]

In France, in contrast to Great Britain, "liberal" thought was constantly called into question both in politics and economics. Say's mediation between Smith, Ricardo and Mill was specific to the French context, just as the recovery of public utilities belonged to the so-called liberals. Finally, Walras remained on the sidelines of French thought for a long time due to his ultra-mathematical approach and his attempt to combine cooperation, socialism and a utilitarian calculus.

Similarly, contrary to standard arguments, for much of the twentieth century, American economists remained faithful to "moral" (Scottish) thought and the classic economics of the early nineteenth century. Smith's position was correctly linked to the connection between

---

[35] John Bartlet Brebner, "Laissez Faire and State Intervention in Nineteenth-Century Britain." *Journal of Economic History*, 8 (1948): 59–73; Kenneth Walker, "The Classical Economists and the Factory Acts." *Journal of Economic History*, 1, 2 (1941): 168–77.

competition and morality and, based on this premise, to the idea that law and government should either abstain from or intervene in economic activity. However, most American economists rejected both Bentham and Ricardo, the first because of his radical utilitarianism, the second because of his theory of annuity which, from an American viewpoint, could only apply when resources were scarce, which was not the case in the United States. For these same reasons, Americans objected to Malthus and his ambition to limit demographic growth. The United States had exactly the opposite problem. American economic observers were ready to accept the suggestions of all those who, like Marshall, emphasised the imperfections of the market and the need to resolve them not by macroeconomic intervention but by using common law and norms to protect competition (such as the Sherman Act).[36]

German economists cannot be identified with encouraging state intervention in the economy as historians of economic thought have often asserted. In the "cameralist" approach at the close of the eighteenth century, there was not so much opposition as interpenetration between the economy and the State. The administrative order was not imposed on the legal order or on the economic order. Instead, these three aspects interacted in such as way as to reconcile economics with ethics. The policing of markets complemented rather than replaced judiciary and contractual law in the strict sense.[37] From this point of view, cameralism was rooted in politics rather than in a desire for bureaucratic control on the part of the state.[38]

[36] Herbert Hovenkamp, "The Political Economy of Substantive Due Process." *Stanford Law Review*, 40, 2 (1988): 379–447; Henry Carey, *Principles of Political Economy*. Philadelphia, Carey, Lea and Blanchard, 1838; Henry Carey, *The Unity of Law, as Exhibited in the Relations of Physical, Social, Mental and Moral Science*. Philadelphia, H. Carey Baird, 1872.

[37] Keith Tribe, "Cameralism and the Science of Government." *Journal of Modern History*, 56, 2 (1984): 263–84; Albion Small, *The Cameralists: Pionners of German Social Policy*. New York, Burt Franklin, 1909; Hans Rosenberg, *Bureaucracy, Aristocracy and Autocracy: The Prussian Experience, 1660–1815*. Cambridge, Mass., Harvard University Press, 1966; Carl William Hasek, *The Introduction of Adam Smith's Doctrine into Germany*. New York, Columbia University Press, 1925; Keith Tribe, *Governing Economy: The Reformation of German Economic Discourse, 1760–1840*. Cambridge, Cambridge University Press, 1988.

[38] Gilbert Garnier, *Etat, économie et territoire en Allemagne. L'espace dans le caméralisme et l'économie politique, 1740–1820*. Paris, EHESS, 2006; Mack Walker, "Rights and Functions: The Social Categories of Eighteenth Century German Jurists and Cameralists." *Journal of Modern History*, 50, 2 (1978): 234–51.

In short, for eighteenth-century authors, utility could hardly be separated from reflections on just price, just as for the marginalists of the late nineteenth century, utilitarian calculus constantly ran up against market "imperfections" that required the intervention of public authorities. This connection would finally be lost in the twentieth century in the ultra-liberal interpretations of neoclassical thought. As nineteenth-century writers adapted the thinking of the previous century to their own requirements, so too twentieth-century economic and political analysts would help invent very peculiar images of nineteenth-century authors who became either liberals close to the "Austrians" or at times Leninists. The complexity of both liberal and socialist approaches in the nineteenth century was thus lost (Walras is a prime example).

In a way, nineteenth-century thought was utopian, staked sometimes on the spontaneous solidarity of individuals and more often on the regulating capacities of markets formed out of selfish, individual calculations. The spontaneous solidarity of society, even in the presence of the market, was associated either with primitive, Robinsonian groups and the state of nature, or with forms of cooperation that had a moral or even religious ideal at their core. This opposition was also presented as self-interest versus charity. From this point of view, the principle of selfishness explained, through the market, the new capitalist, bourgeois society.

Both the defence and the critique of capitalism share these same assumptions and therefore the same explanatory limits. We might sum up these approaches by saying that the image of capitalism and competition proposed by nineteenth-century economists usually came under the heading of regretting a lost world. This title of a famous book by Peter Laslett applies perhaps less to peasants and artisans than to economists. Small, independent producers, covered markets and forced labour provided the reference points and inspiration for numerous economic and social theories, all tendencies combined. Indeed, the operation of the market proposed by the pure theory of competition was largely inspired by the old covered markets. Perceptions inherited from pre-industrial economies influenced these theories. In reality, utopia and nostalgia were intermingled in economic analysis. Such views were in no way "remote from reality" but instead expressed an essential trait of new industrial economies. These nineteenth-century systems were based on structures and institutions inherited from previous periods which actors extended and exploited as far as possible.[39]

The stock market and auctions, present in the minds of economists in the last quarter of the nineteenth century (whether neoclassical, socialist or of another stripe), constituted special cases that have since been presented as examples of the operation of all markets and of the "market" in general. This naturally overlooks the fact that covered markets, stock exchanges and auctions were the least "natural" and most regulated markets since the Ancien Régime. By ignoring these realities, partisans of perfect competition encouraged administrative officials to impose this ideal model from the outside, whereas socialists, Marxists, anarchists and utopians set about attacking a market that did not exist except in these particular expressions. In the following pages, I will explore these topics.

[39] Henry Caton, "The Pre-industrial Economics of Adam Smith." *Journal of Economic History*, 45, 4 (1985): 833–53.

2

CODES, CUSTOMS AND JURISDICTIONS

Beside the ideal types of market and competition, another theoretical type has been present over centuries and generations: It opposes the case law–based common law system to a centralised law system in continental Europe and civil law countries. The former is said to be more efficient and closer to business interests than the latter. In the following pages, I will question these statements. I will compare the role of lawmaking in jurisprudence in France and common law countries. I will argue that while the production of rules and regulations was important both in civil law countries and in Anglo-Saxon countries, conversely, judicial interpretation was essential in both. It was only at the end of the nineteenth century, when legislative production increased in both France and Anglo-Saxon countries, that the theories of no creative jurisprudence in civil law countries and of no positive rules in common law countries were affirmed.

Our first step consists in understanding the historical link between the production and interpretation of rules.[1] Is it true that under the Ancien Régime, multiple jurisdictions made law inefficient, whereas liberal institutions under capitalism built up a strong hierarchical legal order?

In the eighteenth century, the king's authority intervened both in producing and applying rules. The autonomy of judges was often

First draft of this chapter translated by Susan Taponier.

[1] Gunther Teubner (ed.), *Autopoietic Law: A New Approach to Law and Society*. Berlin, DeGruyter, 1988, French translation: *Le droit réflexif*. Paris, LGDJ, 1992; also "Pour une épistémologie constructiviste du droit." *Annales Esc*, 6 (1992): 1149–69; Edward Levi, *Legal Reasoning*. Chicago, University of Chicago Press, 1949.

limited, and in the hierarchy of sources and jurisdictions, administrative authority and the market police dominated.[2] Moreover, there was a multiplicity of jurisdictions: *prévôtés* (first instance), *baillages* and *sénéchaussées* (first instance and appellate), not to mention seigniorial, consular, fiscal, military and ecclesiastical.[3] These jurisdictions often entered into conflicts over their respective scopes, which were settled by the King's Council, a sort of court of cassation, the attributions of which were defined in 1667 and 1738. Finally, actors could bring the same dispute before several jurisdictions, drawing it out indefinitely. In this situation, case law reports, which existed before 1700, sought to respond to the uncertainty weighing on the disputes. However, the judges were sceptical about these reports because the cases analyzed were arbitrarily selected.[4]

From the point of view of the economic actors, the multiplicity of rules and jurisdictions represented not only a cost but also an opportunity. The possibility of calling upon different rules and jurisdictions was important; it not only allowed the actors to "cheat", but also guaranteed them some leeway. Indeed, it encouraged them to reach arrangements to avoid having disputes go on forever.[5]

This observation will serve as the basis for evaluating the breaks and continuities that arose with France's revolution. On this topic, the famous separation of powers (legislative, executive and judicial) discussed by Montesquieu and promoted by the *Assemblée Constituante* has been constantly evoked ever since in legal history.

The principle of non-interpretation of rules on the part of judges is said to be a derivative of this overall institutional architecture. However, this principle should not be considered, as the manuals suggest, as a prohibition imposed on judges, who would consequently be

---

[2] Jean-Pierre Royer, *Histoire de la justice en France*. Paris, PUF, 2001.

[3] François Olivier-Martin, *La police économique*. Paris, les cours de droit, 1944–1945; Jean-Luc Lafon, *Recherches sur la fin des juridictions de l'Ancien régime pendant la révolution: le Châtelet et le Parlement de Paris*. PhD dissertation, University Paris II, 1972.

[4] Evelyne Serverin, *Théorie de la pratique jurisprudentielle en droit privé*. Lyon, PUL, 1985; Benoît Garnot, *Questions de justice, 1667–1789*. Paris, Belin, 2006; Hervé Piant, *Une justice ordinaire. Justice civile et criminelle dans la prévôté de Vaucouleurs sous l'Ancien Régime*. Rennes, PUR, 2006.

[5] Michael Sonenscher, *Work and Wages. Natural Law, Politics and the Eighteenth-Century French Trades*. Cambridge, Cambridge University Press, 1989.

limited to applying rules and interpreting them in accordance with the intent of lawmakers.[6] Initially, the aim of legislators was to produce codes that were as complete as possible. This aim quickly ran up against reality, however: The multiplication of situations and possible cases meant that, by definition, a rule could never be "complete" but merely "general"; this conclusion was especially true for a set of rules, no matter how consistent such as a code. Once it was agreed that concrete situations could pose problems of interpretation and that, above all, as time went by, new phenomena would emerge, making the codes appear inadequate, the question arose as to how the gap between rules and real situations could be bridged. There were two possible solutions: Either the rules were modified, integrated, and completed, or they were maintained and greater interpretive authority was given to judges. Contrary to what is commonly thought, the latter interpretation prevailed from the Restoration to the Third Republic.[7]

Overall, during the first half of the nineteenth century and even afterwards, few new laws were made, and the codes were quite often considered to be self-sufficient. This stability increased the importance of interpretation, which could sometimes prove costly for the actors to acquire.[8] In this context, judicial information and its circulation were highly valued; trade associations and chambers of commerce, particularly in Lille as well as Paris and Lyon, often wondered how to discover the way the law was applied in view of the many court decisions and apparently different or even contradictory opinions of judges.[9] Case law reports served this purpose: to offer reference points, first of all

---

[6] Royer, *Histoire*: 276; Michel Troper, *La séparation des pouvoirs and l'histoire constitutionnelle française*. Paris, LGDJ, 1980; Léon Duguit, "La séparation des pouvoirs and l'Assemblée nationale de 1789." *Revue d'économie politique*, VII (1893): 99–132, 336, 372, 567–75; Serverin, *Jurisprudence*.

[7] Law of 16 September 1807. Discussion in Jean-Louis Halpérin, *Histoire du droit civil*. Paris, LGDJ, 1996: 52. Jean-Marie Carbasse, Louis Depambour-Tarride (eds.), *La conscience du juge dans la tradition juridique européenne*. Paris, PUF, 1990. Archives files: Archives Nationales (hereafter AN), series BB 30, dossiers 524, 525, 527, 534, 540, 541.

[8] On the economic theory of the relation between costs of production and cost of enforcement of a rule: Louis Kaplow, "Rules versus Standards: An Economic Analysis." *Duke Law Journal*, 42 (1992): 557–629.

[9] Correspondence between the Ministry of Justice and professional associations in AN series: BB 18 (criminal department) and BB 30 (civil law cases).

for lawyers, then economic actors and possibly judges for the use and interpretation of the rules. Alongside the decisions of the Court of Cassation and those of most appellate courts, case law reports made their selection on the basis of relatively subjective criteria, which nevertheless ended up influencing the doctrinal and political significance of a given decision and its dissemination within business circles.

During the second half of the nineteenth century, this balance was disrupted. Rules became less stable with the increase in "special legislation" (législation d'exception). Although judicial interpretation still played a central role, it gradually lost part of its importance to legislative action. In addition to reforms of the criminal justice system, territorial organisation of the courts, judges' careers and, to some extent, the jurisdiction of labour courts (prud'hommes), there were significant modifications of positive law. These changes were made partly in response to institutional changes: The Third Republic altered the relationship among the three powers, giving greater weight to legislation and consequently altering the authority of judges.[10]

The accelerated production of rules was also linked to the fact that the Napoleonic codes were henceforth considered outmoded due to economic and social changes. The rise of commerce, industrial concentration, the development of financial relationships – all these elements made existing institutions and rules obsolete, hence the need for reforms. A correlation emerged between stepped-up technological progress and instability in the rules of law, although it is impossible to pinpoint a clear cause–and–effect relationship. Progress in chemistry, particularly organic chemistry, supported the development of new materials and products not only in manufacturing but in food and agriculture as well. Fears began to emerge; public opinion, encouraged by doctors and the economic lobbies concerned, attacked the new techniques and demanded that the laws be changed. This movement, starting with the regulation of specific fields, ultimately led to the conception of new forms of regulation for the economy as a whole. "Special laws" were adopted in the field of labour, products, credit and the stock exchange.

---

[10] Jean-Claude Farcy, *L'histoire de la justice française de la Révolution à nos jours*. Paris, Gip justice, 2001.

Compared to previous periods, there was at once social instability, greater economic uncertainty and accelerated changes in rules.[11] In their earlier (before the 1870s) relationship with the law, the actors and their associations were concerned above all by the high cost of access to case law information, whereas the cost of producing rules remained low. Now, on the contrary, economic and political networks were being expanded and replaced, and a variety of efforts were devoted to the production of rules. In particular, economic actors and the markets demanded rules first of all to control the circulation of economic information: advertising, product labelling, public notification of bankruptcy, credit, mortgage, industrial property and so on. Then the actors focused on the source of instability itself, namely innovation. A number of new rules were also created regarding trademarks, patents, frauds and falsifications, resulting in the emergence of the general category of unfair competition. Finally, many business circles demanded a return to stable rules, which were assumed to foster expectations and business calculation.[12]

In short, the idea that judges did not interpret rules is a political and intellectual invention of the nineteenth century, which was widely expressed in legal manuals; it was not, however, confirmed in the actual workings of justice. If anything, it was precisely at the time when codes and rules changed the least (during the first half of the nineteenth century) that case law counted the most. Post-revolutionary France was highly jurisprudential.

From this point of view, the differences separating civil law countries from Anglo-Saxon countries need to be considerably revised. Jurisprudence and case law were very significant in France, in particular during the first three quarters of the nineteenth century, when

---

[11] Fernand Braudel, Ernest Labrousse (eds.), *Histoire économique and sociale de France*. Paris, PUF, volumes 3 and 4, 1976, 1979; Philippe Ariès, Georges Duby (eds.), *Histoire de la vie privée*. Vol. 4 (by Michelle Perrot), Paris, Seuil, 1987; Yves Lequin (eds.), *Histoire des Français (XIXe and XXe siècles)*. Vol 2, Paris, Colin, 1983; Louis Bergeron, *Les capitalistes en France, 1780–1914*. Paris, Gallimard, 1978; David Higgs, *Nobles in Nineteenth Century France: The Practise of Inegalitarianism*. Baltimore and London, John Hopkins University Press, 1987; Christophe Charle, *Histoire sociale de France au XIXe siècle*. Paris, Seuil, 1991.

[12] AN sery: F 12 (Ministry of Trade and Industry), dossier 7452; AN sery C (parliamentary archives) dossiers: 918, 1023, 1024, 5404; sery BB 18 (criminal department at the Ministry of Justice), dossiers 6603 and 6180.

legislative activity was weak. Conversely, legislative activity in England and the United States was far from negligible. Numerous provisions were made in the eighteenth, nineteenth and twentieth centuries to control the labour market, credit, agriculture, commerce and consumption.[13] A substantial number of such measures were based on the idea that case law alone was not enough to control the economy. Twentieth-century commentators invented the myth of the self-regulating market and the triumph of laissez-faire in the nineteenth century.[14]

Even the idea that case law decisions relied on a precedent was an intellectual and political invention which corresponded only in part to historical reality. Just as French law manuals invented the principle of non-interpretation of rules by judges, similarly, in the United States, the manuals of the last quarter of the nineteenth century preached the principle of "precedent". Indeed, until that moment, multiple judgements and varied decisions from one state to another had been the rule rather than the exception. In the last quarter of the nine-teenth century, however, the lack of uniformity in decisions came under increasing criticism from legal experts as well as certain business circles. The latter were worried about the impact that such inconsist-ent decisions might have on the creation of a genuine national market. Uniform decisions were demanded in order to launch operations on a wider scale. At the same time, another argument was mixed into these considerations. As in France during the same period, the legisla-tive process was accelerating, particularly in the direction of forms of welfare state intervention. Laws on wages, working hours, foodstuffs and railways were adopted. They immediately drew negative reactions from all those who saw the measures as a new form of regulation con-trary to Anglo-American traditions. It was in this context that case law based on precedent was proposed as the genuine "non-regulationist"

---

[13] Herbert Hovenkamp, *Enterprise and American Law, 1836–1937*. Cambridge, Mass., Harvard University Press, 1991; Lawrence Friedman, *A History of American Law*. New York, Simon and Schuster, 1973.

[14] John Bartlet Brebner, "Laissez Faire and State Intervention in Nineteenth-Century Britain." *Journal of Economic History*, 8 (1948): 59–73; Arthur J. Taylor, *Laissez-faire and State Intervention in Nineteenth Century Britain*. London, Macmillan 1972; R. L. Crouch, "Laissez-faire in Nineteenth Century Britain: Myth or Reality?" *Manchester School Economic and Social Studies*, XXXV (1967): 199–215; François Bédarida, "L'Angleterre victorienne paradigme du laissez-faire?" *Revue historique*, 529 (1979): 79–98.

solution and, as such, opposed to state intervention.[15] In other words, this principle was in no way the foundation for the Anglo-Saxon model; rather, it was demanded by certain authors and currents of opinion at a time when the legislative process was speeding up and becoming increasingly intense, especially regarding labour and industrial concentration.

To summarise, the supposed opposition between civil law and Anglo-Saxon law should be nuanced; legislative construction and judicial interpretation were equally important in both systems. To explain different paths to capitalism, we will therefore have to look elsewhere than to the role of jurisprudence for the specificity of civil law countries, especially France, compared with Anglo-Saxon countries. In particular, at least since the twelfth century, market economies have been faced with the question of whether the business world (i.e., trade for several centuries, then industry and labour and today, business in general) should be regulated by common civil rules or special rules for trade.

CIVIL LAW AND COMMERCIAL LAW OR THE SPECIAL STATUS OF TRADESMAN

Two distinct but related problems must be examined; first we must consider the relationship between commercial rules and general civil rules; this will help us understand the degree of equality of social actors before the law. Once I have done this, I must account for the incorporation of trade customs into state (commercial) law to explain the roles of state and lobbies in the making of market economies.

Most analyses by historians of law and neo-institutionalist economists emphasise the fact that trade customs express the market's self-regulating capacities. Taking up the observations of Hayek,[16] these authors consider such rules perfectly suited to the demands of the

---

[15] Hovenkamp, *Enterprise*; Morton G. White, *Social Thought in America: The Revolt against Formalism.* Oxford, Oxford University Press, 1957; Harry Scheiber, "Instrumentalism and Property Rights: A Reconsideration of American Style of Judicial Reasoning in the Nineteenth Century." *Wisconsin Law Review*, 1 (1975): 1–18.

[16] Frederik Hayek, *Studies in Philosophy, Politics and Economics.* Chicago, University of Chicago Press, 1973; Frederik Hayek, *Law, Legislation and Liberty.* London, Routledge, 1973.

economy, unlike state rules which are said to impede competition.[17] This analysis is quite similar to that of numerous legal historians who have attempted to show that until the rise of the monarchy, particularly Colbert's ordinance of 1673, commercial law developed outside the state apparatus, like a form of market self-regulation. Colbert and the absolute monarchy are then said to have incorporated these rules into state law by subordinating them to the monarchy's tax and military requirements. From this point of view, the revolution would have had little impact. The existence of commercial law as separate from civil law is said to be a source of inequality and economic inefficiency.[18]

This question is particularly relevant now in the course of European integration, when the question has indeed been raised as to whether business law is a form of "exceptional" law, as in France and the civil law countries, or whether it should be incorporated into private law, as in the Anglo-Saxon countries.

Historical analysis allows us to clear up some of the misunderstandings that underlie these quarrels. The existence of a special law for trade was not linked to the French Ancien Régime nor did it express a simple state interference in economic matters. Indeed, in modern France, commercial rules were above all linked to the peculiar legal status of merchants. Obtaining the legal status of a merchant (in the eighteenth century) and then of a tradesman (in the nineteenth century) had broad implications; it gave access to consular courts and later commercial courts, and therefore to the special rules provided for "merchants" and "tradesmen" (bankruptcy law, burden of proof, consular judges, etc.). Trade associations and economic actors were thus extremely concerned about the definition of legal status.

In principle, a merchant was identified by his membership in a guild. In reality, already in the eighteenth century, this was increasingly

---

[17] Douglass North, *Structure and Change in Economic History*. New York, Norton, 1981; William Landes, Richard Posner, "Adjudication as a Private Good." *Journal of Legal Studies*, March (1979): 235–84; Bruce Benson, "The Spontaneous Evolution of Commercial Law." *Southern Economic Journal*, 55, 3 (1989): 644–61; Anthony Ogus, "Self-regulation." In Boundewijn Bouckaert, Gerrit de Geest (eds.), *Encyclopedia of Law and Economics*. Aldershot, Edward Elgar, vol. 5: 587–660; Francesco Parisi, "Spontaneous Emergence of Law: Customary Law." In Bouckaert, Geest (eds.), *Encyclopaedia*, vol. 5: 603–30.

[18] Jean Hilaire, *Introduction historique au droit commercial*. Paris, LGDJ, 1986.

called into question,[19] and the definition of merchant status relied more and more not only on guild membership but also on the nature, the continuity and the finality of the transactions performed. A merchant was someone who exercised his activity on an ongoing basis; trade was supposed to be his main activity.[20] A great deal of litigation was thus concerned with the possibility for a craftsman to obtain merchant status, taking interruptions of trade activity into account and, conversely, with the length of trade activity required to be described as customary, and so on.[21] As such, special rules for trade were not synonymous with the Ancien Régime. In fact, they did not disappear with the abolition of guilds and *jurandes*. Even if free trade was the basic principle of the new economic and social order resulting from the revolution, several business circles tried, in the name of free trade and competition, to evoke the right to benefit exclusively from the legal status of tradesman and thereby enjoy the advantages offered by commercial law and commercial courts.[22] There were lively debates on these issues in the Commission assigned to draft the commercial code,[23] and in the courts of justice throughout the nineteenth century. The main case law decisions confirmed that it was not enough to pay the trade tax to be considered a tradesman, nor, by the way, to have engaged in this activity in the past.[24] As the years went by, case law selected three principal prerequisites for entitlement to tradesman status: The trade had to be the person's primary activity;

[19] Joseph de Ferrière, *Dictionnaire de droit et de pratique contenant l'explication des termes de droit, d'ordonnances, de coutumes et de pratique*. Paris, Brunet, vol. 2 : 179.

[20] Hilaire, *Introduction*: 145. Jean Toubeau, *Les institutions du droit consulaire ou les éléments de jurisprudence des marchands*. Paris, Morel, 1700.

[21] Jean-Bernard Denisart, *Collection de décisions nouvelles et de notions relatives à la jurisprudence actuelle*. Paris, Dessaint, 1771.

[22] Henri Levy-Bruhl, *Un projet de code de commerce à la veille de la révolution, le projet Miromesnil*. Paris, E. Leroux, 1932; *Révision du projet de code de commerce, précédé de l'analyse raisonné des observations des tribunaux, par les citoyens Gorneau, Legras et Vital Roux*. Paris, an XI-1803; Jean-Guillaume Locré, *Législation civile, commerciale et criminelle de France*. Paris, Treuttel et Würtz, 31 volumes, 1827–1832 ; Jean-Guillaume Locré, *L'esprit du code de commerce*, 10 vols., Paris, Garnery, 1807–1813.

[23] AN F 12 543 to 546.

[24] Pierre-Claude-Jean-Baptiste Bravard-Veyrières, *Manuel de droit commercial*. Paris, Joubert, 1840: 14. Also decisions by: Court of Cassation, 5 November 1830; Court of Bordeaux, 4 December 1848, quoted in François-Hyppolite Mascret, *Dictionnaire des faillites*. Paris, 1848–1863, vol. XVIII.

the activity had to be carried out on a continuous basis and with a view to making a profit.[25]

This went along with a discriminatory access to special rules. The case law definition of "tradesman" included manufacturers, along with bankers and insurers. On the other hand, solicitors and stockbrokers were excluded from this status and therefore from bankruptcy law as provided for in the commercial code.

Women had a special status; they could not engage in trade without at least the tacit authorisation of their husbands or their parents. A few rare court decisions granted this authorisation, despite the husband's refusal, if the latter was considered unjust or illegitimate and when their marriage contract specified the separation of property. However, both doctrine and case law accepted this solution only when the husband's incapacity was demonstrated.

This state of virtually total subordination of wives to the will of their husbands in nineteenth-century civil law implied that the husband was liable for debts contracted by his wife and that he was often required to stand surety for her activities. Couples often took advantage of this situation to cope with their creditors.[26]

On the whole, the actors who benefited from the legal status of tradesmen were not those who performed "functions" identifiable as trade or intermediation from an economic standpoint. The sole criteria selected were the purpose of the economic activity (it had to be profit making) and its continuity. Wholesale traders, commercial banks and industries enjoyed considerable advantages over those who remained excluded from the legal status of "tradesman", such as women, itinerant merchants, craftsmen, labourers and peasants.

Indeed, the existence of commercial law in France after 1789 indicates the failure of the revolutionary project to eliminate the division of society into "orders".[27] A civil code accessible to everyone was opposed to a commercial code and commercial courts reserved for tradesmen. This distinction set aside a series of privileges for tradesmen alone: the possibility of being judged by tradesmen-judges rather than

---

[25] Marta Torre-Schaub, *Essai sur la construction juridique de la catgégorie de marché*. Paris, LGDJ, 2002.

[26] Cases in: Mascret, *Dictionnaire*.

[27] Francesco Galgano, *Lex mercatoria*. Bologna, Il Mulino, 1991.

by ordinary judges; recourse to special rules regarding sales, protection against non-tradesmen, access to flexible rules in the event of bankruptcy; and the possibility of providing oral evidence to support their case in the event of a dispute, whereas non-tradesmen had to furnish written proof.[28]

Clearly, commercial courts and the commercial code offered significant advantages to the actors who had access to them. These institutions reduced the cost of legal proceedings, thanks to their swift procedures. Commercial courts also facilitated conciliation.[29] These privileges contribute to explaining the success of commercial courts and the commercial code and the attempt to harmonize codes and commercial customs. This seems to confirm the argument of Posner and others who view the existence of a commercial code as a source of inequality and concentration rather than of free competition. This argument is probably accurate in its conclusion, though not in its main explanation, insofar as commercial law did not owe its existence to the state[30] but was strongly desired by certain economic actors and their lobbies. The long process of trade custom codification confirms this argument. Unlike current interpretations, the codification of trade customs was not made by the State against the will of business milieus, but, quite the contrary, was strongly promoted by the latter.

CODES AND CUSTOMS OF TRADE

During the period prior to the development of codification (in the eighteenth century), merchant law was constantly evoked as

[28] Levy-Bruhl, *Projet*; Claire Lemercier, *Un si discret pouvoir*. Paris, La découverte, 2005; Emmanuel Lazéga, Lisa Mounier, "La régulation conjointe du marché: le cas du tribunal de commerce de Paris." *Cahiers lillois d'économie et de sociologie*, 41–42 (2003): 109–35; René Ithurbide, *Histoire critique des tribunaux de commerce*. Paris, LGDJ, 1970. Archival sources on merchant courts in: AN sery BB 7 (Ministry of Justice, trade courts), in particular BB 7 136: observations des tribunaux de commerce sur le projet de code de commerce, an X. Discussions on a special code for merchants in AN F 12 543 to 546.

[29] Statistics in Ministère de la Justice, *Comptes généraux de la justice criminelle*. Paris, Imprimerie nationale, since 1839. On the value of these figures: Gilles Rouet, *Justice et justiciables au XIXe et XXe siècles*. Paris, Belin, 1999; Evelyne Serverin, C. Beroujon, S. Bruxelles, *Classer coder. Une expérimentation sur l'application des nomenclatures d'affaires judiciaires civiles*. GIP Droit et justice, 1987.

[30] Charles Lyon-Caen, Louis Renault, *Manuel de droit commercial*. Paris, LGDJ, 9th edition, 1908; Jean-Marie Pardessus, *Cours de droit commercial*. Paris, 1814.

being based on tacit agreements that were held to be internationally recognised. Although not state-imposed, this law was in no sense informal. The terms of payment and of contract validation, goods inspections, negotiation practices and so on were recognised by the law of municipalities and States and were enforced in the courts provided for that purpose.[31]

The conflict between market customs and official rules was thus, in large part, a historiographical construct inspired by later periods. Case law reports, which multiplied in the twelfth century, testify precisely to the importance merchants attached to the use of the law and the circulation of judicial information (which decisions were made, where, by whom and on which subject).[32] The emergence of centralised states did not substantially change these elements, except that trade customs were increasingly codified and incorporated into state rules. From the fifteenth to the eighteenth centuries, customary practices were distinguished from customs for "a custom was initially an unwritten law introduced by customary practice" which, from that point of view, supplemented and interpreted the formal law. However, since the time of the dukes of Burgundy, customs had become synonymous with customary practices which were written down to give them the force of law.[33]

As in previous periods, it would be simplistic to view this process of formalising customary practices as state intrusion in economic life. No doubt, the constitution and strengthening of the monarchic state were in large part responsible for the codification of trade practices. At the same time, it was not merely an administrative construction that the state imposed on economic actors. The introduction of state rules in these areas expressed the converging desiderata of a substantial portion of tradesmen and political elites. There is evidence for this in,

---

[31] Joachim Hoock, Pierre Jeannin, Wolfgang Kaiser, *Ars mercatoria*, 3 vols. Paderborn, Schoning, 1991, 1993, 2001; Louis Assier-Andrieu, *Une France coutumière, enquête sur les usages locaux et leur codification, XIXe–XXe siècles*. Paris, CNRS, 1990; Jean Escarra, "De la valeur juridique de l'usage en droit commercial." *Annales de droit commercial*, 3 (1910): 17; Carlo Maria Cipolla, *Storia economica dell'Europa pre-industriale*. Bologna, Il Mulino, 1974; Roberto Lopez, *La rivoluzione commerciale del medioevo*. Torino, Einaudi, 1975.

[32] Pierre Huvelin, "L'histoire du droit commercial." *Revue de synthèse historique*, 7 (1903): 328–71; Jacques Le Goff, *Marchands et banquiers du Moyen Age*. Paris, PUF, 1957.

[33] Claude-Joseph De Ferrière, *Dictionnaire de droit*. Paris, 1738, vol. 1: 393.

among others, the rules for establishing produce exchanges (1549) and consular jurisdictions (1563), the ordinance of 1595 on brokers and commission actors, and provisions throughout this period regarding fraudulent bankruptcy, guild constraints in commercial matters, arbitration of disputes between merchants and the recording of transactions with foreign merchants.

These converging interests of the world of business and the Monarchy would later give rise to the commission set up by Miromesnil (the Minister of Justice) in 1774, which continued its work until the revolution. These documents served as a starting point for the work of the commission created by Napoleon to draft the commercial code.[34]

The adoption of the commercial code nevertheless did not solve the question of the role of informal trade customs, that is, those that did not enter into the code. The question was whether or not such practices retained legal validity, and if so, what it was. In 1811, when the State Council was queried on this issue by trade associations and political leaders, it declared that judges should take trade practices into consideration only in the "silence of the code".[35] However, this solution did not answer the question as to how a judge, required by law to take local practices into consideration, was to decide what they were. Naturally, one might assume this was done by referring to the list of trade customs provided by the economic actors and the trade associations concerned, but this interpretation is not confirmed by the facts. When a judge asked a chamber of commerce or any other local trade association for a written statement confirming the existence of a trade custom in a given field, he was often faced with contradictory opinions.[36] As a result, a written statement confirming the existence of such a trade custom and the judge's decision could easily be challenged by one of the parties. Legal archives and case law contain a wealth of challenges of this kind, for example concerning the practices used in making Champagne and Bordeaux wines, producing cloth in

---

[34] Lévy-Bruhl, *Un projet de code.*
[35] Hilaire, *Introduction*: 107–11.
[36] Archives de la chambre de commerce et de l'Industrie de Paris (henceforth: ACCIP) sery III-4.40 (1): commercial customs, 1875–1930; sery VV-3.60 (1): commerce in Paris, reglementation, customs, prices, 1807–1944, butchery, 1822–1975, wines 1805–1843.

northern and central France or even in labour relations.[37] Trade associations not only published and stabilised these customs, they resorted to them in their certifying activity and in settling disputes.[38]

However, different chambers did not express this attitude at the same moment with the same strength. If the Chamber of Lyon, for example, had been ready to list customs and settle disputes since the beginning of the nineteenth century, the Chamber of Paris initially was more cautious. Until the 1820s, *parères* (motivated judgements and advisories) were fundamentally refused in the name of the "freedom of trade" and the independence of merchant law courts. Over time, this attitude evolved, and the main chambers of commerce (including Paris), and later syndicate chambers, introduced arbitration and expertise services for the products most directly concerning their members (e.g., silk in Lyon).[39] It is nonetheless worth noting that in cases such as those of the Chamber of Paris, the legal validity of certificates of product quality required the adoption of a general state rule allowing the chamber to do so.[40] These attestations helped not only to settle possible disputes, but also to anticipate them precisely through a certificate of quality that was ultimately quite similar to the attestations and stamps widely used in the eighteenth century.[41] In case the involved parties still were in disagreement, the chambers provided arbitration. Only in the event that this mediation did not suffice and the parties went to court (justice of the peace, merchant courts, prud'hommes, civil courts), did the latter require a written statement from the same institutions confirming the existence of the trade custom.[42]

[37] Jean-Pierre Hirsch, *Les deux rêves du commerce*. Paris, EHESS, 1991.

[38] Claire Lemercier, "La chambre de commerce de Paris, acteur indispensable de la construction des norms économiques (première moitié du XIXe siècle)." *Genèse*, 50 (March 2003): 50–70.

[39] *Usages du conseil des prud'hommes de la ville de Lyon pou les industries de la soierie*. Lyon, 1872; Pierre Vernus, "Regulating the Activity of a Business Community: Employers' Organizations in the Lyon Silk Industry, 1860s–1939." *Business and Economic History on Line* 2 (2004), at: http://www.thebhc.org/BEH/O4/vernus.pdf

[40] Lemercier, "La chambre": 66.

[41] Philip Minard, *La fortune du colbertisme*. Paris, Fayard, 1998; Gayot, *Les draps*.

[42] Among others, see the factotums (judicial materials) at the BNF: Francisque et Joseph Renard frères, teinturiers à Lyon, 1863, *Affaire du rouge d'aniline, conclusions du ministère public*. Lyon, Imprimerie Renou et Maulde, 1863; *Affaire du rouge d'aniline. Gerber-Keller contre Renard frères et Franc, plaidoirie résumée de Me Arago*, Imprimerie Chaix, 1861; *Mulhouse, opposant-défendeur à la demande principale et à la demande en garantie contre Renard*

However, increasing uncertainties over the content and validity of "local customs" led several trade associations, legal experts and political representatives to suggest that these practices should be written down to reduce the risk of challenges. These views echoed favourably during the Second Empire when a survey was conducted to group trade customs into a code which would be granted legal validity. This ambition took concrete form in the law of 13 June 1866, which was limited to sales practices.[43] However, in the face of the diverse replies from the various trade associations, even in the same town, the project was abandoned.

This outcome testifies to the absence at this time of any agreement among the actors (even in the same region and belonging to the same trade category) regarding trade customs. This means that the economic actors did not oppose local practices and informal agreements to state law. On the contrary, they increasingly called upon state law to fill the void left by the fragmentation of tacit agreements and customs. There was no self-regulating world of business which was, as such, hostile to the intervention of public authorities. Quite the contrary, a strong majority of the business world called for state regulation of business practises and customs.

To sum up, codified commercial law was a source of inequalities and it did not disappear with the revolution. This law did not express interference by the state in the world of business, but was in fact ardently desired by part of it. Customs of trade were systematically included in state rules and code, and this request was sponsored by some business milieus. The question that remains is whether or not this outcome was specific to France.

A LAW FOR COMMERCE: A FRENCH SPECIFICITY?

The adaptation of French codes to the law in Italy, Germany, Austria and other Western countries reveals the interaction between the local

frères. Lyon, Imprimerie Chaix, 1861, *Recherches sur le rouge d'aniline ou rouges d'Hofman par F. Laurent et Casthelaz, décembre 1860*, Paris Baret; *Depoully et Gerber-Keller, utilisant l'oxygène comme agent réacteur, contre M. Renard et M. France utilisant le chlore et ne pouvant donc être coupables de contrefaçon*, Lyon, Imprimerie Renou et Maulde, 1860; *Le rouge d'aniline, tribunal civil de la Seine, 11 février 1860*, Paris, Baret, 1860. Also Natalis Rondot, *L'art de la soie. Les soies*, vol. 1. Paris, 1885.

[43] Hilaire, *Introduction*: 107–11.

law in place and the adaptation to French rules from the point of their formulation as well as their judicial interpretation.[44] In particular, in Italy prior to unification, the codes were introduced in different ways depending on the region. The differences were initially less obvious for the civil code than for the commercial code, which was even eliminated in the Kingdom of the Two Sicilies and considerably amended in Piedmont.[45] In Venetia, Lombardy and Trentino, the Austrian code of 1811 survived until 1865 (and even until 1918 for the regions annexed at that time only). Compared with the French code, the Austrian code was far more rooted in the principles of natural law; it contained no overall control of *negozio giuridico*, and civil liability remained rather limited.

The twofold influence of France and Austria was to be followed during the second half of the century by that of French and German law. The unification of Italian territory was accompanied by the extension of Piedmont rules to other regions. The new civil code was adopted in 1865, whereas the commercial code would have to wait until 1882. As was already the case in France, a commercial code distinct from the civil code was ardently desired by elected representatives and pressure groups with close ties to wholesale trade, banks and, in part, manufacturing.[46]

These borrowings and multiple circulation models came together in the relationship between the civil code and the commercial code. In most European countries (Switzerland was the chief exception), the general trend throughout the nineteenth century was to adopt the French separation between the two codes.[47] In Italy, the aspects debated were much like those I have mentioned in the case of France. It was a question of distinguishing tradesmen from other actors and defining the role of trade customs in relation to written sources. Italy

---

[44] Guido Alpa, *La cultura delle regole*. Bari, Laterza, 2000; Francesco Galgano, *Lex mercatoria*. Bologna, Il mulino, 2001; Jean-Louis Gazzaniga, *Introduction historique au droit des obligations*. Paris, LGDJ, 1992; A.W. Brian Simpson, *Legal Theory and Legal Thought. Essays on the Common Law*. London, Rocenverte, 1987; Harold Berman, *Law and Revolution*. Cambridge, Mass., Harvard University Press, 1983; Rodolfo Sacco, Antonio Gambaro, *Sistemi giuridici comparati*. Torino, Einaudi 1996.

[45] Alpa, *La cultura*: 85.

[46] Galgano, *Lex*: 106.

[47] Francesco Galgano, *Storia del diritto commerciale*. Bologna, Il mulino, 1980.

accepted the French presupposition of a special law for tradesmen. As a result, sales transactions made by tradesmen were controlled differently than sales under the civil code; like its French counterpart, the Italian commercial code established recourse to the civil code and ordinary jurisdiction if one of the parties was not a "tradesman" in the legal sense of the term.

This approach prevailed in Italy until the fascist period, when the separation between the two codes was criticised as being a "class" separation and, as such, incompatible with overcoming class divisions which was promoted by the fascist regime. The process of unification took place above all in the sense of a commercialisation of the civil code rather than the reverse. For example, the control of contracts and obligations, which were separated in the civil code, was now unified, as was already the case in the commercial code.

Another element supported unification in the sense of giving the commercial code precedence over the civil code and defining the role of the head of household. According to the rapporteur, the traditional legal figure of the "head of household" was to be replaced by the entrepreneur, hence the need to control economic and family relationships by the yardstick of commercial law rather than family law.

The outcome in Germany was somewhat similar. The first Prussian commercial code adopted in 1848 resembled the French code; trade transactions gave the actor tradesman status.[48] The commercial code of 1861 assigned priority to the tradesman and thereby controlled all economic relationships. This, too, was a "commercialisation" of law and a subordination of the other forms of trade to business transactions in the strict sense.

However, in the last quarter of the century, this principle was called into question. Many legal experts, supported by the tradesmen and manufacturing groups most concerned with the international market, thought that the civil and commercial codes were overly influenced by economic relationships within the domestic territory. As trade was becoming increasingly international, these commentators concluded that the commercial code had to be adapted to offer better protection

---

[48] Norbert Horn, Hein Kötz, Hans Leser, *German Private and Commercial Law: An Introduction.* Oxford, Oxford University Press, 1982.

to German firms. International contracts, the protection of industrial property and the specific features of business compared with other contracts were the core elements of this thinking.

The new German commercial code (HGB) adopted in 1900 was a compromise between these requirements and those of other pressure groups (small shopkeepers and manufacturers as well as consumer leagues and elected socialist representatives). At first glance, the code appeared to confirm the previous one inherited from the French code, according to which commercial law applied only to tradesmen. However, its novelty lay in strengthening the legal aspect of status definition. Tradesman status was no longer linked to trade transactions, and therefore to economic and legal action, but to the classification of the actor which preceded the transaction. For example, a doctor was not a "tradesman" unless he registered as such and set up a limited liability company.[49]

The implications of this legal definition were both similar to and different from those in France. As in France, tradesman status exempted the actor from providing written evidence in the event of a dispute; but in contrast to France, a contract between one tradesman and another could imply tacit acceptance of the latter's status (which the French civil code rejected).

The important role of travelling salesmen in the expansion of German trade and the rise of department stores encouraged another innovation; unlike English law, the new German code considered that, by definition, a sales agent acted on behalf of the principal. This simplified contracts, especially in the international market, and contributed to the expansion of German firms at the time.

And what of the Anglo-Saxon countries? According to the most widely held position, unlike continental European countries that resorted to codification, the Anglo-Saxon countries did not separate civil law from commercial law and usually relied on common law and case law decisions. Most importantly, traders and businessmen in general did not benefit from any special legal status.[50] In general, in

[49] Horn, Kötz, Leser, German: 214.
[50] John Commons, *Legal Foundations of Capitalism*. London and New York, Macmillan, 1924; Robert Ferguson, "Legal Ideology and Commercial Interests: The Social Origin of Commercial Law Codes." *British Journal of Law and Society*, 4, 1 (1977): 18–38; Keith

the United States and Great Britain, the idea underlying the criticism of commercial codification was not to oppose special business law to civil law that was valid for everyone. On the contrary, the ideal of judges and commentators was to permeate civil law, considered to be local and particular, with commercial law, held to be universal.[51]

At the same time, tendencies towards codification of rules acquired increasing weight over the nineteenth and twentieth centuries. In Great Britain, the .debate over codification took place above all between the last quarter of the nineteenth century and the First World War. Codification was supposed to reduce legal and economic costs.[52] This ambition found support in Great Britain in managing the Empire in order to increase the uniformity of rules and the stability of their interpretation throughout the dominions. The adoption of labour, credit and company codes in India, Australia and other places at the time[53] gave concrete form to this aim. The little-known history of commercial codes in the British dominions reveals a close relationship between Empire and codification. Consistent rules were sought not to overcome legal pluralism, which was highly tolerated, but rather to give it a hierarchical, institutional framework (with priority to English rules in certain areas and the possibility of resorting to local customs and jurisdictions, but only in the cases provided for by English law). Thus, the contract code adopted in India reproduced English law and case law pertaining to contracts and obligations. English rules were adopted for the other dominions, above all Australia and Canada. In South Africa, Ceylon and British Guyana, on the other hand, Dutch-Roman law was used as the source of English-style common law.

Renner, *The Institutions of Private Law and Their Social Functions*. London, RKP, 1949; J. Milnes Holden, *The History of Negotiable Instruments in English Law*. London, Athlon Press, 1955.

[51] Roscoe Pond, "Uniformity of Commercial Law on the American Continent." *Michigan Law Review*, 8, 2 (1909): 91–107.

[52] Robert Ferguson, "Legal Ideology and Commercial Interests: The Social Origins of the Commercial Law Codes." *British Journal of Law and Society*, 4, 1 (1977): 18–38; David Wilson, "Unification of the Law of Bills of Exchange." *Law Quarterly Review*, 2 (1886): 312; David Wilson, "The Recent Progress of Codification." *Juridical Review*, 3 (1891): 103.

[53] John Macdonell, "The Codification of the Commercial Law of the Empire." *Journal of the Society of Comparative Legislation*, 16, 2 (1916): 265–82.

At the turn of the century, the ambition to achieve a commercial code for the Empire also responded to issues that arose when companies operated in several territories of the Empire. The criteria for the transfer of shares and bankruptcy and credit law were mentioned as creating problems for transactions within an Empire that was increasingly integrated from an economic standpoint.

In the United States, the origin of the movement in support of codifying commercial law was altogether different. Here, the debate was part of broader discussions concerning the organisation of the federal government. Thus, in the middle of the nineteenth century, several judges and trade associations raised the issue of how to reconcile the priority of case law over legislation with the demand for common control, above all with regard to certain economic instruments. The case arose in particular for letters of exchange, an area in which federal case law solutions could create problems: Indeed, the lack of uniformity NOT the uniformity of judicial decisions and judges' approaches, combined with the legislative autonomy of the individual states, made it difficult to circulate letters of exchange within the American territory. Consequently, the Supreme Court assimilated letters of exchange negotiated between actors of different states to international circulation and hence, the rules were subject to "general commercial rules" rather than to local case law.

Commercial law thus became synonymous with uniform common law. As time went by, the decisions of the Supreme Court created a list of the areas of private law over which case law lost some of its autonomy.[54] This movement accelerated towards the end of the nineteenth century and even more in the twentieth century. Beginning in the 1930s and particularly after the Second World War, a vast movement of legal experts and lobbies pushed for the drafting of a "uniform commercial code" which would ensure consistency among the rules of the various states of the Union to be identified as genuine "commercial" law. The movement succeeded in 1962 with the adoption of a new code designated as "commercial law" which, in fact, is business law. It was a set of laws governing professionals, as opposed to

[54] Hovenkamp, *Enterprise*: 86–8; Tony Freyer, *Forums of Order: The Federal Courts and Business in American History*. Greenwich, Conn., JAI Press, 1979; Joseph Story, *Commentaries on the Conflicts of Law, Foreign and Inland*. Boston, C. C. Little and J. Brown, 1834.

relationships between professionals and consumers who did not come within this scope.[55]

To sum up, unlike civil law countries, common law countries experienced the first and to a given extent the second industrial revolution without a commercial code; a special legal status for "tradesman" was lacking. These disparities intervened much more than the celebrated opposition between jurisprudence and positive law (quite non-existent as such) in the institutional and economic dynamics of different areas. We have to understand how this general principle worked in the historical construction of markets in France and in the main Western countries.

---

[55] Roy Goode, "The Codification of Commercial Law." *Monash University Law Review*, 14 (1988): 135–57; Zipporah Batshaw Wiseman, "The Limits of Vision: Karl Llewellyn and the Merchant Rules." *Harvard Law Review*, 100, 2 (1967): 465–519.

PART II

TRADE AND MARKETPLACE

It is commonly held that in a market economy, market freedom implies that everyone can engage in trade and business. I have already questioned this assertion in examining how the status of economic actors was determined. Now I shall complete this analysis by looking first at the locations and then the methods of exchange. These three levels of the market and of capitalism have been masterfully described in the work of Braudel who amply demonstrated their complexity and interaction. He gives overall recognition to the various stages of capitalism without neglecting specific national or even regional and local features.[1] But why were markets organised in one particular way rather than another? How can we account for certain common traits (e.g., recourse to administrative regulations), whereas other aspects differ (e.g., the organisation of trades and professions)?

It is precisely because marketplaces did not take shape spontaneously and their transactions were not overseen by a supreme power (either God, Walrasian auctioneer or anyone else) that it is important to understand the rules of their construction and operation. A market was, first and foremost, a meeting place, as well as an area comprising shops, stalls and warehouses, tradesmen and goods. Each of these components needed to be defined and redefined before, during and after the exchange for the latter to take place. I will show that closed markets and shop regulation were not specific to

---

[1] Fernand Braudel, *Civilisation matérielle, économie et capitalisme, XVe–XVIIIe siècles.* Paris, Armand Colin, 1979.

pre-industrial economies or to France, but could be found in most Western countries. This was due to the fact that the political and social order of the cities heavily influenced market organisation. I shall begin by studying closed markets, before going on to shops and produce exchange.

3

COVERED MARKETS

The theory of pure, perfect competition presupposes freedom to enter the market. When barriers exist to prevent entry, prices rise at the expense of consumers and in favour of the virtual monopolies present in the market.

In contrast, partisans of regulation emphasise the unequal strength of the actors and the imperfect circulation of information; excessive competition is said to lead to reduced quality and company concentration. Hence they evoke the need to control entry into the market. This control concerns two main aspects: the type of barrier and how to ensure compliance with it. With regard to the first point, several types of barrier are possible; one solution, for example, is to assign places on a first come–first served basis; *numerus clausus* is often practiced by European universities and for determining the location of shops in cities.

The second solution consists of charging a fee to enter the market – for example, a license or a deposit. The higher the fee, the fewer actors there will be in the market. This solution is used today for taxis, whereas in the past it was applied, for example, to commodities brokers which we are going to study here. Another form of barrier consists of requiring a diploma; this is the case today for most "liberal" professions and in the past for guilds and apprenticeship contracts.

The fourth way of regulating entry into the market consists of requiring that the actor comply with certain terms – for example, charge a certain price or provide uninterrupted service. In general, license

First version of this chapter translated by Susan Taponier.

contracts contain such clauses. Each of these solutions, as well as combinations of them, has been adopted. For example, chemists are subject to restrictions regarding diplomas, access to shops and retail outlet regulations. Economic theory specifies the criteria for ensuring that a solution will be effective; different professions have different rules.[1]

These rules should be distinguished from the methods of applying barriers. In particular, mechanisms are required to detect and punish cheaters[2] such as circulating information regarding compliance with regulations by a given actor. For some, these ex-post controls (certification, sanctions) are still preferable to entry barriers, because they avoid monopoly positions while guaranteeing the services offered to the end consumer.

Others have observed, however, that certification and sanctions alone are not enough, partly because they do not exclude cheating and partly because they are difficult to put into practice and evaluate. Indeed, control mechanisms can be interior (e.g., through guilds or professional orders) or exterior to the group. In the first case, a profession – let us say the order of dentists – verifies compliance with entry norms (diploma) and operating norms (pricing, ethics). In the second case, an outside authority (a certifier, the state, municipalities) oversees the actors' activity and calls upon the same institution or another mobilised for the occasion, such as the courts, to pronounce sanctions in the event of a failure to comply with the norms. The first solution is more effective than the second only when the particular trade involved manages to avoid any form of cheating or collusion. For some, this objective is achieved through market pressure, because the entire profession or group of producers can be punished for the bad conduct of a few (this has been the case for winemakers which we will

---

[1] Shirley Svorny, "Licensing, Market Entry Regulation." In Boundewijn Bouckaert, Gerrit de Geest (eds.), *Encyclopedia of Law and Economics*. Aldershot, Edward Elgar, 2000, vol. 5: 296–328; Roger Blair, Stephen Rubin (eds.), *Regulating the Professions: A Public-Policy Symposium*. Lexington, MA, Lexington Books, 1980; J. L. Berlant, *Profession and Monopoly. A Study of Medicine in Great-Britain and the USA*. Berkeley, University of California Press, 1975; Corinne Glib, *Hidden Hierarchies: The Professions and Government*. New York, Harper and Row, 1966; Lucien Karpik, *Les avocats. Entre l'Etat, le public et le marché, XIXe–XXe siècles*. Paris, Gallimard, 1995.

[2] Jan Der Hartog, "General Theories of Regulation." In *Encyclopaedia of Law and Economics*, vol. 5: 223–70.

examine later). However, this argument becomes questionable when we recall the problems that end consumers face when they try to have an effect on the producer's reputation. Critics of the *Appellation d'Origine Contrôlée* use the same argument to challenge the legitimacy of these quality labels as a component of certification.[3]

In reality, these outcomes depend on the relationships that the actors (professions, institutions, economic actors) establish between professional opportunities and the public interest. It is generally agreed that due to the danger of malpractice, an entry barrier (a diploma) is necessary for doctors but less so for taxi drivers. Of course, the same profession may be subject to varying regulations in different contexts. For example, entry into the butchery market can be of major importance due to fears related to meat consumption. On the contrary, regulation of the butchery trade becomes less important in contexts marked by safe meat supply and quality.

In the following pages, we will look at the way in which market access was determined between the end of the eighteenth century and the early twentieth century in three marketplaces: covered markets, shops and produce exchanges. None of these three markets took form spontaneously nor were their operations left to market self-regulation. We will see that in all three cases, there was considerable regulation over the long term in all the countries studied. This regulation relied on economic factors and ethical considerations, even in the context of advanced capitalism.

Covered markets are an important reference point in neoclassical thought which used them as an example of a competitive market involving a uniform group of actors and undifferentiated products. The models of general market equilibrium proposed by Walras[4] and Edgeworth[5] were clearly inspired by this type of market.

---

[3] Alessandro Stanziani, "Wine Reputation and Quality Controls: The Origins of the AOC in Nineteenth Century France." *European Journal of Law and Economics*, 18, 2 (2004): 149–67.

[4] Léon Walras, *Éléments d'économie politique pure ou théorie de la richesse sociale*. Lausanne, Corbaz, 1874.

[5] Francis Ysidro Edgeworth, *Mathematichal Psychics. An Essay on the Application of Mathematics to the Moral Sciences*. London, Kegan Paul, 1881.

The neo-institutionalist approach, on the other hand, associates fairs and markets with pre-industrial economies in which trading took place occasionally and merchants met only periodically.[6] The rise of capitalism is said to have gradually eliminated this logic and thus deprived such markets of their *raison d'être*. This argument has been challenged by demonstrating the importance of fairs and markets in the eighteenth and nineteenth centuries without necessarily interpreting the phenomenon as proof of a "delay" in capitalist development.[7] Even today, as a number of economic and sociological studies show, consumers go to covered markets to have contact with tradesmen, which is lacking in supermarkets. This goes hand in hand with purchasing products of non-standardised quality.

In many respects, these conceptions of the marketplace are opposed; for some, such markets are the expression of the pre-industrial world, for others, of industrial and post-industrial societies. Some maintain that covered markets imply undifferentiated actors and products; others say they imply produce classification and personal contact.

There is some truth in each of these interpretations, but all of them leave out an essential aspect, namely that covered markets have always been strictly controlled, not only in pre-industrial times but afterwards and even today. When viewed over the very long term, they have probably been the most regulated markets in history. Rules govern access to stalls as well as transactions and goods inspection. It is only after the actors had been selected and product quality determined that transactions could take place and relationships established between the actors. Regulation of covered markets has played an important role over the very long term, before and after the rise of industrial capitalism. In order to articulate this point, we are going to study, at first, covered market regulation in some areas of Ancien Régime France; we will then consider covered market regulation in nineteenth-century France; finally, we will compare these features to those of other countries and municipalities outside France.

---

[6] Paul Milgrom, Douglass North, Berry Weingast, "The Role of Institutions in the Revival of Trade: The Law Merchant, Private Judges and the Champagne Fairs." *Economics and Politics*, 2 (1990): 1–23.

[7] Dominique Margairaz, *Foires et marchés dans la France préindustrielle*. Paris, EHESS, 1988; Jack Thomas, *Le temps des foires. Foires et marchés dans le Midi toulousains de la fin de l'Ancien Régime à 1914*. Toulouse, Presses universitaires du Mirail, 1993.

Let us look at covered markets under the Ancien Régime. Even though all the studies of these markets have emphasised regulatory power, they have only recently tried to clarify its meaning and scope in a given city. As a general rule, access to a covered market was a multilateral game between the municipality, the professional order and individual traders (and their networks).

For example, butchery was a free trade in Toulouse from the standpoint of apprenticeship and stall acquisition. In the butcher's contract with the municipality, he was required to buy and sell in a specific place. The butcher received an exclusive lease; he had a monopoly in the neighbourhood, but in exchange, he had to get his supplies from certain markets and sell to the city population as a matter of priority. He was also required to have a stock of meat on hand. Exclusive contracts were given not only to supply sources but also to slaughterhouses. The licensee did not necessarily own the butchery.[8]

Licenses provided for prior definition of the respective liabilities of the municipality and the licensee. In Toulouse, before 1779 (the date of the return to a system of exclusion, after an attempt to liberalise butchery), in the event of a famine or epizootic, if the butcher was unable to get his meat supply, the municipality could terminate his contract. Starting in 1779, licensing rules came to resemble those we know today: The licensee assumed sole liability when signing a tender contract (*contrat d'ajudication*).

In Paris, most trades relating to food and beverages were governed by the guild system; as in Toulouse, the guild and the municipality engaged in a selection process to award a stall or shop, particularly for the sale of bread and meat.[9] This system was in fact quite complex, and the guilds by no means controlled the market. The different places of trade were organised into a hierarchy both by the actors (Parisians, non-Parisian [*forain*] and itinerant stallholders, legal and illegal, guild members or not) and products. Several qualities of meat were available in butcher shops, but meat that was less fresh,

---

[8] Jeanne-Marie Tuffery, *Ebauche d'un droit de la consommation. La protection du chaland sur les marchés toulousains au XVIIe et au XVIIIe siècles*. Paris, LGDJ, 1998: 148–50, 159, 172.

[9] Steve Kaplan, *Le meilleur pain du monde*. Paris, Fayard, 1996; Sidney Watts, "Boucherie et hygiène à Paris au XVIIIe siècle." *Revue d'histoire moderne and contemporaine*, 51–3 (2004): 79–103; Louis-Sebastien Mercier, *Tableau de Paris*, Amsterdam, 1, 1783.

if not nearly rotten, was only available at certain markets or from forain stallholders.

The same complexity characterised the relationship between retail outlets (shops, covered markets, open markets) and wholesale outlets. The authorities designated and controlled the location of wholesale markets; thus, in Paris, beef merchants and butchers met in Poissy and Sceaux. Lots were drawn for places, as some had greater visibility than others, and trading started at the sound of a bell. Merchants were required to sell the meat and return any unsold animals the following day. In theory, there was free access to these markets, at least as regards the actors (product acceptance, on the other hand, was more complex, as we shall see); however, the authorities were careful to keep watch over ties between merchants to prevent any collusion or coalition that might harm the working of the market.[10]

This hierarchical world was not exclusively defined by regulation. Regulated markets were predominant, but unregulated markets sprang up alongside them and were officially or informally approved by the authorities. Such formal and informal rules were aimed at controlling markets, notably food markets, for a specific purpose: to ensure a sufficient quality of the product concerned, in precisely identified qualities and at fair prices.[11] This latter aspect rules out the possibility of interpreting regulations under the Ancien Régime based on later economic analyses. The choice between a barrier to entry and certification, as well as between self-certification and control on the part of an outside authority, cannot be evaluated solely on the basis of cost-effectiveness in keeping with the objective of maximising profit. On the contrary, extra-economic criteria played an equally important role in public policies. Their aim was not to maximise the utility of undifferentiated consumers by minimising prices (the criterion of the pure competitive model), but to ensure a correspondence between price, quality and actors in a hierarchical order, which, although not rigid, was nevertheless supposed to remain relatively stable.

[10] Raynald Abad, *Le grand marché*. Paris, Fayard, 2004: 208.
[11] Monica Martinat, *Le "juste" marché. Le système annonaire romain au XVIe et XVIIe siècles*. Rome, Ecole française, 2005.

Did this aim and these forms of regulation disappear with the revolution? The answer is no, at least as regards closed markets. Local authorities – the municipalities and prefectures – were in charge of applying market rules.[12] Covered markets belonged to municipalities or to long-standing owners who were required to rent them to municipalities.[13] The rental price was controlled: It was calculated *ad valorem* or on the basis of the rented surface area (the latter criterion was established during the Second Empire under pressure from trade associations).

This is the legal framework in which conflicts over assigned places in the markets should be analysed. The question is whether the limited number of places in closed markets still came under the public licensing system, as it did in the previous period, or whether other factors entered into the picture. In theory, the municipality was free to assign places through a tender procedure. However, this solution was rarely used in practice, particularly as it often gave rise to conflicts between the municipality and the tendering merchant on the one hand and between the municipality and other merchants or their trade association on the other. As a result, municipalities preferred to rely on customary trade criteria – that is, they took into account suggestions from trade associations or even those of the merchant who was releasing his stall. In the latter case, it was the merchant who indicated his successor, usually one of his children, but it could also be a member of his extended family or even an apprentice.[14] In 1868, however, a municipal ordinance prohibited these "inherited" forms as outside

---

[12] Laws of 16 August 1790 and 28 March 1790.

[13] Decree 27 March 1814; ordonnances 27 May 1819 and 2 June 1829; Alfred de Cilleuls, *Histoire de l'administration parisienne au XIXe siècle*. Paris, Champion (1900), 2 vol. Vol. 2: 14–15. Archives documents: at the National Archives (AN): closed market regulation, years 1702–1823: F 12 1228–1286; years 1829–1867: F 11 2846; years 1902–1940: F 10 2174. Police regulation in F 2, 2764–2770 (years 1871–1938). ACCIP (archives de la chambre de commerce and de l'industrie de Paris): sery II-2.11: Halles and markets; sery II-2.13 (1): wheat markets 1901–1913; sery II-2.13 (2): wheat markets 1914–1926; sery II-2.14 (1): oil market 1883–1940; II-2.17 (1): and (2): sugar, regulation, classifications, grades, prices etc., 1838–1907. On stocks: ACCIP, II-3.10 (1): 1853–1891, II-3.10 (2): 1890–1952; on Magasins généraux, ACCIP, II-3.20 (1): 1859–1894, II-3.20 (2): 1883–1907, II-3.20 (3): 1908–1929.

[14] ADS (archives départementales de la Seine), DU.2 F 4, DA 380.

the scope of public licensing, as well as outside any control by trade associations.[15]

The interests of municipalities and trade associations also converged in the controls to which covered market merchants were subject. As before under the Ancien Régime,[16] the municipality could always reproach the stallholder for providing only intermittent service.[17] It often happened that merchants who had to run an errand or who temporarily abandoned their stalls, left the neighbour in the next stall in charge. However, the town hall and the prefecture intervened when such absences were repeated and ended up being tantamount to subletting the stall. This prohibition was extended to apprentices in 1868.[18] There appear to have been two considerations behind these provisions; firstly, it was in the interest of the municipality to have merchants in covered markets offer continuous service. This continuity requirement was a legacy from the license system, but it was also justified by the legal definition of tradesman which, as we have seen, included continuity of activity as one of its justifications. Secondly, continuity was also demanded by trade associations which feared they might otherwise lose control over places in the market as well as over the flow of merchants and apprentices.

Merchants, trade associations and municipalities did not always agree on the public order of the market. The merchants thought that in exchange for their continuous presence at the market, as well as their lease and paid trade tax, they should have a right to a position of oligopoly. In other words, when a municipality decided to open a new covered market, the tradesmen at the markets already in place demanded compensation. This confirms the fact that, from the point of view of the economic actors, free competition was supposed to be exercised within a predetermined group and hence did not preclude other forms of protection and exclusion. However, most of the judges who ruled on these cases refused to grant this demand insofar as the

---

[15] *Moniteur universel*, 17 November (1868); ADS, APP DA 380.

[16] Tuffery, *Ebauche*; Abad, *Le grand marché*; Kaplan, *Le meilleur*.

[17] AN F 11 (subsistance), dossier 2846, several documents; Maurice Block, *Dictionnaire de l'administration française*. Paris, Berger-Levrault, 1855, vol. 1: 258–9.

[18] Victoria Thompson, "Urban Renovation, Moral Regeneration: Domesticating the Halles in Second-Empire Paris." *French Historical Studies*, 20, 1 (1977): 87–109.

lease or payment of the trade tax were not considered equivalent to the purchase of a position under the leasing system or a monopoly (as was the case for notaries and brokers).

In short, unlike most economic theories, covered markets were not free markets, because access to places and rules of exchange were strictly regulated. This was so not only because authorities associated public order with a regulated market, but also because well-identified economic lobbies wanted it. For example, unlike other trades and the butchery trade in other cities, Parisian butchery was regulated until 1858. There was free access between 1791 and 1811, whereas *numerus clausus* was adopted between 1811 and 1825 which, following a short period of deregulation, was reintroduced in 1828. It was not until 1858 that opening a butcher shop was finally liberalised.[19] To do so, authorities and lobbies called upon two different models. The partisans of *numerus clausus* considered competition to be synonymous with speculation, price increases and fraud regarding quality;[20] conversely, their opponents maintained that it was precisely the butchers' monopoly that caused such distortions.[21]

In general, wholesale merchants were opposed to *numerus clausus* in the hope of thereby taking advantage of competition among butchers. The latter, on the contrary, were usually favourable to market regulation, above all if it was accompanied by the introduction of a system of privileged financing (the Poissy "caisse"), inherited from the Ancien Régime.[22]

However, these measures did not depend solely on the relative strength of pressure groups, but also on administrative orientations. As in the eighteenth century, during the first half of the nineteenth century, the aim was not to maximise efficiency and minimise costs nor thwart the imperfections of the market, but rather to ensure a sufficient supply of good quality meat at a given price to give the entire urban population access to the product. This objective was combined with the other which consisted of maintaining equivalencies

[19] AN F 11 2846; M. Joubert, *De la viande à bon marché et du commerce de la boucherie.* Paris, Garnier, 1851: 33, 34.
[20] Joubert, *De la viande*: 29, 46–7.
[21] Albert Menant, Emile Caullet, "Boucherie." In Yves Guyot, Alexis Raffalovitch, *Dictionnaire du commerce, de l'industrie et de la banque.* Paris, Guillaumin, 1901, vol. 1: 599–606.
[22] AN F 11 2835, 2846.

and relatively stable hierarchies between prices, qualities of meat and classes of consumers.[23] However, this model came under fire during the Second Empire, when a majority of political leaders henceforth considered that only the free market led to satisfying the needs of the population, while at the same time respecting the relationship between price and quality.

On the basis of all this, changeover of liberalisation and regulation should be qualified; liberalisation in 1858 officially marked the end of *numerus clausus* and the opening of the meat market. In reality, the number of butchers and markets had been growing for several decades by then. Hence the change in prices hardly corresponded to phases of "freedom" and "regulation". Free markets did not always bring lower prices while regulation did not always stabilize prices. Again, we must ask whether this trend reflected a specificity of French capitalism.

REGULATING COVERED MARKETS:
A FRENCH SPECIFICITY?

The orientations we have studied were not specific to France but were found in the main European countries and the United States throughout the period under study. In all these countries, access to places and transactions in covered markets were regulated.[24] Licenses

---

[23] AN F 11 2846, in particular: "Rapports du ministère des travaux publics, de l'agriculture et de l'industrie au ministère des affaires étrangères, 28 décembre 1837"; *Mémoire sur le commerce de la boucherie*, par Lepecq (syndic), Ingé, Dolbel, Parget, Evrard, Roux and Fayel, adjoints. Paris, Imprimerie de Lebegue, 1838; Jean de la Pilorgerie, *De la viande de boucherie and de la taxe sur les bestiaux à Nantes*. Nantes, Imprimerie Camille Mellinet, 1841; *Journal de la chambre syndicale de la boucherie de Paris*, several years (1841–1854).

[24] Gary Libecap, "The Rise of the Chicago Packers and the Origin of the Meat Inspection and Antitrust." *Economic Inquiry*, 30 (1992): 242–62; Robert Dupré, "If It Is Yellow, It Must be Butter: Margarine Regulation in North America Since 1886." *Journal of Economic History*, 59, 2 (1992): 353–71; Donna Wood, "The Strategic Use of Public Policy: Business Support for the 1906 Food and Drug Act." *Business History Review*, 59, 3 (1985): 403–32; Alain Olmstead, Paul Rhode, "The Tuberculosis Cattle Trust: Disease Contagion in an Era of Regulatory Uncertainty." *Journal of Economic History*, 64, 4 (2004): 929–63; Edward J.T. Collins, "Food Adulteration and Food Safety in Britain in the Nineteenth and Early Twentieth Centuries." *Food Policy*, April (1993): 95–108; Peter Atkins, "Sophisticated Detected, or the Adulteration of the Milk Supply, 1850–1914." *Social History*, 16, 3 (1991): 300–21; John J. Burnett, *The History of Food Adulteration in Britain in the Nineteenth Century, with Special Reference to Bread, Tea and Beer*. PhD Dissertation (University of London): 1958; John Burnett, *Liquid Pleasure*. London and New York, Routledge, 1999;

and authorisations were omnipresent, and generally speaking, covered markets were among the most highly regulated. Thus, in London, in the nineteenth century, the opening of new markets, particularly meat markets, systematically generated protests from the merchants already in place and had to be negotiated between the various trade associations and the municipality. As in Paris, access to the market was also conditioned on the availability of slaughterhouses. The prohibition of private slaughterhouses made access to slaughterhouses crucial, and in this context, the presence of one or more slaughterhouses and their type (municipal or private) naturally influenced stockbreeders' access to city markets, along with the rise of wholesalers and specialised butchers (capable of cutting up meat) for new butchers who lacked the skill.[25] In London, too, closed markets were looked upon as a public service,[26] and ethical factors entered into their regulation in the eighteenth and nineteenth centuries.[27]

Even in the United States, the number of norms in this sector was constantly increasing. In the municipality of Philadelphia alone, 150 ordinances concerning covered markets were adopted between 1789 and 1889.[28] Let us take the case of regulation most widely discussed at the time and since then by legal experts and economic historians. It involved the creation of a municipal slaughterhouse in New Orleans

Frederick Arthur Filby, *A History of Food Adulteration and Analysis*. London, Allen and Unwin, 1934; Michael French, Jim Phillips, *Cheated Not Poisoned? Food Regulation in the United Kingdom, 1875–1938*. Manchester, Manchester University Press, 2000.

[25] Richard Perren, "The Meat and Livestock Trade in Britain, 1850–1870." *The Economic History Review*, 28, 3 (1975): 385–400; William A. Robson, *The Government and Misgovernment of London*. London, Allen and Unwin, 1939; Rob A. Atkinson, Graham Moon, *Urban Policy in Britain*. Basingstoke, Macmillan, 1994; James Schmiechen, Keneth Carls, *The British Market Hall. A Social and Architectural History*. New Haven, Yale University Press, 1999.

[26] Don Shakow, "The Municipal Farmer's Market as an Urban Service." *Economic Geography*, 57, 1 (1981): 68–77.

[27] Edward P. Thompson, "The Moral Economy of the English Crowd in the Eighteenth Century." *Past and Present*, 50 (1971): 70–136.

[28] William Novak, "Public Economy and the Well-Ordered Market: Law and Economic Regulation in Nineteenth Century America." *Law and Social Enquiry*, 18, 1 (1993): 1–32. Also: Susan Henderson, "Out of the Ashes: The Great Fire and the Transformation of London's Public Markets." *Radical History Review*, 21 (1979): 119–30; Jon Teaford, *The Municipal Revolution in America: Origins of Modern Urban Government, 1650–1825*. Chicago, University of Chicago Press, 1975; Thomas De Voe, *The Market Book: A History of the Public Markets of the City of New York*. 1862, reprint New York, Augustus M. Kelley Publishers, 1970.

in 1867. This measure came after years of expanding meat consumption, accompanied by a multiplication of private slaughterhouses and of health accidents, notably poisoning but above all, yellow fever. An investigating commission discovered that the epidemics were due to slaughterhouse dumps located in Mississippi upstream from the city. Drinking water had been affected. The solution was found in building a municipal slaughterhouse in keeping with the norms adopted during the Napoleonic period in France, which had once again become topical with the Villette slaughterhouse construction project.[29] The monopoly was immediately challenged by the managers of other slaughterhouses and some consumer associations that thought the measure was aimed more at raising the price of meat than protecting the health of consumers. In 1873, the case was brought to the Supreme Court which legitimated the possibility of an institutional monopoly. The Court's decision, often interpreted as the result of lobbying or even corruption, in fact responded to the principles of a large percentage of American judges at the time, who believed that public services justified a monopoly position precisely in the name of public utility. In any event, the rise of municipal regulations clearly shows that the process of urban expansion and the marketing process related to it were based on rather tight control of markets and that this control was viewed not only as compatible with but even indispensable to a competitive order.[30] The federal government, the states of the Union and the municipalities intervened considerably in the control of markets, according to a logic that was shared by business lobbies, consumer movements, judges and public opinion which was increasingly favourable to these measures.[31]

Market regulation for health reasons and social equilibrium was a form of regulationism that ultimately proved to be negative for the economy as a whole and therefore also for the main categories it theoretically sought to protect (the poorest).[32] In other words, in Western

---

[29] Hovenkamp, *The Transformation*: 118–25.

[30] Novak, "Public Economy".

[31] J. Willard Hurst, *Law and the Condition of Freedom in the Nineteenth Century United States.* Madison, Wis., University of Wisconsin Press, 1956; Morton Horwitz, *The Transformation of American Law, 1780–1860.* Cambridge, MA, Harvard University Press, 1977.

[32] Marc Law, "The Origin of State Pure Food Regulation." *Journal of Economic History*, 63, 4 (2003): 1103–30.

countries, public control over covered markets was a common phenomenon not only during the pre-industrial period but even afterwards. Regulating access of actors to covered markets and monitoring
their operations responded to common concerns about reconciling
markets with social hierarchies and food safety. In no case was the free
market viewed as the sole solution to these problems; on the contrary, inadequate circulation of information, the importance attached
to qualitative classification and the link between ethics and the market
led administrative, political and court officials to view flexible regulation as the best way to control the markets. Of course, to ensure that
control was effective, it had to be extended to other marketplaces,
beginning with shops.

4

THE WORLD OF SHOPS

Historians often associate shops with the growth of cities, and literary works from Molière to Zola frequently seized the opportunity to attack the profit-oriented mentality of shopkeepers in a "moralising" tone. There were of course less stereotyped and more favourable images of the world of shopkeeping; they became widespread at particular moments, for example in the late nineteenth century, when department stores appeared to be swallowing up traditional shops, or nowadays, when the small neighbourhood grocery shop is seen as the last rampart against supermarkets.[1]

But what were the rules that governed the colourful world of shops over time? Was the shop level the expression of free market capitalism?

The criteria for access to shops were important: The possibility of renting or buying shop premises, the capital invested and hence the financing of the business were essential factors. This is where marriage and dowry (at least in continental Europe) contracts

[1] Franco Angiolini, Daniel Roche, *Cultures et formations négociantes dans l'Europe moderne.* Paris, EHESS, 1995; Louis Duclos, *Des transformations du commerce de détail en France au 19e siècle.* Paris, L. Boyer, 1902; Alain Faure, "L'épicerie parisienne au 19ᵉ siècle ou la corporation éclatée." *Le mouvement social*, 108 (1979): 89–104; Jacques Marseille (ed.), *La révolution commerciale en France. Du "Bon marché" à l'hypermarché.* Paris, Le Monde-éditions, 1997; Barrie M. Ratcliffe, "The Business Elite and the Development of Paris: Intervention in Ports and Entrepôts, 1814–1834." *The Journal of European Economic History*, 14, 1 (1985): 95–142; Natacha Coquery (ed.), *La Boutique et la ville. Commerces, commerçants, espaces et clientèles, XVIe–XXe siècle. Actes du colloque des 2, 3 and 4 décembre 1999 organisé par l'université François Rabelais de Tours.*Tours, Centre d'histoire de la ville moderne and contemporaine/Publications de l'université François Rabelais, 2000; Geoffrey Crossick, Heinz-Gerhard Haupt (eds.), *Shopkeepers and Master Artisans in Nineteenth Century Europe.* London, Meuthen, 1984.

entered in: Their rules strongly interacted with the evolution of small capitalism. In the following pages, after discussing the general dynamics of the world of shopkeeping in France, we will study the link between shops and marriage contracts. We will also show that, over time, namely during the second half of the nineteenth century, these traditional forms of financing business and family units declined. New forms of capital then emerged, in particular intangible capital: goodwill and reputation. We will study their features and identification and the rules governing their circulation. The final section of this chapter will seek to explain the evolution of the world of shops at the turn of the nineteenth and twentieth centuries.

Retail trade in France has been studied at the regional and nationwide levels; these studies demonstrate the importance of display, contact (i.e., shops as a place for sociability) and business growth, which can be summed up by long-term stability with peaks of success and periods of crisis when bankruptcies increased. The trend remained upwards throughout the nineteenth century. Around 1900, there were about 13 small shops for every 1,000 inhabitants.[2] In terms of specialisation, food sellers, off-license managers and hoteliers were the most numerous. Towards the end of the nineteenth century, family-owned businesses clearly dominated the world of shops in France: about half of the 1,129,000 trade establishments had neither salaried workers nor employees, and in establishments that did have personnel, there were, on average, just three employees or salaried workers.[3]

At the same time, shops were threatened by instability and polarisation. In Lyon, in 1911, half of the small shopkeepers bequeathed less than 5,000 francs − the value of a mediocre business. Again in 1911, an estimated 21 per cent of Parisian shopkeepers had suffered a loss in revenue over the ten previous years, 27 per cent found their situation

[2] Jean-Pierre Daviet, *La société industrielle en France. 1814–1914*. Paris, Seuil, 1997: 237.
[3] Heinz-Gerhard Haupt, "Les petits commerçants et la politique sociale: l'exemple de la loi sur le repos hebdomadaire." *Bulletin du Centre d'histoire de France contemporaine*, 8 (1987): 20; Jean Lalouette; "Débits de boisson et discours bourgeois". In Lion Murard, Patrick Zylberman (eds.), *L'haleine des faubourgs. Ville, habitat et santé au 19e siècle*. Fontenay-sous-bois, Ed. Recherches, 1978: 346–7.

unchanged, 38 per cent noted a certain improvement and only 14 per cent had grown rich.[4]

This data appears to back up the view of observers at the time and historians since then, who point to department stores as one of the main causes of the decline of shops. Although this is true, the picture must be qualified. Department stores are said to profit from advertising more than small shops. However, the effect of advertising remains uncertain because it may contribute to better informing consumers and making the market more competitive or on the contrary, push in the opposite direction.[5]

Yet competition involves not only selling and marketing strategies, but also, and mainly, access to credit. The latter can be divided into three main components: 1) initial capital which, in the world of nineteenth-century shops, was basically equivalent to the dowry contributed by the shopkeeper's wife; 2) credit properly speaking, which consisted primarily of commercial loans granted by other shopkeepers and above all by the shopkeeper's wholesale suppliers; 3) the possibility for the shopkeeper to pledge his know-how and clientele, hence his reputation (or goodwill). The history of shops is linked to the history of these three sources of financing. In the following pages, we are going to examine them in detail; we will look at the evolution of the marriage contract with the slow decline in the role of dowries in the nineteenth century and, from there, the increased importance of other sources of financing.

[4] Pierre Léon, *Géographie de la fortune et structure sociale à Lyon au 19e siècle*. Lyon, Presses universitaires de Lyon, 1974. Also Parliament enquiries in archives: AN sery C (parliamentary archives) dossiers 7455 (*Grand commerce de détail*), 7456 (*Petit commerce*), 7457 (*coopératives, chambres de commerce*); 7458, 7459 (*Commerce*).

[5] Roy Church, "New Perspectives on the History of Products, Firms, Marketing, and Consumers in Britain and the United States since the Mid-Nineteenth Century." *Economic History Review*, LII, 3 (1999): 406–35; Nicholas Alexander, Gary Akerhurst, "Introduction: The Emergence of Modern Retailing, 1750–1950." *Business History*, 40 (1998): 1–15; Patricia Baird, *Advertising Process: American Business and the Rise of Consumer Marketing*. Baltimore, John Hopkins University, 1998; Stanley D. Chapman, *Merchant Enterprise in Britain: From the Industrial Revolution Until World War I*. Cambridge, Cambridge University Press, 1982; Philip Kotler, *Marketing Management*. Upper Saddle River, NJ, and London, 1976, 1988; Terry R. Nevett, *Advertising in Britain: A History*. London, Heinemann, 1980; Richard Schmalensee, *The Economics of Advertising*. Amsterdam and London, North-Holland, 1972; Susan Strasser, *Satisfaction Guaranteed: The Making of the American Mass Market*. Seattle, Washington, University of Washington Press, 1995.

THE SHOP AND THE MARRIAGE CONTRACT

For shops, the contribution of capital was linked to both the credit market and the marriage contract;[6] one was inconceivable without the other. For example, in nineteenth-century Paris, the sons of shopkeepers sought to marry the daughters of shopkeepers in nearly 60 per cent of cases,[7] whereas the chances of this occurring dropped to 25 per cent for the sons of domestics or labourers. This was often the only way an apprentice could open his own shop. Conversely, there was a greater chance for a shopkeeper's son to lose social status when he married the daughter of a domestic, a factory worker or a labourer.

However, marrying the daughter of an established tradesman was not merely a matter of luck; whereas the attitude and above all the income and possible capital of the suitor were important, the definition of marriage contract clauses also entered into these negotiations. The contracts sought to anticipate the possible pitfalls the family and its business might face.[8] This process was complex, for not only were forecasts often proved wrong by events, but also because the drafting of the marriage contract could not always be reconciled with the various anticipated needs (to have sufficient resources and maintain the family and its business in the present and future). Thus, movable property (shares, a business) could either be contributed by one of the spouses or acquired by both in the course of their marriage. In the first case, a decision had to be made as to whether this property would enter into the community of property between spouses.[9] In nineteenth-century France, when the dowry system was declining,[10] community

---

[6] Jean-Pierre Hirsch, *Les deux rêves du commerce*. Paris, EHESS, 1992; Yves Guyot, *Le commerce et le commerçant*. Paris, Douin, 1909; Jean-Claude Daumas, *L'amour du drap, Blin and Blin, 1827–1975. Histoire d'une entreprise familiale*. Besançon, Presses universitaires franc-comtoises, 1999; Pierre Lamard, *Histoire d'un capital familial au 19e siècle*. Belfort, Société belfortaine d'émulation, 1988.

[7] Jean Le Yaouanq, "La mobilité sociale dans le milieu boutiquier parisien au 19e siècle." *Le mouvement social*, 108 (1979): 88–112.

[8] ADS (archives départementales de la Seine) D11 U 3 (bankruptcy files).

[9] ADS D 11 U 3. Also Faure, "L'épicerie parisienne"; Florence Laroche-Gisserot, "Pratiques de la dot en France au XIXe siècle." *Annales ESC*, 6 (1988): 1433–52.

[10] Hirsch, *Les deux rêves*. Also Madeleine Faucheux, *Le choix du régime matrimoniale*. PhD dissertation (University of Paris II): 1979. Raoul Raymond, *Le déclin du régime dotal*. PhD dissertation (University of Aix): 1942.

of property remained the rule in marriage contracts in general and in those of shopkeepers in particular. The solution increasingly practiced during the nineteenth century consisted of limiting the community to after-acquired property.[11] Let us take the case of a shop that was contributed in the woman's dowry. In this case, with simple community of property or community limited to after-acquired property, the husband claimed his right to administer and therefore control the business. Countless disputes over this point gave rise to considerable case law development: The husband systematically won.[12]

At the same time, in the course of the nineteenth century, the role of dowries was diminishing in trades as well as in other sectors. Thus, towards the end of the century, in Parisian grocery stores, only 15 per cent of the capital contributions from wives enabled the takeover of a business.[13] This dynamic was linked to the erosion and differentiation of family assets, growing liquidity requirements on the part of shops and, in general, the decreasing value of dowries. As a result, attention shifted from the amount of the initial contribution to enhancing its value in the course of activity. This involved determining the respective portions of initial capital, later financial contributions and the work of family members in increasing the value of the business. The wife contributed the shop and the initial capital; her husband and possibly the children contributed to the success of the family business through their work and their decisions; in this case, how should the profits (or losses) be distributed?

There were two possible scenarios. The first case was when the value of the shop depended primarily on its location. Once this point had been demonstrated, barring a clause to the contrary in the marriage contract, the value of the business fell within the community of property and the profits were to be distributed proportionately.[14]

On the other hand, when the qualities of the shopkeeper were recognised as contributing to the value of his shops, the problem of how to assess them between the spouses arose. The nineteenth century

[11] ADS D11 U3.
[12] Pierre Vignancour, *Le fonds de commerce dans les rapports entre les époux*. Gournay-en-Bray, Imprimerie Letresor, 1928.
[13] Faure, "L'épicerie parisienne."
[14] Decisions by the appeal law court in Alger, 22 October 1907 and 13 January 1908.

presented no clear, definitive solution to this subject; in the event of a dispute, the judge made this assessment according to the particular situation but naturally within the scope of family law, which was largely favourable to the husband. Consequently, it was rather difficult for a wife to win; her work was recognised only insofar as it was provided within the scope of the family business managed by her husband, and it was very hard for her to produce tangible evidence of her contribution. The items most frequently taken into account by judges, such as business correspondence, invoices, letters of exchange and the like, were almost always in the husband's name. Thus, the most the wife could hope for was to recover her initial dowry (and again only if the chosen marriage contract so permitted).[15]

Of course, the economic role and the rules governing the shopkeeper's wife were closely tied to those pertaining to the children. In nineteenth-century trade, children frequently took over the shop and continued their father's business. In the event of the latter's premature death, the transfer sometimes took place through the intermediary of the mother who managed the business until the children reached adulthood. The transfer was not automatic, however, and in any case, it occurred less often than is usually asserted. Thus, in nineteenth-century Paris, only one-third of the grandsons of shopkeepers became shopkeepers themselves, whereas the rate rose to about 50 per cent for the first generation. This phenomenon was linked to family size and composition; succession was more easily ensured in small families than in large ones: The probability of succeeding one's father dropped to 25 per cent for families with three children.[16]

Other factors also influenced the outcome; the premature death of the father entered into 50 per cent of cases of social decline, whereas bankruptcy played a lesser role (25.3 per cent of cases of lower status). To keep the business, the shopkeeper's legitimate sons often went to court to fight other prospective successors, such as apprentices and shop assistants.[17] In any event, whether the outcome was a sale or a

[15] Alain Burguière, Christiane Klapisch-Zuber, Martine Segalen, *Histoire de la famille*. Paris, Colin, 1986, in particular: vol. II (Michelle Perrot, ed.); Pierre Daveaux, *La femme et les contrats qu'elle passe pour les besoins du ménage*. PhD dissertation (University of Paris): 1908.
[16] Le Yaouanq, "La mobilité sociale."
[17] Cour impériale de Paris, 1866, plea for D. Borgnis, J.-A. Borgnis and A.-A. Borgnis against Mr. Fradelizi, factum BNF. The factum are typographical reproductions of

succession, the valuation of the shop was fundamental. The issue was whether it could be reduced to the shop building and inventory of goods or whether the shopkeeper's reputation and clientele, known as goodwill or intangible capital, could be taken into account.

THE DEFINITION OF A BUSINESS (*FONDS DE COMMERCE*): GOODWILL AND INTANGIBLE CAPITAL

Beginning in the second half of the eighteenth century, the documents drawn up by solicitors for Parisian merchants included the overall value not only of the shop building, the lease and the inventory, but also goodwill and trade name.[18] However, despite the obvious advantage for the tax office, this solution provoked negative reactions from creditors and consular courts that considered goodwill as a way to inflate the business assets, which furthermore could not be seized by creditors. For this reason, incidentally, the shop's goodwill and intangible items did not appear in bankruptcy balance sheets except as a negative value (business without value, no goodwill, etc.).

The revolution did not solve these problems; on the contrary, the notion of business (*fonds de commerce*) was absent both from the civil code and the commercial code.[19] However, in the course of the nineteenth century, the increasingly frequent acceptance of the notion of business by ordinary judges[20] opposed the hostility of consular judges who thought that taking intangible items of the business (clientele, goodwill) into account did not provide sufficient guarantees either to creditors or to the buyer.[21]

litigation documents (pleas, supports, etc.). They are available at the BNF (Bibliothèque Nationale de France).

[18] Jean Hilaire, *Introduction historique au droit commercial*. Paris, LGDJ, 1986: 153.

[19] Procès-verbaux du Conseil d'Etat (Proceedings of the State Council). 5 vols. years VIII–XII reproduced in *Archives parlementaires*. 2e série, Paris, 1862–1866, vols. I–VIII; Pierre-Antoine Fenet, *Recueil complet des travaux préparatoires du Code civil*. Paris, Imprimerie Ducessois, 1827, 15 vols.; Jean-Guillaume Locré, *La législation civile, commerciale et criminelle de France*. Paris, 1827–1832, 31 vols.

[20] Cours de Paris, 26 February 1895, *Sirey* 1897, 2, 23; Lyon, 14 March 1895, *Sirey*, 1897, 2, 89. The most widespread collection of French jurisprudence is the yearly Sirey and Dalloz general jurisprudence (hereafter: *Sirey* and *Dalloz*). Cases and court decisions are quoted as follows: name of the court (for example: Court of Paris); year (often resumed: 82 stands for 1882), then the section, and finally the case number.

[21] ADS D11 U3 dossier Gautier, 1882, dossier Meyer Demoget, 1882.

At the same time, as was already the case in the eighteenth century, legal reticence did not prevent economic actors from using the notions of business and goodwill in their transactions. Goodwill intervened in two distinct but related transactions, that is the selling of a business and its pledging. In the lack of clear legal protection, traders could always include intangible capital and clientele in the sale price, but if problems arose, they would have no legal parachute.[22] Indeed, as movable property, the business was not subject to any form of public notice concerning its sale and above all, the sale could be recorded in a private document, without going through a solicitor. Notice limitation encouraged takeovers within the same family group or family network because it increased the risk for the buyer, the creditors and even for the seller. Thus, the buyer ran the risk of not being informed of the seller's business debts; creditors in turn risked losing their right to payment of debts and privileges; and finally, a seller would have no guarantee of payment, especially as the buyer could resell the business without having paid for it.[23]

To remedy these contractual problems in certain cities (Lyon, Marseille, Paris, Rouen), notice of the sale of a business, while ignored by the code, was accepted as a trade custom. However, in this area, as with trade customs in general, judges were uncertain about the content of notices and the scope of the territory on which they would be applicable. For example, did a customary practice in Paris mean Paris *intra muros*, Paris and its immediate suburbs or the Seine *département*?[24]

The judges' uncertainty appeared to have been all the more justified as, beginning in the last quarter of the nineteenth century, local trade associations were themselves divided about these customs, which consequently fell into disuse.[25] In this context, business transfers declined and were often limited to one or more items, often the most "tangible"

[22] *Discours de M. Jean-Baptiste Verdun acquéreur à M. Jean-Hubert Verdun, vendeur du fonds de commerce de papeterie.* Paris, 1846, factum BNF.

[23] Trib. Commerce Seine, 18 January 1897, 26 February 1895, *Sirey*, 1897, 89; Cour de Cassation, 29 December 1875, *Sirey* 1876, 1, 109.

[24] Tr. Civ. Seine, 8 October 1869, *Dalloz*, 1870, 3, 87; tribunal Civil de la Seine, 31 March 1868, *Sirey*, 1869, 2, 56.

[25] M. A. Bernus, *De la vente et du nantissement des fonds de commerce.* Lyon, Rey and c., 1909; Annexes: M. Cordelet, *Rapport au Sénat, 1905*: 35.

ones, such as goods for example. However, business sellers increasingly sought to exclude from the sale a trademark or even the trade name. In general, the judges refused this solution and considered that the business and its component items constituted a whole.[26] This solution protected the shopkeeper's buyers and creditors but it remained partial as long as the entire business did not receive legal recognition. This obstacle was to be surmounted by the end of the century when the financing needs of shops raised the issue of taking their reputation into account from an economic and legal standpoint.

HYPOTHECATION OF MOVABLES

Hypothecation was a relatively well-established practice consisting of obtaining credit by pledging an object as security. In theory, hypothecation was possible only through the concrete transfer of the object into the hands of the creditor. This was also why mortgage was allowed only for immovable goods and forbidden for movable. Hypothecation of business and namely of its goodwill and generally speaking of intangible property thus broke with this tradition.[27]

The possibility of using the company's clientele and reputation as a guarantee is absolutely essential in the history of capitalism; when applied to shops and small firms, mortgage of goodwill turns small shopkeepers into capitalists. However, in the eighteenth and much of the nineteenth century, judges were opposed to this transaction because they thought it failed to protect creditors and favoured speculation. Indeed, it led to multiplying the transfer of the same business

---

[26] *Raymond Chevalliers Contre Auguste Prieur*, plea at the Cour Royale de Paris, 1847, factum BNF; *Dorvault contre Grimault*, plea at the Cour impériale de Paris, 1864, factum BNF; Cassation req. 14 January 1845, *Dalloz* 1845, 1, 115; Cass. Req, 22 May 1889, *Dalloz* 1889, 1, 370; Paris, 29 January 1902 and Cour de Nancy, 21 March 1902, *Dalloz* 1903, 2, 169. Among the few decisions admitting separate selling for different business assets: Cours de Paris, 28 November 1896, *Gazette du palais*, 1897, 1, 383; Paris 4 Augusts 1896, *Dalloz*, 1897, 2, 477; Grenoble, 16 April 1886, *Sirey*, 1888, 1, 303. On the exclusion of debts and credits from the evaluation and transmission of business: Cour de Cassation, 13 December 1842, *Sirey*, 1843, 1, 22; Cour de Cassation, 13 March 1888, *Dalloz*, 1888, 1, 351; Cours de Aix, 12 March 1878, *Sirey*, 1878, 2, 265; Cours de Bordeaux, 28 October 1896, *Journal des tribunaux de commerce*, 1897, 794; Trib. Civ. de la Seine, 16 April 1902, *Dalloz* 1902, 2, 239.
[27] ACCIP, III-3.44(1).

to the sellers' creditors. The situation changed during the last twenty years of the nineteenth century for legal, economic and political reasons. The first impetus came from the tax office, which had been favourable to the recognition of goodwill and intangible capital since the eighteenth century. In the early 1870s, tax measures aimed to facilitate the declaration of these items and explicitly recognised goodwill. This orientation coincided with that of civil court judges: A decision by the Court of Cassation in 1883 confirmed the position of the civil courts in favour of legal recognition of mortgages of movables.[28] The decision received widespread attention due to a favourable political and economic climate: The drop in prices and the crisis of small shopkeepers were at the centre of the political debate. Trade associations repeatedly demanded recognition of goodwill hypothecation.

In the early 1890s, their cause earned the unexpected support of the powerful wine merchants' lobby which was also facing business problems and increasingly making use of hypothecation of goodwill. The lobby proposed a bill to regulate this practice, first in 1893 and again in 1898.[29] The bill was adopted in 1898 with immediate results. At the registry of the Seine Commercial Court, 728 hypothecation of business were recorded in 1898, 1,089 in 1899, 1,269 in 1900, 1,492 in 1901, 1,065 in 1902, 1,649 in 1903 and 1,807 in 1904.[30]

However, the new law and the success of the hypothecation did not put an end to disputes between economic actors or between ordinary and consular courts; the latter considered it a form of mortgage without a sale and without public notice, this was impossible.[31] In other words, in contrast to the preceding decades, consular judges were no longer strictly opposed to the legal recognition of a business or goodwill and, hence, to their mortgages. However, they demanded that the

---

[28] Cassation 13 March 1888, *Dalloz*, 1888, 1, 351.

[29] "Chambre des députés, Documents Parlementaires." *Journal officiel* (1897), annexe 2716: 663, and 1898, annexe 3034: 680; "Sénat. Documents parlementaires. "*Journal officiel* (1892), annexe 94: 809; M. Bergeron, "Nantissement sur fonds de commerce. " *La revue vinicole*, 24 July (1892): 114.

[30] M. Cordelet, "Rapport au Sénat sur la proposition de loi relative à la vente and au nantissement des fonds de commerce. Sénat, Documents parlementaires." *Journal officiel* (1905), annexe 73.

[31] Trib. de Commerce de la Seine, 21 November 1895, *Gazette du Palais*, 1896, 1, 194; Trib. de Commerce de la Seine, 18 January 1896, *Sirey*, 1897, 2, 89.

TABLE 4.1. *Sales of Businesses, Paris* Intra Muros, *1901–1914*

Years	Number of Businesses Sold	Revenue From the Sales (in Hundreds of Millions of Francs)	Average Price of the Business
1901	9,274	100	11,000
1902	11,368	117	10,300
1903	11,802	114	9,700
1904	11,522	113	9,800
1905	11,021	113	10,250
1906	12,061	122	10,100
1907	12,677	149	11,800
1908	14,054	154	11,100
1909	16,850	208	12,300
1910	15,133	183	12,100
1911	14,340	180	12,500
1912	13,434	198	14,700
1913	12,273	185	15,100
1914	7,842	145	18,000

Sources: Statistics Directory of the City of Paris, several years; Albert Buisson, *Le statut légal du fonds de commerce*, Paris, LGDJ, 1934: 30.

transaction be accompanied by legally controlled notice to avoid speculation and protect creditors. Despite the reticence of certain chambers of commerce and employers' federations[32] as well as all those (authorised brokers, arbitrators and liquidators) whose livelihood was derived precisely from the uncertainty weighing on the sale of businesses,[33] a majority of actors now emerged in favour of notices concerning businesses. The new law was adopted on 17 March 1909; it regulated the selling of business and their hypothecation. Its effects were immediate, as the statistics of the Seine Commercial Court show in Table 4.1.

This table shows the rise in the number of transactions, despite and sometimes thanks to increased prices. The circulation of businesses outside the (extended) family network continued to grow[34] due to

[32] Bernus, *De la vente*: V–VI; F. Rouvière, *Rapport and vœux présentés à la réunion amicale des tribunaux de commerce de la cour d'appel de Montpellier, 17 février 1900*. Montpellier, Imprimerie Firmin and Montane, 1900; Michel de Pindray, *Etude sur l'utilité d'une réforme de la législation en matière de fonds de commerce*. Paris, administration du répertoire général pratique du notariat et de l'enregistrement, 1905.

[33] Eugène Saulnier, *De la nécessité de la probité commerciale*. Paris, Imprimerie Duval, 1884: 7.

[34] Pierre Bercot, *La cession des fonds de commerce du point de vue économique*. PhD dissertation (University of Paris), Imprimerie G. Subervie, 1933: 52.

the decline of dowries and improved guarantees that the law offered to buyers and creditors of businesses.

Indeed, business mortgages were much less successful, at least with regard to banks. These last still considered hypothecation of goodwill an insufficient guarantee and continued to require traditional mortgages. Business hypothecation was practised above all by wholesalers, who were quick to finance shops in this manner. The practice allowed them to maintain control over the retail trade without obviously taking it over. By financing shopkeepers through goodwill hypothecation, wholesale merchants sought to protect themselves from both department store expansion and the integration of retail, wholesale and production. The strength of French shops during the first half of the twentieth century was in large part linked to commercial mortgages, as well as to family law which was still strongly favourable to the head of the household. Notwithstanding their portrayal by Zola and some of the press during this time, French shops ultimately withstood the rise of department stores rather well. In 1965, in the food sector, 90 per cent of retail outlets were still made up of small, family-based shops.[35]

Legal admission of hypothecation also contributed to the recognition of the goodwill after decades of uncertainty and discussions. Goodwill and the sale of clientele were now perfectly legitimate. Indeed, when a business was sold, the seller agreed not to exercise unfair competition against the buyer. Yet, this commitment was difficult to appraise; if the buyer saw his clientele go elsewhere, he would accuse the seller of having inflated his clientele or drawing it away after the sale. The seller would answer by asserting that the buyer's lack of ability was the source of customer migration. Judges would attempt to sort out these elements by identifying the seller's new activity, its location and his contacts with his former customers.

Then, from the start of the twentieth century and especially after the First World War, judges began to distinguish stable clientele from occasional clientele; only the latter were included in the notion of goodwill. This meant that regular customers were held to be linked

[35] Claude Martin, "Le commerce de détail alimentaire en France. Facteurs d'évolution." *Revue économique*, 21, 4 (1970): 660–99.

more to the shopkeeper than to the shop, and hence it was perfectly legitimate for them to follow him elsewhere. In other words, precisely because customers were not obliged to continue giving the business their custom, the sale of clientele was in a sense the price that the buyer was ready to pay to keep the seller from competing with him on his own turf. This price served to reassure the buyer that the seller had no niche in the market, rather than to give precedence to an acquired reputation. This was the legal construction of a form of monopolistic competition, that is, competition based not on the uniformity and lack of differentiation of the actors, but, on the contrary, on their differentiation and classification.

To sum up, in France the evolution of shopkeepers and retail trade was linked not only to broader market dynamics, but also to the evolution of the marriage and credit market. The decline of dowry as a source for financing business was compensated by the persistent refusal to admit the full legal personality of trading women and the opening up of new sources of credit, above all hypothecation of goodwill. These elements together sustained a long-term alliance between retailers and wholesalers at the expense of *grands magasins* and consequently the long-term resistance of small shops. Personal and family links still stood at the root of business activity, alliances and networks. Before drawing some general conclusion, it is worth comparing this issue to that of other countries: To what extent was the legal recognition of goodwill admitted? Were the timing and content of this recognition responsible for the size of commercial units and the relations between retailers, wholesale traders and producers?

GOODWILL AND BUSINESS RECOGNITION IN A COMPARATIVE PERSPECTIVE

Small shops and artisans worried about the development of large retail and manufacturing units during the last quarter of the nineteenth century not only in France, but also in Germany, Britain, Italy and the United States. For a long time, these fears have been accepted in historiography; for example, in Great Britain, economic historiography dated successful urban distribution from 1850 onwards, whereas more recent analyses maintain that this trend was already visible in the last quarter of the eighteenth century and did not accelerate before the twentieth century.[36] In any case, department stores did not appear until the second half of the nineteenth century, and then only to a limited extent; they primarily targeted the middle and upper classes.[37]

As in France, the role of food stores and foodstuffs at the shop level and forms of credit played a crucial role in Britain. Foodstuffs were essential in British department stores (much more than in France), in connection with the rapid integration of agriculture and distribution on the one hand and of the food industry and distribution on the other.[38] This encouraged concentration upstream rather than downstream, as in the United States and France.

At the same time, this process differed according to the trade involved. For example, on the milk market, despite a general tendency for developing forms of producer retailing, this outcome was much less important in London than in the countryside.[39] Quite differently, the origin of grocery multiples, which were to become the most important focus of price competition by the end of the nineteenth century, may be traced to the fiscal changes in the 1860s.[40]

Despite this process, small independent shops did not disappear. In some cases, they tried to improve their competitive position by pooling their purchases to get the benefit of quantity discounts. The increase in the range of branded goods stimulated the entry of new retailers, and the growing number of shops added to the cutting of

[36] John H. Clapham, *An Economic History of Modern Britain*. Cambridge, Cambridge University Press, 1926; James B. Jeffreys, *Retail Trading in Great-Britain, 1850–1950*. Cambridge, Cambridge University Press, 1954; David Alexander, *Retailing in England during the Industrial Revolution*. London, Athlone Press, 1970; Gareth Shaw, M.T. Wild, "Retail Patterns in the Victorian City." *Transactions of the Institute of British Geographers*, 4, 2 (1979): 278–91; F. G. Pennance, B. S. Yamey, "Competition in the Retail Grocery Trade 1850–1939." *Economica*, 22, 88 (1955): 303–17; Peter J. Atkins, "The Retail Milk Trade in London, 1790–1914." *The Economic History Review*, 33, 4 (1980): 522–37; Janet Blackman, "The Development of the Retail Grocery Trade in the Nineteenth Century." *Business History*, 9, 2 (1967): 110–17; John Benson, Laura Ugolini, *A Nation of Shopkeepers. Five Centuries of British Retailing*. New York and London, Tauris, 2003.

[37] Benson, Ugolini, *A Nation*: 227; G. M. Lebhar, "The Story of the Chains." *Chain Store Age*, June (1950): 15–60.

[38] Carlo J. Morelli, "Information Costs and Information Asymmetry in British Food Retailing." *Service Industries Journal*, 19, 3 (1999): 175–86.

[39] Atkins, "The Retail Milk Trade."

[40] Pennance, Yamey, "Competition."

prices. Access to credit was important: Small shopkeepers had trouble finding resources due, for one, to family law, which was less favourable to dowries, and to the reluctance of banks to lend money on trust. As in France, mercantile credit played a crucial, although declining role;[41] but, unlike France, reputation and goodwill had been legally admitted since the eighteenth century. This issue gave support to small business during most of the nineteenth century.

However, as in France, the decades after 1870 in Britain were unfavourable to small commercial units faced with decreasing prices and credit. Even if jurisprudence began paying increasing attention to the transfer and definition of goodwill in an attempt to avoid speculation and protect small units, the lack of any antitrust rule, as in the United States, put small retailers under pressure from big units, wholesalers and producers.[42] Thus, unlike France, the legal recognition of goodwill was not a strong enough tool in defence of small retailers and small units in general.[43]

The situation was still different in the United States, where wholesale trade seemed to be having problems in the face of industrial concentration on the one hand and the early rise of department stores on the other.[44] Contrary to the situation in Great Britain, department stores in the United States were oriented more towards ordinary products, especially because such large outlets were more widely found in small centres and in the country than in large cities.[45] The extension of the internal market and the development of transport contributed significantly to this process. The arrival of department stores was not, however, immediately accompanied by the disappearance of small shops. On the contrary, on the eve of the First World War, about 90 per cent of retail outlets belonged to their managers, 86 per cent comprised a single store and these outlets accounted for

---

[41] C. A. Cook, "English Law and the Monopolistic Process." *Journal of Industrial Economics*, 2, 1 (1953): 1–31; Sidney Simon, "Courts Decisions Concerning Goodwill." *The Accounting Review*, 31, 2 (1956): 272–7.

[42] Morelli, "Information Costs."

[43] Shaw, Wild, "Retail Patterns."

[44] Nathanael Engle, "Chain Store Distribution vs. Independent Wholesaling." *Journal of Marketing*, 14, 2 (1949): 241–52.

[45] Ron Bellamy, "The Changing Pattern of Retail Distribution." *Bulletin of the Oxford Institute of Statistics*, 8, 11 (1946): 237–60.

65 per cent of all retail sales.[46] The process of concentration did not become widespread until after the war.

Distribution within the territory and the difference between city and country help to explain this complexity; other factors also entered in, especially the rules regarding competition, goodwill and credit.[47] These rules supported the spread of mass marketing along with downstream integration rather than upstream as in Great Britain.[48] Agreements between firms were affected, but not the development of department stores and large retail outlets, as long as they did not seek to impose their prices. In the lack of dowry support, attempts to obtain legal recognition of goodwill were made very early, since the first half of the nineteenth century. In the face of the reluctance of banks to lend to small shopkeepers and include the business and goodwill among guarantees, wholesalers were ready to step in once they had obtained the necessary guarantees from retailers. This is why, still in the 1950s, mercantile credit dominated the American economy (about 90 per cent of sales).[49]

This went along with numerous legal conflicts and important debates over goodwill and mortgages of movables in the United States from the last quarter of the nineteenth century and increasingly in the twentieth century. In general, American judges were rather favourable towards accepting goodwill, and problems arose solely with regard firstly to its appraisal, accounting and taxation, and secondly to protection for creditors in the event of sale.[50] In the United States, the first attempts in this direction were made in the 1890s in the form of bulk sales laws. The legal system concentrated on transfers of specific assets rather than on the business as a whole, as in France. It is thus not

---

[46] U.S. Bureau of Census, *Sixteenth Census of the United States, 1940. Census of Business, vol. 1, Retail Trade, 1939, part 1.* Washington, DC, 1941–1943: 63, table 3A.

[47] Koch, "Methods of Regulating." For a synthesis of case law on this: United States, *Annual Reports of the Federal Trade Commission,* Washington, DC, Government Printing Office, 1919–1930.

[48] Morelli, "Information Costs"; R. D. F. Bromley, C. Thomas (eds.), *Retail Change: Contemporary Issues,* London, University College London Press, 1993.

[49] Hedwig Reinhardt, "Economics of Mercantile Credit: A Study in Methodology." *The Review of Economics and Statistics,* 39, 4 (1957): 463–7.

[50] "An Inquiry into the Nature of Goodwill." Special issue, *Columbia Law Review,* 53, 5 (1953): 660–731.

surprising that litigation multiplied the more the subject matter of the transfer moved from specific chattels to the whole enterprise.[51]

At the same time, although the tax office was favourable to including goodwill in company assets, in practice, it was accepted only for goodwill that had been purchased and excluded any value linked to the activity of company members. This accounting solution created problems not only at the tax office, but also in relationships between husbands and wives who, as in France, became intransigent about their respective contributions to the success (or bankruptcy) of the business.[52] This issue was especially important in the United States where, in contrast to France (at least until the reforms of the family code after the Second World War), wives had full legal capacity to engage in trade, and their husbands could not be held liable for their debts.[53]

The American notion of goodwill as it emerged in case law included capital gains for the company or the business compared with the value of its fixed asset items, clientele and the privilege of continuing the activity. The problem for the judges, as in France, consisted of translating this relative qualitative advantage into quantitative terms. Again as in France, the solution was found firstly in the idea that assets are indivisible and goodwill cannot be transferred without all the assets, and secondly by defining several asset items that were easily identifiable from a legal and accounting standpoint (trademarks, patents, trade name, etc.) as intangible capital. At the same time, in contrast to France, the legal debate in the United States was far more concerned about whether or not notice expenses could be included in the business capital, along with its potential (in terms of goodwill) as a factor in retaining its clientele.[54]

The dynamic of retail trade depended not only on urbanisation, industrialisation and demographic variables, but also on the forms of available credit. In general, retailers had little access to bank financing, and then only belatedly. In France, until around the middle of the nineteenth century, dowries and commercial credit were the main

---

[51] Stoyan A. Bayitch, "Transfer of Business. A Study in Comparative Law." *The American Journal of Comparative Law*, 6, 2/3 (1957): 284–301.

[52] Grace Blumberg, "Identifying and Valuing Goodwill at Divorce." *Law and Contemporary Problems*, 56, 2 (1993): 217–72.

[53] "Husband and Wife: Liability of Husband where Credit Is Extended to Wife." *Michigan Law Review*, 10, 1 (1911): 66–7.

[54] Henry W. Ballantine, *On Private Corporations*. Chicago, Callaghan and Co., 1927.

source of this financing. However, as time went by, dowries appeared increasingly insufficient; yet the head of the household's control over his wife's dowry and income persisted until the 1950s. An attempt was made to propose mortgages of movables and the economic recognition of goodwill as new sources of shopkeeper financing, but once again, these practices had to overcome the law's reluctance to accept them. This reluctance was mainly linked to that of the shopkeeper's principal creditors – wholesalers. The obstacle could be overcome only if information on the business was circulated institutionally. In France, this was accomplished with specific rules aimed at legally recognizing goodwill while imposing a whole set of publicity (public advertisement, published in local bulletins and hung at the local law court) on units' credit, reputation and the like.

In Britain, on the other hand, early legal recognition of goodwill compensated the lack of dowries until close to the end of the nineteenth century. At this moment, increasing concentration of retailing and vertical integration put small units in trouble, above all in the lack of any antitrust regulation as in the United States. Here, the recognition of goodwill and antitrust rules played an important role in the defence of small units which coexisted beside new department stores at least until the mid-twentieth century.

These conclusions on the subject of shops can be compared to the ones we reached concerning covered markets. The most important difference was that access to places in covered markets remained, on the whole, strongly embedded in a regulatory system, whereas in the case of shops, although municipal and prefectoral ordinances also played a role, financing was the main barrier to entering the market. The covered market system involved regulating competition with the aim of reconciling food safety and urban food supply with the hierarchical classification of goods and social groups. The control of shops was complementary to the process, at least as far as foodstuffs were concerned. The license system disappeared in France after the revolution, but the notion of retail sales as a public service survived in the nineteenth century, at a time when the health safety and commercial quality of the product was of a much greater concern than the tradesman's skill. Shopkeeping activity was influenced more by ties to the family and to the wholesale trade than to the municipality.

At the same time, an important factor unified hierarchical control over these two places of trade – the value assigned to the tradesman's know-how. In the case of closed markets, this factor affected stall assignment and monitoring sales activity. Similarly, the increased value of a shop depended on the worth of its clientele.

A significant change took place towards the end of the nineteenth century, when the intangible capital of shops received full legal and economic recognition. This outcome was thought to be in keeping with the continuity of the liberal market order, for it involved supporting small family shops and giving them a source of credit. In reality, however, the market order was shaken, because the recognition of intangible capital called into question the almost exclusive role immovable property had played until this moment in financing capitalism. This trend was widely recorded in every capitalist country and linked to the same phenomena, beginning with the decline of land as the privileged object of ownership and a form of collateral. This evolution accompanied that of social hierarchies, with the slow decline of the landed aristocracy and farm owners in favour of urban groups. The world of shops evolved within this scope. The recognition of goodwill was an acknowledgement of intangible capital. The price of goodwill was crucial, for it was related to the dynamics within the family (the contribution of the husband and wife), between families (the role of the dowry, the contribution of funds to society) and finally, the relationship between retail and wholesale trade and banks. Different issues in market hierarchies in France, Britain and the United States were related to this process.

These issues have little to do with free competition; on the contrary, the limitation of places in markets as well as the constraints on intangible capital and later its recognition come under strategies of non-competition (exclusion from other markets, disputes within families or between families, the increased value of capital).

There remains a third type of market; after the covered markets and shops, we are going to study the produce exchange. Two aspects distinguish it from the other two marketplaces examined thus far. From the point of view of the actors involved, we know that covered markets were dominated by retail tradesmen, whereas shops, although still in the retail field, owed much of their existence to wholesale traders. Produce exchanges were the privileged place for the activity of wholesale traders (often through intermediaries). Similarly, from the standpoint of the purpose of transactions, covered markets and shops dealt with existing objects, whereas produce exchanges were concerned with future products.

5

INTANGIBLE TRADE AND THE
PRODUCE EXCHANGE

Until now, we have studied the first "floor" of markets, that is, physical places of trade, limited to retailing. We now pass to wholesale markets. The very definition of "trader" – as presented in Chapter 2 – and the distinction between retail and wholesale trade was historically and institutionally differentiated. In this chapter, I am not going to focus on wholesale trade as such, but rather a particular expression of it, that is, the history of produce exchanges and the emergency of virtual markets.

At first glance, the history of produce exchange can be easily summed up: Such markets were already in existence under the Ancien Régime; then, after a short disappearance during the revolutionary period, they resurfaced in the nineteenth century when they enjoyed rather limited fortunes until the 1880s, for both economic and institutional reasons that will be discussed later. From then on, they expanded considerably.[1] These are interesting organisations to

Parts of this chapter were translated by Susan Taponier.

[1] Louis Repoux, *La bourse des marchandises.* Paris, Rousseau, 1909; Yves Guyot, Alexis Raffalovitch, *Dictionnaire du commerce, de l'industrie et de la banque.* Paris, Guillaumin, 1901, vol. 1: 618; Yves Guyot, *Le commerce et les commerçants.* Paris, Octave Doin et fils, 1909; Jacques Dumortier, *La bourse de commerce de Lille et ses marchés réglementés.* PhD, Tourcoing, imprimerie Debisschop, 1932. Archives: AN (Archives Nationales) F 12 4554 through 4616, several files on brokers and exchanges in several towns (AN IX-1870); files on brokers also in AN F 12 1760 and 946–78. For the years 1907 to 1910: AN F 12 6176; on brokers' compensation after liberalisation in 1867: F 12 8491. On produce exchanges: F 10 2174; F 12 979A, 979D, 980. On foreign produce exchange: F 12 979F. ACCIP (Archives de la Chambre de commerce et de l'industrie de Paris): produce exchange: 1889–1933 (II-2.10 (1), II-2.11; II-2.13 (1–2)).

study because they reveal the connection between product markets and the credit market as well as between production and the retail and wholesale trades. At a higher level of abstraction, produce exchanges and their internal logic expressed the transition from real to virtual trade. Transactions involving wheat, flour and cooking oil markets were no longer solely concerned with supplying cities but became an integral part of capital trading. The real subject of the exchanges was information on future products and transactions. In this chapter, I will discuss first the general rules of the produce exchange and then the brokers and traders' activities and the qualification of goods. Forward transactions will be analysed in the last part of this book, when I discuss speculation and the general rules of competition.

According to a mid-nineteenth-century interpretation (Coquelin), produce exchange saves time by bringing supply and demand together through brokers.[2] Exchanges as physical meeting places were also the meeting place of supply and demand and reduced the cost of research and negotiation, and therefore transaction costs.

This image was based on the assumption that the physical meeting of the actors led to the meeting of supply and demand, as if the mere fact of assembling the various actors in the same place would create a mechanism for market equilibrium. It is the same faith in the market as a place and as a regulating mechanism that animated most liberal thinking during the period. We may question, however, how far this image is confirmed by the actual workings of the produce exchange.

As at closed markets, the opening and closing of transactions at produce exchanges was signalled by the sound of a bell. And as in the case of closed markets, this apparently ideal image of perfect competition concealed, in reality, strict regulation. The rules concerned trading, the actors, the products involved and the operating methods.[3] Since the very beginning and up to our day, access to the exchange has never been free. In post-revolutionary years, access was free only

[2] Charles Coquelin, *Dictionnaire d'économie politique*. Paris, Guillaumin, 1864: 207.
[3] Arrêté of 29 Germinal year IX (19 April 1801) and law of 28 Ventôse year IX (19 March 1801).

for tradesmen (legally defined); then, when chambers of commerce were introduced, it was extended to all their members and finally, following the recognition of associations in 1884, the exchange was open to all members of recognised federations. Producers were few and far between, whereas the mass of participants was made up of wholesale tradesmen and brokers. Unlike the model of perfect competition, actors were not undifferentiated but performed different economic functions.

At the same time, wholesale merchants seldom intervened directly in trading at the exchange; instead, they had recourse to commission actors and brokers. This was primarily for legal and economic reasons: Until 1866, brokers enjoyed a legal monopoly over exchange transactions. It was therefore normal that merchants did not take part directly. But would they have wanted to participate?

To answer this question, we have to trace the history of the brokerage system. Brokers were granted a privilege until the revolution, and they lost it in 1791. A return to regulation occurred with the law of *28 Ventôse Year IX* (19 March 1801), which distinguished commodities brokers from stockbrokers. The code of 1807 recognised four categories of brokers: commodities brokers, insurance brokers, brokers for ship captains and brokers for land and waterway shipping. In 1813, the category of wine brokers was added. Brokers could be merchants, bankers or persons who had worked for at least four years for a solicitor.[4] Towards the middle of the century, there were 60 stockbrokers in Paris, each of whom was supposed to contribute 125,000 francs in guarantees, and 60 commodities brokers and 8 insurance brokers who contributed only 15,000 francs. Considerable variations were recorded in other exchanges, although they were less marked than in Paris. There were more commodities brokers in Marseille and Le Havre than in Paris or Lyon.[5]

---

[4] AN F 10 2174.

[5] Sources record 30 exchange brokers (15,000 francs' deposit each), 20 silk brokers (15,000 francs) and 10 goods brokers (9,000 francs) in Lyon. Marseille: 20 exchange actors (15,000 francs of deposit) and 140 goods brokers (8,000 francs' deposit). Bordeaux: 20 exchange actors (15,000 francs' deposit), 70 brokers, of whom 43 were goods brokers (8,000 francs). Source: M. Mollot, *Bourse de commerce, actors de change et courtiers*. Paris, Librairie Cotillon, 1853, third edition (first edition 1831): 757. Also AN F 12 from 4554 through 4604.

The number of brokers was linked to regulations on the one hand and to the required guarantee on the other. Thus, brokers were public officers who were authorised to choose their successors beginning in 1816. However, they had to apply for authorisation for the succession to take place. From a legal standpoint, the successor had to provide the ordinary guarantees (property, mortgage), as well as demonstrate a solid financial, professional and, of course, legal reputation.[6]

The brokers' federation and the produce exchanges sought to manoeuvre between these two pitfalls: On the one hand, the transfer of offices had to be assured, for otherwise they would not have any return on their investment and the price of offices would collapse. On the other hand, increased circulation of offices had to be avoided to prevent suspicion of speculative behaviour on the part of brokers. The decisions adopted by the federations regarding successions testify to the attempt to reconcile these two requirements.[7]

However, the question arose as to whether the appointment of new brokers should require compensation for the current brokers.[8] The question is analogous to the one raised during the same period by merchants at covered markets when the municipality decided to open a new market. Yet, in contrast to the refusal given to merchants at covered markets, most judges and even the Court of Cassation answered the brokers' demand in the affirmative.[9] Brokers, therefore, enjoyed a monopoly or at least the benefits of a highly regulated market, but in exchange they had to pay a guarantee for their office and future transactions. This rule also applied to stockbrokers at the stock exchange.

Public authorities as well as wholesale tradesmen interested in commodities market transactions and ultimately the judges that were called upon to decide disputes concerning those transactions agreed that the monopoly was justified by the uncertainty of the transactions and the opacity of the markets – in other words, by the difficulties in obtaining information.[10] It was necessary, however, to specify the

[6] AN F 12 from 4554 through 4604.
[7] AN F 12 from 4554 through 4604, several files, in particular 4594.
[8] AN F 12 4593.
[9] Court of Cassation, 28 November 1827 and 16 February 1831, *Sirey* 1827, 1, 43 and 1831, 1, 74.
[10] AN F 12 4593.

characteristics and limits of the monopoly, that is, the rights and obligations of brokers and how they differed from auctioneers on the one hand and ordinary commission actors on the other. As public officers, brokers were supposed to bring buyers and sellers together and certify the honesty of the subsequent transactions. However, brokers were not held liable for fraud committed by one of the contracting parties. Brokers could not refuse to provide their service, and unlike commission actors, their rights could not be invoked against third parties.[11] At the same time, brokers remained tradesmen (in its legal meaning) and performed exchange transactions that could be prosecuted before a commercial court.[12] Enjoying the mixed status of public officer and tradesman was quite unusual. This influenced the way brokers intervened in producing and then circulating information. They were supposed to verify that trading prices corresponded to the rates set by the chamber of commerce. They did not dictate the price to the parties but were limited to transmitting the price fixed by the local chamber of commerce. Conversely, they could not withhold this information, for, as the Court of Cassation asserted in a dispute between a broker and merchants, the broker did not own information on prices.[13] Consequently, brokers could not accuse newspapers or bulletins that published these prices of infringing on their rights.

For this same reason, brokers were not the only intermediaries legally appointed; auctioneers and commission actors − that is, the other trading intermediaries who were supposed to reduce transaction costs − provided the same information in newspapers and trade bulletins. In particular, brokers competed with auctioneers with regard to bankruptcies. The commercial code gave brokers the possibility of selling the property of the bankrupt person. However, auctioneers were theoretically supposed to sell the same property. Conflicts sprang up between brokers and auctioneers during the Empire period; several appellate courts, and then the Court of Cassation (28 February 1813) decided that auctioneers had priority over these transactions

[11] AN F 12 4595.

[12] Ernest Chabrol-Chaméane, *Dictionnaire de législation usuelle*. Paris, Bureau du Fb Montmartre, 1833 volume I, 279.

[13] Court of Cassation, 12 August 1843, in *Pandectes chronologiques, tome 2, 1830–1844*. Paris, Plon, 1891, volume I, 370.

and brokers could intervene only in their absence.[14] The auctioneers reacted to this demonstration of brokers' strength by demanding not only to retain their priority in bankruptcy cases, but to eliminate altogether the brokers' status as public officers.

Brokers and their monopoly came under criticism from another category of intermediary – the commission actors. The latter were not public officers; they intervened in transactions through a single mandate contract, according to which the commission actors advanced money and the commercial court gave them the exclusive privilege over the value of the goods shipped and stored or consigned to them. Commission actors also had a right to retain these goods, which was valid over third parties. In time, naturally, the commission actors accused brokers of taking advantage of their monopoly to contribute more services; the brokers replied that, as private intermediaries, commission actors did not guarantee the transparency and fairness of transactions beyond the ordinary contractual guarantees.

However, pressure from auctioneers and commission actors was not enough as long as the main parties in the market – the wholesalers – continued to have an interest in seeing the brokers play an active role at the exchange. This interest was justified as long as the brokers provided useful information or even information unavailable elsewhere at a lower price. However, this support decreased from the 1860s onwards when trade associations emphasised that the arrival of the telegraph and the rise of the business press had made much information available without pay. Transaction validity could be ensured by the chamber of commerce and, if need be, before a commercial court.[15]

Wholesalers and commission actors therefore accused brokers of taking advantage of their monopoly position by increasing transaction costs rather than reducing them through improved access to information, as well as subcontracting their activity to unqualified brokers. The latter were unofficially employed by official brokers when a new product was introduced. Later, when the transactions on this commodity became sufficiently stable and sizeable, the brokers took over.[16]

[14] AN F 10 2174; F 12 8491.
[15] ACCIP II-2.10 (1).
[16] AN F 12 2174, "Rapport fait à la commission extraparlementaire."

Political leaders did not immediately respond favourably to pressure from wholesale tradesmen, partly due to the resistance of the brokers and partly owing to the fact that certain chambers of commerce were not convinced of the need for reform. In the end, the authorities themselves were still not sure that speculation and monopolies on essential goods were no longer a threat, and that forward transactions in the commodities market could therefore be liberalised.

Finally, in 1866, the brokers' privilege was eliminated. From that moment, any licensed tradesman could be a commodities broker. However, market transactions did not necessarily have to be carried out by a broker (even though recourse to one was not prohibited). But was it necessary to compensate the brokers, and if so, at what rate?

This question is important for it sheds light on the way liberalisation was conceived and implemented on the ground. Administrative representatives and judges ruled in favour of compensation; this was justified by the fact that the brokers had to pay a guarantee to be able to engage in their profession. Compensation thus corresponded to both reimbursement and damages. This confirms, as we saw in the case of market stalls, that the brokers in fact constituted an institutionally defined form of oligopoly.

Next, the amount of compensation had to be determined. The issue was discussed at length during the debates prior to the adoption of the 1866 reform law. The discussions concerned two points: the period to be taken into account and the inclusion of clientele in the price of the office. With regard to the first aspect, the price of offices, which rose steadily in the 1850s, dropped sharply during the following years. As a result, broker representatives insisted that their compensation should take into account the price over at least a fifteen-year period, whereas other trade associations and the ministry of finance proposed to take only the last years prior to the reform into consideration. A compromise was reached by excluding the two years preceding the reform (when the prices declined steeply in anticipation of the reform) and limiting the calculation to the years 1857–1864.[17]

However, once this interval was determined, the question arose as to whether all the brokers in the same *département* should be

---

[17] AN F 12 8491.

compensated in accordance with the average price of offices sold in that *département* over the last seven years or if the clientele should be taken into consideration. I have discussed the lengthy debate that went on over this subject relative to businesses. In this case, the intermediary status of brokers – between public officers and tradesmen – called for a solution midway between the assessment of businesses and of solicitors.[18] Some commissions working on this issue referred explicitly to solicitors, by the way. In general, most commissions did not favour including clientele in the assessment of the office and therefore of compensation, as the law abolishing the brokers' monopoly proposed. They argued that in local trade practices, clientele was not taken into consideration in the sale of the office.[19] This solution was adopted and the amount of broker compensation was thus lower than the assessments put forward by the brokers themselves.

The liberalisation of brokerage activity had important consequences. Transactions at the commodities market could be carried out directly between wholesale merchants who would call upon intermediaries according to the information they could provide. But in any case, the intermediaries were bound by private law contracts, which meant that, aside from situations of demonstrated bad faith, they were not liable for the information they delivered. This means that to make a market possible and reliable, rules governing forward transactions had to be identified. In the following pages, I will develop this point and study criteria of identification of virtual goods.

THE IDENTIFICATION OF FUTURE PRODUCTS AND MARKET COORDINATION

The evaluation of products brought to the market, particularly wheat and flour, was an old practice which had already yielded a body of regulations in the seventeenth and eighteenth centuries concerning

[18] On solicitors in France: Gilles Postel-Vinay, *La terre et l'argent*. Paris, Albin Michel, 1997; Jean-Paul Barrière, "La formation professionnelle des notaires au XIXe-XXe siècles." *Revue du Nord*, 17 (2002): 339–65; Paul Barrière, "Notaires des villes et des champs: les origines sociales d'une profession au XIXe siècle." *Le mouvement social*, 181 (1997): 73–104.

[19] AN F 12 8491, in particular commissions of departments of Hérault, Rhône, Nord and Bouches-du-Rhône.

these products, as well as the actors in charge of their inspection and the criteria for the actors' expertise. Wheat measurers, for example, had to have specific skills; they were akin to sworn experts, and detailed provisions were made regarding their training and activity.[20] The abolition of guilds and regulated markets did not lead to the elimination of measurers, because false weighing and measurement offences were sanctioned. In the course of the nineteenth century, however, measurers often worked for trade associations and chambers of commerce, even when municipal inspection services had their own actors. The classification of wheat and flour by type were thus included in contractual documents.

However, as the nineteenth century wore on, especially in the second half, these practices were also developed at the produce exchange, where they were less concerned with ex-post transaction verification than with specifying the ex-ante content of contractual agreements on future goods. This was most often carried out for international contracts. Indeed, the actual development of forward transactions at produce exchanges owed a great deal to the control of international transactions. It was no accident that the method per "filière", that is, model contracts for standardised products, was developed at the Le Havre market in the 1870s. The filière was a written document which could be transferred by endorsement. It indicated the name of the trader and the characteristics (grades) of the product, the date of delivery and the place at which the produce was stored. On this ground, it became synonymous with a product of a given kind and quality, exchanged on forward markets.

The American Civil War and its aftermath posed problems for Le Havre merchants in evaluating the quality of cotton, especially as different types were often mixed. This difficulty could result in lower profit margins for importers who frequently faced complaints from manufacturers. In 1869, Le Havre merchants reached an agreement requiring deliverers to pay a price per bale rather than one based on the average value per lot. Two years later, the system was perfected by setting a price for each quality of cotton. Importers and spinners were thus forced to develop forward transactions to protect themselves against

---

[20] Reynald Abad, *Le grand marché*. Paris, Fayard, 2002.

price fluctuations and introduce a system of equivalencies between price and quality to ensure proper production, sales and contractual terms. A final improvement was added in 1883, when tradesmen had the chamber of commerce of Le Havre adopt a rule imposing a specific weight for each lot of cotton and penalties in the event of deviations.

The system rapidly spread to other produce exchanges (Lyon, Paris, Lille) and to domestic transactions. The commodities accepted on the Paris market included wheat, rye, oats, flour, cooking oil, alcohol and sugar. All these goods had two possible uses, as end consumer products or as intermediary products. There was an international market for these products, in which wholesalers traditionally played a more predominant role than the other actors. The list of accepted products was gradually drawn up on the basis of negotiations between wholesale merchants' associations and the public authorities.

There were six syndicates corresponding to the six products mentioned; each syndicate appointed a commission to set the rules for the transactions concerned, which included the characteristics of the goods, methods of expertise, transaction practices and the settlement of possible disputes. The acceptance of goods at the market required detailed classification involving a statement that the commodity received was identical to the previously recorded specified standard. There were legal as well as economic reasons for this regulation. From the legal standpoint, both the civil and commercial codes required a statement of the purpose of the contract and the identification of the "types" of products in the case of forward transactions.

Another legal argument explains why products presented at the exchange were classified and standardised. Exchange transactions were not sales based on samples, which required the presence of the sample when the contract was signed and allowed the buyer to certify the correspondence between the delivered commodities and the sample. Such a procedure would slow down exchange transactions enormously and therefore rob them of any advantage. Certifying that goods were identical to the standard for every transaction at the exchange was therefore to be avoided. For this reason, product characteristics were listed in detail, and expertise was required both before and after the transaction. The presentation of typical products, the presence of a suitable sample, expertise on both the sample and stocks – in short the definition of product quality, which made the transaction possible – were ensured by the syndicate of the trade association concerned. This was everything but an impersonal, anonymous market of unspecified goods as suggested by the theory of perfect competition.

From a more strictly economic standpoint, the need to determine a market price, and therefore a correspondence between price and quality, required the definition of the types of products. As an analyst explained at the time, "if each speculation contract specified a different quality of goods, the resulting multiplicity of prices would not in any way achieve the aim of the speculative market, namely to determine a price and provide that information to the actors".[21]

In other words, the definition of quality by product type was the prerequisite for the very possibility of trading on the produce exchange. Such detailed quality definitions were not necessary in other markets and, above all, products did not need to be standardised in as much as the transactions were usually bilateral and not always repeated. At the commodities market, on the other hand, where products were not visible and multilateral payments were made on several transactions per actor, these two components – quality definition and standardisation – were indispensable.

Generally speaking, forward transactions on commodities modified the aim of the contract and the nature of the exchange; since the commodities were virtual, fungibility pertained less to the goods exchanged than to the contract itself. The actors exchanged promises on virtual goods and afterwards, unlike other contracts, bought and sold those promises. At the same time, unlike securities, which are fungible intangible objects, it was necessary to specify the "types" of goods to which the promises referred – hence the need for "filière".[22]

Product standards were filed at warehouses and storage facilities and grouped into lots corresponding to the minimum quantities fixed by the rules to serve as basic units for forward transactions. For example, 250 *quintaux* for grain, 150 for flour, 100 for sugar, 50 for cooking oil, 25 *pipes* (or 155 hectolitres) for alcohol. The trade

---

[21] Repoux, *La bourse*: 132.

[22] BB 18 6603, "Chambre des députés, n. 2234, séance du 29 mars 1901: rapport de la commission chargée d'examiner la proposition de Claude Rajon; rapport par Honoré Leygue."

associations defined the accepted quality of each product. Thus, in 1907, the rules of the wheat trade syndicate indicated 22 sources of white, yellow and red wheat.

The oats market accepted high-quality black oats from all countries, grey oats from La Beauce and so on. Russian oats were accepted at a reduced price of 0.75 francs per *quintal* because of inferior quality.

Flour had to be produced in France in compliance with the standard type known as twelve-trademark flour (so called because, according to the rules, flour accepted for delivery came from eleven millers selected by the trade as typical manufacturers, along with the flour of another miller-producer after prior acceptance and expertise). Each "type" of flour came from one of these millers; the expertise performed on their flour was perfunctory, based on the premise that, since they were included in the elite, it was not in their interest to cheat. In contrast, the flour of other millers who sought to have it traded at the exchange was subject to much more serious expertise.[23]

Products for delivery, samples and accepted products were examined by both sworn experts and by the market police (police ordinance of 1 October 1889, modified by that of 9 July 1891). Thus, a preliminary expertise was required for acceptance, along with expertise on conservation.

Types were determined for each marketplace for a specific period of time. For example, in Paris, the typical producers of twelve-trademark flour had to deposit a 159-kg bag of their top-quality flour, as it was delivered to Parisian bakeries, between the first and the fifth of each month. The bag had to indicate the name of the producer, the year and the month. Flour types were classified by a commission of experts. Several characteristics for each product were used to identify the various qualities. In the case of flour, for example, the experts checked to ensure that it was top-quality flour; then they examined the grade of texture and bread-making properties, the gluten content and the amount of humidity. If these measurements did not correspond to accepted standards, the product would be refused; however, the producer could always request a counter-opinion.

[23] ACCIP: wines and alcohols: II-2.11; wheat: II-2.13 (1–2). Also AN F 12 2174, several documents.

Trade associations also had to see to it that sufficient stocks of commodities were available in the designated quality; in the event that the stocks fell below a predetermined threshold, trading of the product would be suspended.[24]

Of course, all these precautions concerning product characteristics did not prevent challenges, which arose when a typical product, particularly in the list of products mentioned earlier, did not measure up to the standard. A certain type of flour might spoil or its characteristics change from one month to the next; hence the delivered product might be somewhat different from the promised product without necessarily involving fraud. However, these contractual uncertainties did not prevent the produce exchange from developing. In Paris alone, according to the syndicate of the produce exchange, every year between 1885 and 1914, 5 million tons of sugar, 7 million–8 million tons of wheat, 3 million–4 million tons of oats and 160,000–180,000 hectolitres of alcohol were negotiated.[25]

To sum up, at least during the first half of the nineteenth century, the produce exchange was an institution that met the requirements of the public authorities seeking to control forward transactions; the system, inherited from the Ancien Régime, involved intermediaries, whose status was midway between tradesmen and public officers, who were assigned to circulate information, ensure compliance with the rules and avoid speculative phenomena. These interests were in large part shared by wholesalers who wanted to maintain control over both producers and retailers and trade on the international market in a context characterised by considerable market uncertainty and opacity.

In the course of the century, the increased circulation of information and the interests of tradesmen, who were more focused on the international market than on the domestic market, brought about changes in trading and forward transactions. The advent of steam on

---

[24] Guyot, Raffalovitch, *Dictionnaire*, vol. 1: 618; ACCIP, II-2.11, II-2.13 (1–2). Similar rules were adopted by other chambers of commerce (Lille, Roubaix, Havre, Lyon, etc.): M. Mussault, *Histoire du marchés à terme sur laines peignées de Roubaix-Tourcoing.* Paris, A. Rousseau, 1909; Dumortier, *La bourse de commerce de Lille et ses marchés réglementés*; Robert Lacombe, *La bourse de commerce du Havre (marchés de coton et de café).* Paris, Sirey, 1939.

[25] A. de Lavergne, F. Cyril James, "Commodity Exchanges in France." *Annals of the American Academy of Political and Social Science*, 155, 1 (1931): 218–22.

the ocean; the extension of railroads on the land; improved financial conditions and facilities; refrigeration and the improvement of storage methods; the invention of the telephone and the telegraph – all of these contributed to this change. Indeed, the abolition of the brokers' monopoly and the subsequent acceptance of a plurality of information sources and transaction managers were accompanied by the introduction of forms of verification and control by trade associations. The latter offered a detailed classification of products, product quality and main suppliers. As a result, forward contracts were less concerned with the products than with the transactions themselves, which were regulated to ensure their fungibility. From that point on, transactions at produce exchanges took off and with them the international transactions capable of moving huge quantities of wheat, cooking oil and other products, influencing present and future market prices. This explains the simultaneous interest in produce exchange, their dynamics and regulation in different countries.

PRODUCE EXCHANGE OUTSIDE FRANCE

This history and control of produce exchanges were not specific to France. A similar chronology can be found in other countries. In the United States, Great Britain, Italy and Germany, a series of laws were adopted to facilitate intermediary operations. In Great Britain, an 1860 law repealed the 1733 law prohibiting speculation at exchanges, and a series of Factors acts (1823, 1825, 1842 and 1877) strengthened the rights of third parties when acquiring a representative. Similarly, the commodities market, although a long-standing institution, did not begin to grow rapidly until the second half of the nineteenth century, with the development of forward transactions and consequent increased circulation of information and products (the latter was linked to improved conservation techniques). In general, the enthusiasm for produce exchanges in the various countries stemmed from common phenomena (concentration of the wholesale trade, increasing international trade, accelerated circulation of information), as well as genuine competition among the main markets.

In Paris, London, New York and Berlin, wholesale tradesmen hastened to ask for regulatory support for their forward transactions; they obtained the agreement of their respective governments precisely on the grounds that increased international competition required expanded commodities exchanges, or they would be excluded from, or at least occupy a subordinate position in, international trade. The demands of wholesale merchants did not meet with the same support from other pressure groups. In the United States, agricultural expansion and mechanisation encouraged farmers to enter into forward transactions, even at the cost of increasing dependence on wholesale tradesmen. Competition from Canadian and Russian wheat and the size of the domestic market had considerable influence on relationships between farmers and merchants and hence on the dynamics of the produce exchanges in New York and Chicago. From this standpoint, taking into account the question of market size, the situation in the United States was no doubt closer to the one in Paris than the one in London where, due to significant dependence on food and cotton imports, forward transactions on agricultural products were mainly of interest to importers and manufacturers rather than to farmers and exporters.

With these considerations in mind, we can attempt to describe the organisation of produce exchanges. In London, brokers did not enjoy a monopoly; access to a position was open and rather inexpensive, whereas in New York and in France, new membership was possible only when one broker relinquished his position to another. London therefore always had outside brokers who transacted in the exchange, whereas New York and Paris had numerous brokers operating outside the exchange. The initial outlay and guarantee requirements were higher in New York than in London; a brokerage firm had less value in London than in New York or Paris (prior to 1866), and consequently, American brokers and their Parisian counterparts were quite favourable to self-regulation by the profession, which they considered more effective in protecting their asset (the price of membership) than public regulation. Hence, American brokers concentrated rather quickly into firms, whereas this occurred less often in London, at least initially.[26] Unlike the American stock exchanges, which were private, voluntary,

[26] John Coffee, "The Rise of Dispersed Ownership: The Roles of Law and the State in the Separation of Ownership and Control." *The Yale Law Journal*, 111, 1 (2001): 1–82; Ranald

unincorporated associations, produce exchanges were incorporated bodies. Their rules, organisations and methods resembled one another, hence a tendency towards cooperation and the founding, in 1909, of a "Council of North American Grain Exchanges". The main aims of this organisation were to promote uniformity in customs and usages, to render enforceable the principles of justice and equity, to encourage the enactment of wise and helpful legislation – in a word, to push the government to adopt new rules of the game which had been previously identified by traders' associations.[27]

As in France, the American authorities considered trading virtually as a public service, namely, the dissemination of economic information[28] – hence, the need to adopt clear rules. At the same time, the analogies between Paris and New York should not obscure the main differences between them prior to the 1866 reform in France, in particular the joint responsibility of commission actors and state authority for any transfer of membership at the exchange. The 1866 reform eliminated these restrictions and brought the Paris commodities market closer in line with that of New York. In New York, organisation into groups quickly led to an agreement between the main firms on the price of intermediation, which was relatively fixed, whereas it varied more widely in London. Commission actors at the New York commodities market, like those in Paris, were more interested in large contracts and the business of major wholesale tradesmen than in many small contracts, which were often traded in London. The Civil War created the same problems in London and New York that it did in Paris, namely increased speculation on cotton and wheat and more mixed products that were difficult to identify straightaway. Standardised contracts and products thus became the rule in Chicago and in Liverpool.[29]

C. Michie (ed.), *The London and New York Stock Exchanges, 1850–1914*. London, Allen and Unwin, 2000.

[27] Stephen E. Huebner, "The Functions of Produce Exchanges." *Annals of the American Academy of Political and Social Science*, 38, 2 (1911): 1–35.

[28] Edward R. Carhart, "The New York Produce Exchange." *Annals of the American Academy of Political and Social Science*, 38, 2 (1911): 206–21.

[29] Jeffrey C. Williams, "The Origin of Futures Markets." *Agricultural History*, 56, 1 (1982): 306–16; Thomas Odle, "Entrepreneurial Cooperation on the Great Lakes: The Origin of the Methods of American Grain Marketing." *Business History Review*, 38 (Winter 1964): 439–55.

Classification of grains, cotton, sugar and other products into grades developed very rapidly in the United States. The adoption of grades responded to two requirements: first, interstate trade suffered from the lack of uniform rules for trading grains; second, export traders wished to prevent European importers' complaints about American grains and possibly to reverse their contractual power by imposing a uniform quality of grain. From this point of view, increasingly formalised transactions at these exchanges supported rather than impeded market globalisation and product standardisation.[30] Finally, as we shall show in the chapter devoted to speculation, the English laissez-faire attitude in commodities market organisation, contracts and the definition of product characteristics played a very different role in the regulation of speculative phenomena than in Paris or New York.

In short, produce exchanges grew rapidly during the second half of the nineteenth century. These places of exchange marked the supremacy of wholesale merchants above all those experienced in handling forward contracts in international markets. Produce exchanges reflected first of all the possibility of mobilising large quantities of virtual goods and were more concerned with transactions than with the goods themselves. Hence, information was the essential variable in this market, to such an extent that the real protagonists were in fact the information dealers. As institutions, produce exchanges had nothing to do with real exchange and thus with the making of prices of commodities dealt in on their floors. By gathering information, they simply enabled their members to come to a quick decision on price. The result was that their quotations, which were simply a record of trades made, represented the average opinion of all those interested in a given article.[31] At the same time, for these markets to be possible, it was necessary for wholesale merchants to take control of the segment at the expense of the farmers through forward transactions and product standardisation. An open market in which all the world might trade was just what traders' associations did not want.

Negotiations began at the international level concerning the terms of the exchange. *Lex mercatoria* was, of course, at its height here, in as

[30] Harold Irwin, *Evolution of Future Trading*. Madison, Wisconsin, Mimir Publishers, 1954.
[31] Carhart, "The New York Produce Exchange."

much as the exchange syndicates and trade associations mainly determined the goods and terms of exchange and made international trade possible (or restricted it). At the same time, produce exchanges wished to promote uniformity of customs and usages, that is, a coordinated *lex mercatoria* that could respond to the new economic and institutional environment. In other words, produce exchanges were much less the "rational response" of trade milieus to the increasing uncertainty and changing environment than the opposite of this, that is, the attempt to impose new rules of the game onto farmers, producers and foreign traders. Of course, at the international level, product classification criteria, like the payment systems that were introduced, relied on the diplomatic action of the countries involved along with national or even local lawmakers to impose a given system of expertise and contract definition.

CONCLUSION OF PART II

We can draw a few conclusions about the market as a place of exchange. This institution was characterised neither by free entry nor spontaneous transactions. The existence of the markets as well as access and operations were strictly controlled, not only in the modern age, but even afterwards. From this standpoint, traditional administrative-type regulations were found over the very long term, as the rules governing access to stalls in covered markets, licenses for shops and membership in produce exchanges testify. Neoclassical economists are correct when they point to similarities between covered markets and produce exchanges; however, the similarities are not due to the perfect, spontaneous nature of the competitive system, but on the contrary, to their form of regulation. It was precisely this tension between speculation on essential goods and speculation on virtual products that underlay the organisation of markets in the nineteenth century.

It would therefore be a mistake to view the historical development from covered markets through shops to the commodities market as a linear progression. On the contrary, these places of exchange coexisted rather than succeeded each other, and their hierarchical ordering was far from predetermined. The rise of virtual markets took place slowly; it was a late-nineteenth-century phenomenon. It was only then that transactions involving future goods took precedence over those concerning real products; during the same period, financing based on reputation and goodwill increasingly became an alternative to mortgage loans. This also means that the first industrial revolution relied on markets with highly regulated access and transaction methods. Regulations were imposed on butchers' supply contracts, on shopkeepers' credit, marriages and mortgages and on forward transactions.

Within this scope, the uncertainty characterising the world of the eighteenth and nineteenth centuries cannot be compared to that of later periods. Uncertainty during the first industrial revolution concerned the strategies and financial contributions of the actors and product characteristics and was conditioned by so-called natural risks. It was regulated by measures aimed at controlling access to the market and its operations. In contrast, with the rise of forward transactions, the second industrial revolution and the stock exchange, this framework was to undergo a radical transformation, and the relationship between socio-economic stability and capitalist dynamism would be based on new market and non-market institutions, namely institutional control over economic information (the rules of disclosure concerning capital, companies, products and patents) and intangible capital (reputation, goodwill and innovation). I am going to examine this evolution in detail by studying the two market stages after the marketplace, namely the market as transactions followed by the overall ordering of the market and control of competition.

PART III

MARKET AS TRANSACTION

6

CONTRACTS AND THE QUALITY OF GOODS

I have shown that the market as a place of exchange was characterised neither by free entry nor spontaneous transactions. The existence of markets as well as access and operations have been strictly controlled. To what extent may this conclusion be made for transactions?

The theory of perfect competition argues that anonymous actors exchange products according to their price, which in turn expresses its cost of production (for the seller) and utility (for the buyer). Two alternative schemes are available; a first argument holds ... that personalised exchange minimises the gain from shirking and opportunism because of both repeated dealings and personal contact. Moreover, social ethics intervenes in guaranteeing coordination. In contrast to this, impersonal markets replace informal agreements with formal contracts. Some have identified the first situation with pre-capitalistic markets[1] whereas others have associated informal agreements to market stability and contracts to periods of crisis or transition.[2]

I will advance an alternative approach. I will begin by discussing the evolution of economic and legal thought from the eighteenth to the twentieth century regarding contracts and trade in order to understand the meanings attached to these notions. From there, I will go on to examine how transactions were carried out in specific institutional and historical contexts. In particular, I will focus on a specific aspect of the contractual relationship, namely the definition of the quality of

[1] Douglass North, *Structure and Change in Economic History*. New York and London, Norton, 1981.
[2] Neil Fligstein, *The Architecture of Markets*. Princeton, NJ, Princeton University Press, 2001.

goods. Doing so will shed light on the historical relationship between economic and legal thought with regard to trade, as well as other contract components (contractual freedom and will) in their historical dynamics. Indeed, an important change took place in contracts and the classification of goods both in economic and legal thought and in practices. The rise and decline of contractual freedom was the most significant modification affecting trading and selling during this period.[3]

However, alongside these changes, considerable continuities can also be detected. In particular, the ethical aspects (fair price), while central in the eighteenth century, did not disappear altogether afterwards; conversely, contract components were also important in the eighteenth and nineteenth centuries. Hence, it would seem difficult to compare ex-ante regulation under the Ancien Régime to ex-post contractual agreements in the following centuries. All the same, I will maintain some distance from North's argument identifying informal agreements with personal, pre-capitalistic trade. On the contrary, these various instances and forms of contractual regulation can be found in every period. I will stress the link between transition ("crisis") periods in society and the economy with the production of new formal rules. At the same time, as I have already observed in the chapter devoted to commercial customs and rules, that informal rules are consistently included in a formal legal framework. To demonstrate these points, I will begin by looking at the way economic thought today approaches contracts and the quality of goods. Next, I will verify the relevance of these approaches to the study of eighteenth- and nineteenth-century economies. I will discuss the rise and fall of free will in contracts and then devote special attention to contract failure, in particular to frauds and counterfeiting. I will demonstrate that these practises cannot be taken as synonymous to economic and legal pathologies, but, on the contrary, express the real functioning of capitalism, aiming to conciliate innovation with social stability. In the ensuing sections, I will discuss the other two tools for market coordination (beyond contract), labels and product standardisation. Finally, reputation and information will also be discussed.

[3] Patrick S. Atiyah, *The Rise and Fall of Freedom of Contract*. Oxford, Clarendon Press, 1979.

CONTRACTS AND THE QUALITY OF GOODS IN CONTEMPORARY ECONOMIC THOUGHT

Historical analyses of the economy usually resort to notions of trade and the quality of goods explicitly or implicitly borrowed from economics. Indeed, the neoclassical economic approach paid little attention to contracts insofar as information was said to circulate perfectly and trade did not require legal constraints to take place. Neoclassical thought was interested in the quality of goods only if it could be translated into utility.[4]

The renewed importance attached to the quality of goods on the one hand and contracts on the other is a recent phenomenon which has taken two different paths. The theory of information asymmetry has brought information back into prominence in economic thinking. Imperfect circulation of information generates sub-optimal solutions compared with the pure, perfect balance of competition. As a result, and to rule out the possibility of a "failure of the markets", it is necessary to resort to institutions that thwart information asymmetry.[5] This approach relies on particular assumptions, the first one being that the actors share the same conventions with regard to quality; if this was not the case, opportunistic behaviour that seeks to exploit the ignorance of the other contracting party would not even be thinkable. Thus, when selling a car, it makes no sense to cheat on its fuel consumption rate if the buyer is interested in something else, like the design or the speed. Another hypothesis, linked to the first, is that information coincides with knowledge: Once one gets the appropriate information, the rational actor will make the best decision, and this does not change from one individual to another. Subjective perceptions and individual values are not taken into account by rational actors.

[4] Kevin Lancaster, "Operationally Relevant Characteristics in the Theory of Consumer Behaviour." In Kevin Lancaster, *Modern Consumer Theory*. Aldershot, Edward Elgar, 1991: 53–68. Critics of Lancaster's theory: Peter Bowbrick, *The Economics of Quality, Grades and Brands*. London, Routledge, 1992; Shaun Hargreaves Heap, Martin Hollis, Bruce Lyons, Robert Sugden, Albert Weale, *The Theory of Choice*. London, Blackwell, 1992.

[5] Gary A. Akerlof, "The Market for Lemons: Quality Uncertainty and the Market Mechanism." *Quarterly Journal of Economics*, 84 (1970): 488–500.

French so-called economy of conventions has challenged these assumptions and managed to account for actors' subjective assessments while succeeding in coordinating the markets precisely through quality conventions.[6] The basic idea is that several forms of product quality definition are possible; therefore, neither prices nor contracts alone furnish a reliable indicator of quality. The solution that is actually adopted requires a "reality check"[7] which is based on quality conventions, past behaviours and path dependency.[8] Over the long term, the extension of new quality definitions presupposes the construction of normative frameworks which give them widespread application.[9]

On these questions, the conventionalist approach remains fundamentally irreducible to standard neo-institutionalism as expressed in the work of Williamson, Coase and North.[10] These authors have shown that, in the presence of imperfect markets, both macroeconomic and public institutions as well as microeconomic ones such as contracts improve the system's efficiency. Defining the quality of goods in a contract enters into this strategy: To avoid surprises or conflict, rational actors first seek to optimise contractual clauses and secondly to reduce ex-post conflicts. All types of contracts will therefore have to contain the threat of legal action and the possibility of an out-of-court settlement. The latter is encouraged by the presence of appropriate institutions (e.g., chambers of commerce), but also by the threat of non-legal sanctions (e.g., loss of reputation in the market).[11] Contrary to the

---

[6] François Eymard-Duvernay, "Convention de qualité et forme de coordination." *Revue économique*, 2 (1989): 329–59; Pierre-Yves Gomez, *Qualité et théorie des conventions*. Paris, Economica, 1994; Marie-Thérèse Letablier, Claire Delfosse, "Genèse d'une convention de qualité. Le cas des appellations d'origine fromagères." In Gilles Allaire, Robert Boyer, *La grande transformation de l'agriculture: lectures conventionnalistes et régulationnistes*. Paris, Inra-Economica, 1995: 97–118; Lucien Karpik, *Les avocats. Entre l'état, le public et le marché*. Paris, Gallimard, 1995.

[7] Luc Boltanski, Laurent Thévenot, *Les économies de la grandeur*. Paris, PUF, 1987.

[8] Michael Storper, Robert Salais, *Les mondes de production*. Paris, EHESS, 1993.

[9] François Eymard-Duvernay, "La qualification des biens." *Sociologie du travail*, 44 (2002): 267–72.

[10] Ronald Coase, *The Firm, the Market and the Law*. Chicago, University of Chicago Press, 1988; Oliver Williamson, *The Economic Institutions of Capitalism*. New York, Free Press, 1985; Douglass North, Robert Thomas, *The Rise of Western Civilization: A New Economic History*. Cambridge, Cambridge University Press, 1973.

[11] Benjamin Klein, Keith Leiffer, "The Role of Market Forces in Assuring Contractual Performance." *The Journal of Political Economy*, 89, 4 (1981): 615–41.

conventionalist idea, in this approach, the formal elements situate and specify the informal aspects. Conventions regarding quality as well as trust and reputation are determined by the institutional organisation of the markets, and not the reverse.[12]

It is interesting to note that, despite their opposition, conventionalist thinking and the neo-institutionalist view have at least one aspect in common: Markets are imperfect and contracts are incomplete. However, for the former, this insufficiency is overcome through conventions and informal elements, whereas the latter considers that only formal constraints make it possible to overcome market limitations. In reality, the debate over the respective roles of formal rules and conventions and beliefs as factors in market coordination is not a new one – it dates back to the eighteenth century. I am now going to develop this history, taking into account both economic and legal thought and its relationship to public policies and individual economic action in the areas of trade and the definition of the quality of goods.

DEFINING CONTRACT AND THE QUALITY OF GOODS UNDER THE ANCIEN RÉGIME

Until the seventeenth century, scholastic economic thought and legal doctrine took into account both sales contracts and exchange.[13] Towards the middle of the seventeenth century, economic thought focused its attention on exchange, whereas, in contrast to the Romanist tradition, legal experts accentuated the difference between contracts of sale. Although trade gradually lost its original specificity and became more like sales (the model of the consensual contract), the relationship between the two notions remained problematic. Indeed, the uses of banknotes and, more generally, of bills of exchange and promissory notes had a major impact on modes of exchange. Before property rights came to be seen primarily in terms of their exchange value, the law of property had grown far more sophisticated than the simple concept of use-value would suggest. The value of paper notes

[12] Oliver Williamson, "Calculativeness, Trust and Economic Organization." *Journal of Law and Economics*, 36 (1993): 453–502.
[13] Jean-Marie Poughon, *Histoire doctrinale de l'échange*. Paris, LGDJ, 1986; Jean-Yves Grenier, *L'économie d'Ancien Régime*. Paris, Albin Michel, 1996.

rests entirely on expectations.[14] Legal protection of expectations thus becomes crucial. According to Domat, the notion of exchange is broader than that of selling which emerged only with the acceptance of money guaranteed by the State.[15]

The seller who accepted banknotes had been paid and the contract executed; the buyer had wholly performed his contractual obligations. And yet the seller held in his hand merely a few pieces of paper; he could expect to exchange these pieces of paper for gold, but that was a mere expectation.[16]

The process of defining quality responded not only to legal and economic concerns but also moral and religious ones. The quality of goods and its connection to fair price played a central role in Thomistic thought. A fair price reflected a qualitative hierarchy of goods that referred to a determined social hierarchy.[17] But this approach was not opposed to contracts; ethics, religion, economics and law did not propose different definitions of exchange, but referred to one and the same practice.

Economists in the eighteenth century viewed fair price not as an intrinsic value (related to work or production costs, i.e., the classical approach, or to the market price, i.e., the utilitarian and later neoclassical approach), but rather as a regulator of social order.[18] In this approach, the quality of goods reflected individual and social hierarchies. For example, low-quality meat was to be sold to poor people at accessible price. Hence, the importance of classificatory tables for both goods and people, as well as the debates over luxury products, on the one hand and essential foodstuffs on the other. The quality of goods was essential to defining the contract: It raised the question of the force of the contract and its validity. To detect possible fraud and decide disputes over goods received, a judge would inquire into the origin of the contract and its binding force.

---

[14] Atiyah, *The Rise*: 104.

[15] Jean Domat, *Les lois civiles dans leur ordre naturel; le droit public et legum delectus*. Paris, Le Clerc, 1777: 60

[16] Jean Domat, *Les lois civiles dans leur ordre naturel; le droit public et legum delectus*, Paris, Le Clerc, 1777, vol. I, part III, section II: 19–23.

[17] Jean-Yves Grenier, "Une économie de l'indentification. Juste prix et ordre des marchandises dans l'Ancien Régime." In Alessandro Stanziani (ed.), *La qualité des produits en France, XVIIIe-XXe siècles*. Paris, Belin, 2003: 25–54.

[18] Grenier, *L'économie*.

This system does not coincide with the way it was described by liberal critics in the eighteenth and nineteenth centuries: Rules did not impede trade but rather provided a solid basis for trade negotiations. They served less to prohibit than to negotiate the qualities of products at the time of manufacturing (work reports) instead of in sales contracts. At the international level, the provisions were aimed precisely at reducing the cost of negotiating qualities, then checking them upon delivery and finally settling disputes that arose on the subject.[19] If all this is true, then the breaks and continuities between the Ancien Régime and succeeding periods should be called into question; can we assert that the revolution and the Napoleonic codes modified the definition of contract and product qualities, and if so, how?

THE LIBERAL ORDER OF THE FIRST HALF OF THE NINETEENTH CENTURY: THE DEFINITION OF TRADED GOODS AS THE EXPRESSION OF CONTRACTUAL FREEDOM?

Recent economic thought, especially the neo-institutionalist and law and economics currents, favour a particular approach to contracts. Assuming that all contracts are incomplete, these authors show that rational actors try to identify the optimum scope and type of pre-contractual information in order to minimise the danger of ex-post surprises. This approach to contracts (and to the law in general) is profoundly different from the one that predominated in the nineteenth century. At that time, the classical English authors, socialists and utilitarians, gave little importance to contracts; their attention was focused on production (classical thinkers) or on exchange (utilitarians and neoclassical thinkers). According to utilitarian thought, if cheating occurred, market sanctions would re-establish equilibrium.[20]

At first glance, the so-called classical English thought (from Ricardo to Senior and Mill) appears to have adopted a different approach insofar as it posed the problem of the equivalence between ex-ante and ex-post values, that is, the value of goods determined by their

---

[19] Philip Minard, "Réputation, normes et qualité dans l'industrie textile française au XVIIIe siècle." In Stanziani, *La qualité*: 69–92.

[20] Jean-Baptiste Say, *Cours complet d'économie politique*. Bruxelles, 1852: 552.

production cost (or by labour alone) and set by the market. However, although it accounted more fully for monetary phenomena than utilitarianism, the analysis aimed to understand the relationship between value and prices rather than to question contractual commitments. In addition, unlike utilitarian and neoclassical approaches, classical thought considered the product market as dependent upon the labour market. Product specifications therefore reflected production relationships, whereas use-value was only important if it could be translated into exchange value. For Marx, as for Ricardo and Mill, contracts and the law in general served merely to confirm the rules of exchange as defined by economics.

Indeed, economic thought neglected contracts precisely when they acquired a privileged status in law and economics practices as a factor in market coordination. This gap between economics and law can be interpreted in two different ways. An initial reading might consist of saying that, in the end, law and economics gave different names to one and the same thing, and their dominant approaches in the nineteenth century were ultimately compatible. Economics looked at competition, whereas law saw contractual freedom as the mechanism of economic and social equilibrium. Contractual freedom would thus correspond to market freedom and to the play of competition.

Even if this interpretation is tempting, we may wonder whether it reflects legal thought and economic practices. During the first half of the nineteenth century, the civil code gave no particular definition of the characteristics of the goods that were the subject matter of contracts. At the time, no special law sought to fill the gap and offer an institutional definition of goods. Only general rules governing trade and contracts provided specific definitions of quality. All through the nineteenth century, legal specialists debated the question of knowing whether contract performance was achieved with the definition of promises or only with the material execution of the exchange.[21]

It was only with the July Monarchy that the interpreters of the civil code clearly indicated that they thought judges should in no way be

---

[21] Raymond Théodore Troplong, *De la vente*. Paris, Hingray, 1834. *Répertoire général de jurisprudence générale Dalloz 1860*. Paris, Dalloz, 1860, vol. XXXIII, entry n. 132, "Obligations."

involved in setting prices. Although prices did not always express quality (as in the case of perfect competition), at the same time, variations did not necessarily mean deceit or fraud.[22] This approach shows how far removed the law had become from the fair price doctrine, which legitimated intervention by the authorities in price setting, even in the event of an agreement between the parties, when social equilibrium was threatened. On the contrary, judges could now intervene in prices only in the event of proven fraud. In other words, as long as the seller did not conceal product characteristics from the buyer, any transaction that might be otherwise unlawful (against customs, the State or for public health reasons) was legitimate.

These measures were based on a particular notion of the qualities of goods: "[T]he nature of goods is different from their qualities strictly speaking, i.e., their accessory, descriptive qualities. This distinction is crucial, for deception concerning the stated qualities as opposed to deception concerning the nature of the goods, is not liable to criminal prosecution when it occurs in the sale of goods. It could only occur if it were exercised with regard to foodstuffs or medicinal products or if the goods were consumed due to falsification."[23] The notion of quality mentioned here is far removed from the one stated by economic theories at the time, which emphasised either the exchange value (classical thought) or the utility of the goods (neoclassical thought). The law, on the contrary, looks at the qualities of the product, which cannot be separated from its use. This is not so much the notion of use-value cherished by economists as the idea that use itself modifies the qualities of a product. The distinction between the substantial qualities and the accessory qualities of a product was to be made on a case-by-case basis by judges who would not take into account the intrinsic characteristics of the product concerned (defined in pre-classical, classical or neoclassical terms), but rather its use recommended by the buyer and approved by the seller. Free will in contract took precedence: A buyer could therefore legitimately acquire watered-down wine provided he was informed by the buyer.

---

[22] Pierre Antoine Merlin, *Répertoire universel et raisonné de jurisprudence.* 5th edition, Paris, J. P. Roret éditeur, 1827, vol. 7, entry "Fraude": 94.

[23] Charles Robé, *De la falsification des denrées alimentaires.* Paris, A. Pedone éditeur, 1902: 60–1.

However, this approach ceased at the moment public health was at stake; substances that were harmful to health were prohibited even if the buyer had been informed.

A widespread interpretation maintains that, in the nineteenth century, in contrast to the Ancien Régime,[24] the qualities of traded products were not specified by referring to guild regulations but to the terms of the contract. Disputes could be settled by comparing the business correspondence with the product actually delivered. On this ground, Reddy[25] contrasted the Ancien Régime, when product qualities were defined prior to trade, to later periods in which the process of definition took place during or after trade. We are going to question this assertion. For, although disputes about quality indeed arose under the Ancien Régime, similarly, in the nineteenth century, proof of fraud required a comparison between the product characteristics defined prior to trade and those resulting from contract performance. Hence, there was a possibility of negotiating and changing some of these characteristics, even after an agreement was reached. This also means that the uncertainty about the quality of traded goods did not necessarily imply information asymmetry, but it could also result from shared uncertainty. For example, the use of new animal crossbreeding techniques or importing certain hybrid fibres from the colonies created problems for both wholesale and retail merchants. In this case, the uncertainty was radical, and neither the prices nor informal agreements or official, formalised definitions of product qualities were enough to ensure market coordination. In this context, the competitive model and the principle of contractual freedom were called into question. In the following pages, I am going to detail this process. I will start with foodstuffs and beverages and then continue on to manufactured products.

[24] Jean-Claude Perrot, "Les dictionnaires du commerce au XVIIIe siècle." In Jean-Claude Perrot, *Une histoire intellectuelle de l'économie politique*. Paris, EHESS, 1992: 97–126; Pierre Jeannin, "Distinction de compétences et niveaux de qualification: les savoirs négociants dans l'Europe moderne." In Franco Angiolini, Daniel Roche, *Cultures et formations négociantes*. Paris, EHESS, 1995: 363–97.
[25] William Reddy, "The Structure of a Cultural Crisis: Thinking About Cloth in France Before and After the Revolution." In Arjun Appadurai (ed.), *The Social Life of Things: Commodities in Cultural Perspective*. New York, Cambridge University Press, 1986: 261–84.

ATTACKS ON CONTRACTUAL FREEDOM:
DISPLAYING PRODUCT INFORMATION

Some believe that quality regulation is enacted to advance specific producer interests (rent seeking), whereas others see consumer protection as the main aim of regulation.[26] A quite common notion, though not necessarily implied by the former position, is that market forces and producer self-regulation are more effective than government regulation and third-party certification in guaranteeing quality. Opponents reply that market forces alone cannot solve the problem of quality information and determination, and that external regulation is required.

Economic historians have largely followed the terms of these debates in their own writings. On the one hand, we find those who support the idea that food regulation is mostly a lobbyist's tool, whereas others take into account the aims of consumer protection.[27] However, even among those who believe public interest is at stake, we find some who believe that regulation has failed to protect the consumer because it creates market distortions.[28] Some British historians have supported a more nuanced position, maintaining that food regulation originates with self-seeking behaviour but is influenced by consumer associations, medical professionals and government bureaucrats.[29] The final

[26] George Stigler, "The Theory of Economic Regulation." *Bell Journal of Economics and Management Science* 2, 1 (1971): 3–21; Stephen Peltzman, "Toward a More General Theory of Regulation." *Journal of Law and Economics* 19, 2 (1976): 211–40; Edward Glaeser and Andrei Shleifer, "The Rise of the Regulatory State." *Journal of Economic Literature* 41, 2 (2003): 401–25.

[27] Gary Libecap, "The Rise of the Chicago Packers and the Origin of the Meat Inspection and Antitrust." *Economic Inquiry* 30, 2 (1992): 242–62; Robert Dupré, "If It Is Yellow, It Must Be Butter: Margarine Regulation in North America since 1886." *Journal of Economic History*, 59, 2 (1992): 353–71; Donna Wood, "The Strategic Use of Public Policy: Business Support for the 1906 Food and Drug Act." *Business History Review*, 59, 3 (1985): 403–32. For the latter view, see Marc Law, "The Origin of State Pure Food Regulation." *Journal of Economic History*, 63, 4 (2003): 1103–30.

[28] Alain A. Olmstead and Paul Rhode, "The Tuberculosis Cattle Trust: Disease Contagion in an Era of Regulatory Uncertainty." *Journal of Economic History*, 64, 4 (2004): 929–63; Edward J.T. Collins, "Food Adulteration and Food Safety in Britain in the Nineteenth and Early Twentieth Centuries." *Food Policy*, 18, 1 (1993): 95–108.

[29] Peter Atkins, "Sophisticated Detected, or the Adulteration of the Milk Supply, 1850–1914," *Social History*, 16, 3 (1991): 300–21; John J. Burnett, *The History of Food Adulteration in Britain in the Nineteenth Century, with Special Reference to Bread, Tea and Beer*, PhD diss.,

impact of regulation depends on the relative strength of these groups. An historical appraisal of French food regulation is particularly interesting because, as a major example of a national system based on civil law, it will offer a chance for comparison with existing historical studies, which have largely been confined to common law countries.[30]

In the following pages, I am going to test these approaches. Contrary to the standard economic approach, we will not find any historical evidence that efficiency was the main aim of food regulation or that the market was able to overcome the problem of information asymmetry. Instead, economic lobbies were mostly responsible for originating regulatory rules, although they needed occasional strategic alliances with other groups to achieve their aims. At the same time, the outcome of the struggle between industry, medical authorities, the state and consumer advocates depended heavily on rules and procedures.

The economic and legal system introduced along with the revolution experienced its first setbacks between 1835 and 1845, when technological progress, changes in economic networks (colonies, internationalisation of the economy) and monetary and speculative fluctuations in France and Great Britain generated a high degree of uncertainty in the markets. As a result, several economic actors and their institutional representatives brought up the need to change the rules of the game. Lively debates took place within trade associations and the Chamber of Peers concerning rampant fraud, particularly in wine and textiles,[31] as well as commercial companies and their effects on trade. In the first case, they pertained to new fabrics and new winemaking techniques; in the second, an attempt was made to protect unfortunate debtors from their creditors, but there was also concern about stock exchange speculation (see bill of 1838 on the prohibition

University of London, 1958; Michael French and Jim Phillips, *Cheated not Poisoned? Food Regulation in the United Kingdom, 1875–1938*. Manchester, Manchester University Press, 2000.

[30] Marcel Lachiver, *Vins, vignes et vignerons*. Paris, Fayard, 1988; Rémy Pech, *Entreprise viticole et capitalisme en Languedoc Roussillon*. Toulouse, Université le Mirail, 1975; Philippe Roudié, *Vignobles et vignerons du Bordelais, 1850–1980*. Paris, CNRS, 1988; Pierre Guillaume, *Histoire sociale du lait*. Paris, Editions Christian, 2003. An exception in the literature is James Simpson, "Cooperative and Conflicts: Institutional Innovation in France's wine markets, 1870–1911." *Business History Review*, 79, 3 (2005): 527–58.

[31] AN F 12 7452, "Lettre du consul de France à Valparaiso au ministre des Affaires Etrangères, 1 mai 1835."

of limited partnerships with shares). The actors' strategies were questioned and stricter rules to control markets were discussed. The issue was how the principle of contractual freedom could be maintained without encouraging fraud. It was precisely innovation that caused problems and led to a desire for standardisation among merchants and producers who "would like the government to be able to require a single manufacturing method", although they were aware "that in the current state of things, such a measure would not have a satisfactory effect".[32]

Thus, several new rules were introduced to control trade and competition: the law on weights and measures (4 July 1837), the law on bankruptcy (28 May 1838) and finally, the law on food fraud of 1851. According to this law, fraud constituted a violation of private property. Protecting the quality of foodstuffs encouraged the growth of labour productivity and preserved the reputation of national products. The law introduced a distinction between fraud and adulteration. The first category referred to the behaviour of the actor and the act of deception, whereas the second focused on the product and its characteristics. This solution confirms that, for more than half of the nineteenth century, the consumer did not exist from the standpoint of the law, which limited itself to talking about the general "purchaser", in keeping with the idea that the final consumer, like any professional buying products, should be protected by ordinary contractual rules. There were no special provisions regarding consumption.[33]

Among other things, these rules and their interpretation account for the extent and characteristics of agricultural development and the production of foodstuffs under the Second Empire. This development was marked by increased quantity at the expense of quality. Thus, a vineyard in the south of France used grape varieties with increasingly high output and specialised in the production of diluted wine and then table wine intended for labourers, which was made without paying much attention to its organoleptic or even health characteristics.

---

[32] AN F 12 7452, "Rapport du consul de France à Beyrouth du 20 mars 1838."
[33] Raymond Théodore Troplong, *De la vente*. Paris, Hingray, 1834; Jean-Marie Pardessus, *Cours de droit commercial*. Paris, 1814.

The addition of plaster, which stabilised mediocre wine without using cellars,[34] was widely practised in the south of France and was not prohibited by the laws of 1851 and 1855.[35]

Similarly, phosphates and nitrates were used to increase the output of the soil, without questioning their impact on health and the quality of the final products. Contractual rules emphasising free will, and product information display supported the process of massive agricultural production, which found its strong point in the converging interests of producers and tradesmen. The growth of the Second Empire was rooted in the institutional construction of competition that released the seller from any liability outside of fraud while giving free rein to product standardisation. The widespread availability of certain products, such as wine, foodstuffs and clothing, would have been impossible without a legal structure open to any kind of innovation which would reduce production costs. Yet this apparently stable model was to vacillate during the last quarter of the nineteenth century. Why did this occur and what were the consequences?

INNOVATION, ADULTERATION AND THE END OF FREE WILL IN CONTRACT

During the last quarter of the nineteenth century and until the First World War, the control of sales contracts and the specification of product qualities in particular underwent important changes as a result of a complex process; the second industrial revolution and the rise of new techniques, especially progress in synthetic chemistry, posed considerable problems in product labelling for trade: Should artificial fibre be defined as a textile or as something else?[36] And could wine that

---

[34] Gérard Fox, "Rapport sur le plâtrage des vins." *Bulletin du Ministère de l'agriculture*, 5 (1887): 483–522.

[35] Edouard Petit, "Du plâtrage des vins au point de vue pénal." *La France judiciaire*, 4 (1877): 73–9; AN BB 18 6023.

[36] Some passages in the following pages are from: Alessandro Stanziani, "Negotiating Innovation in a Market Economy: Foodstuffs and Beverages Adulteration in Nineteenth Century France." *Enterprise and Society*, 8, 2 (2007): 375–412. I am grateful to Oxford University Press and *Enterprise and Society* for having granted permission to reproduce here.

contained chemical products from vineyards that were also chemically treated still be described as an agricultural product?

Moreover, urbanisation and the rise of national and international networks increased intermediary transactions and, with them, information asymmetry. All this considered, between 1870 and 1914, the business world was very concerned with the increase in fraud and counterfeiting in beverages and foodstuffs, notably in areas such as artificially coloured wines, wines made from raisins, margarine passed off as butter or watered-down milk.

This process can be easily interpreted by saying that adulteration was linked to an increasing demand for food among low-income classes in highly imperfect markets as these developments increased intermediation and raised information asymmetries. Such an argument is based upon long-standing assumptions that demand determines supply rather than the reverse, that quality is an objective, if sometimes difficult to observe characteristic, and that rules can correct imperfect markets. Against this, I adopt a radically different approach and question some usually unquestioned categories, starting with that of adulteration. Why and by whom are particular technical processes and the ensuing products qualified as adulteration? How is innovation defined and perceived in a market economy? Why does one speak of innovation for manufactures but evoke adulteration when food and drinks are concerned?

These questions go beyond the French case, as food adulteration was a principal item on the public agendas of most European countries and the United States during the second half of the nineteenth century and up through 1914. It involved power relationships between producers, traders, retailers and consumers, as well as between the central State and municipalities, and between public authority, business and science. Contemporary conflicts within the European Community (EC) and between the EC and the United States on food quality reflect these same questions.

Let us take the example of the wine market. French wine production increased throughout the nineteenth century, in particular after the adoption of free trade policies in 1860. Forty million hectolitres were produced that year, and between 50 and 70 million per year until 1865, reaching the record production of 84.5 million in 1875. After that, output declined abruptly due to the phylloxera infestation. It fell to 30 million hectolitres in 1880, 25–30 million during the rest of the 1880s, reaching a low of 23 million hectolitres in 1889. Recovery was gradual and uncertain until the Belle Époque, when annual production stabilised at around 60 million hectolitres.[37]

Consumption mostly followed the same path: Between 76 and 86 litres of wine per capita were consumed each year on average between 1831 and 1860, increasing to 107 litres in 1860–1864, 148 litres in 1865–1869, and then falling to 93–104 litres during the 1880s. It rose again to 108–122 litres during the following decade but was subject to violent fluctuations between 1900 and 1914.[38] The general rising trend of consumption was mostly due to increasing urban consumption, which added to the consumption in the traditional winegrowing areas. Urban demand was not only due to the bourgeoisie; workers contributed to it as well. In fact, wine provided cheaper energies than meat. These dynamics reveal an increasing gap between wine demand and supply during the 1880s. As a consequence France imported grapes and blended wine from Mediterranean countries, Spain and Italy at first, Algeria later.[39]

Prices rose constantly during the Second Empire, and, because of phylloxera, price increases accelerated from the end of the 1870s through the following decade. This trend was reversed in 1893. Prices for ordinary wines from Midi decreased more than wines from Gironde and Champagne. Falling or static prices of wine from Midi were due less to a decrease in consumption (despite temperance campaigns) than to intensive cultivation in the Midi and a sharp fall in transportation costs, which lowered the price of imported wines.[40] The question of wine adulteration was raised in relation to different processes: the making of wine with raisins or even chemical products instead of grapes; the fraudulent use of a label or a name; and the use of new grape varieties and techniques in Burgundy, Champagne or Bordeaux. Although related, these practices expressed different problems. One was the adulteration of a generic product (wine), whereas

[37] *Annuaire statistique de la France.* Paris, years 1875–1914.
[38] Didier Nourrisson, *Le buveur au XIXe siècle.* Paris, Albin Michel, 1990: appendix 1.
[39] *Annuaire statistique de la France.* Paris, years 1880–1905.
[40] Lachiver, *Vins*: 64, 410; *Annuaire statistique*, years 1885–1905.

another was the counterfeiting of a brand. For the sake of clarity and also because such distinctions were clearly perceived by actors at the time, I will focus only on wine adulteration.[41]

Watering down wine (*mouillage*) was widespread in large cities, and the municipal taxation based on volume (*octroi*) encouraged it. High-alcohol wine was transported to towns where retailers diluted it with water. According to the statistics of the Parisian *octroi*, in the early 1880s watering counted for at least one million hectolitres out of the six million consumed annually in Paris. Plastering, on the other hand, was a traditional practice widespread in the Midi, Spain and Italy. It prevented wine spoiling on long trips or because of sharp shifts in temperature. Plastering thus particularly concerned the Midi production, which comprised between 25 and 40 per cent of French production between 1875 and the 1910s.[42]

Sugar wines were made either by adding sweetened water on the marc or sweetening the first vintage product when it was not very alcoholic. This practice was increasingly widespread from the 1870s, mostly in Burgundy and in the central-northern areas of France. Until 1897, it was not forbidden but had to be practised in accordance with a prior declaration to the tax department. Production of dry grape (raisin) wines also increased during the 1880s and then started to fall after 1891. This can be partly explained by the evolution of commercial and diplomatic relationships with Greece (from where most of the raisins were imported) and partly by the evolution of French legislation. From 1891, raisin wines were subjected to increasingly heavy fiscal and legal constraints. During the second half of the 1880s, whereas national wine production oscillated between 25 and 30 million hectolitres, officially declared sugar and dry grape wines accounted for at least 5 million to 6 million hectolitres, and watering accounted for about one million hectolitres in Paris alone.

The answer to adulteration was the adoption of criminal rules strongly limiting free will in contract. In 1889, the Griffe law defined wine as a product made from only fresh grapes; beverages made from

---

[41] On brand and counterfeiting on the wine market, see Alessandro Stanziani, "Wine Reputation and Quality Controls: The Origins of the AOC in Nineteenth-Century France." *European Journal of Law and Economics*, 18 (2004): 149–67.

[42] Lachiver, *Vins*: 453; Pech, *Entreprise*: 496–7.

raisins had to be indicated as such.[43] However, the law did not ban using the term "vin" for products derived from the fermentation of raisins because, as explained in a parliamentary report, an excess of information lowers the reputation of French produce and economic development.[44] Even though the report initially justified this law as a tool in defence of the "labouring population", it did stress its primary aim – to help southern winegrowers faced with heavy burdens of post-phylloxera reconstruction avoid damage by fraudulent practises. The law was mainly supported by the Midi winegrowers aiming to exclude from their market segment the raisin wines, which they accused of unfair competition. This gave the Midi producers a comparative advantage over other French producers of ordinary wines, above all, sellers of low-quality Bordeaux. As a form of compensation, Bordeaux producers obtained in 1891 the interdiction of plastering (mainly practiced in the Midi) above two grams per litre. Imports of wine from Spain declined over the next decade.

In the early 1890s, in response to the Bordeaux attacks on plastering, Midi producers asked for a new rule forbidding watering down, mostly practiced by retailers. This was achieved by the law of June 1894 in which watering down was forbidden and the seller was held responsible for fraud even if the buyer and the seller had reached a previous agreement and the product (watered wine) was not dangerous for the health. This new law went against ordinary contract rules and widened the scope of application of the penal code for cheating and falsification.[45] However, judges and courts met increasing difficulties convicting under this law because it was extremely difficult to prove who had added water – the retailer, the wholesale trader, or the winegrower.[46]

---

[43] AN F 12 6873: *Sénat*, n. 400, session of 22 June 1888.

[44] "La fraude dans la vente des vins." *Journal des chambres de commerce*, 9 (1889): 1–2; "Chambre des députés, session of 16 October 1888." *Journal Officiel*, 17 October (1888): 1344; "Chambre des députés, session of 23 Oct. 1888. "*Journal Officiel*, 25 October (1888): 1381.

[45] On the law of 1894, see AN F 12 7432, "Projet de loi sur la réforme des alcools. Session of 19 May 1894"; "Chambre des députés, session of 16 June 1894." *Journal Officiel*, 17 June (1894): 1029 ff and in particular the whole excerpt AN, BB 18 6025.

[46] AN, BB 18 6024 (salt wine), 6026 (raisin wine), several files.

This was a major innovation compared with previous laws, according to which no rule of law could infringe the contractual free will unless the contract involved substances hazardous to health. In this case, the contract could be in breach through the action of a public ministry even if water was not harmful and the buyer knew it had been added to wine.

The last and final step of this process consisted of adopting a general law on adulteration supposed to coordinate and generalise all previous existing rules. Different lobbies and governmental agencies were involved in its gestation. The hygienist movement found that existing rules did not offer a strong enough protection to consumers' health. Agrarian protectionist interests considered France insufficiently protected by tariffs and duties and wanted non-tariff forms of protection. The result – the law of 1905 – was fundamental not only because it was the result of a long debate on fraud (on wine in particular), but also because it survived until it was replaced as recently as 1993 by new European Community norms (which were largely inspired by it).

This law had two objectives – to offer a definition of all products and to assure the evolution of norms in relation to procedures of adulteration. In both cases, the law was limited to defining a general framework (definitions of falsification, "cheating", etc.) and referred to public administrative rulings for the definition of products and permissible techniques. In this context, the defence of the consumer was marginal. During the preliminary discussions in Parliament, in which Edouard Vaillant (former member of the Paris Commune) criticised adulterated alcohols as "poisons" which "filled up the insane asylums", the Minister of Agriculture, Leon Mougeot, stated that "we are discussing a law on fraud not a law on public health... At the same time, I would be pleased if certain provisions of the project could fight against fraud and also protect public health."[47] He added several days later that a law on health was not to be formulated at the Commission of Agriculture but at the ministries of the Interior and Commerce. The reporter thus concluded that "it is certain that the act of fabricating and selling a liquor which presents a risk to public health constitutes neither fraud nor falsification. It is simply an act of

---

[47] "Chambre des Députés, session of 17 Nov. 1904." *Journal Officiel*, 18 Nov. (1904): 2485.

commerce. However, we are only legislating with reference to fraud and falsification. If the consumer wants to drink an absinthe which is damaging to health, it is of his concern alone. We cannot make a law on public health at this moment."[48]

This was a clear explanation of the link between norms and the market in the eyes of the creators of the law of 1905. This law essentially aimed to discipline the economy by ensuring legitimate transactions. Protection of public health was only an incidental consequence of these measures. The law was devised to ensure the circulation of product information, after which the consumer was free to buy what he or she wished. From this perspective, if the norms were clear and commercial fraud punished, the consumer would be automatically protected.

These rules sought to reduce contractual uncertainty by proposing a pre-established grid of product characteristics. Except in the case of products that were hazardous to health, it was up to the buyer to demonstrate the seller's liability. Naturally, consumers have a better chance of imposing their point of view when they act through associations, but such associations did not exist in the nineteenth century and when they were finally permitted by the general law on free association in 1884, they did not acquire the right to take part in court proceedings until 1913, and even then, that right was narrowly interpreted by the courts.

To sum up, in France, between the eighteenth and twentieth centuries, there were continuities as well as breaks in the orientation towards contractual freedom and the definition of the quality of goods featured in contracts. The continuities reside in the fact that, contrary to standard arguments, there is no reason to contrast the eighteenth and twentieth centuries with the nineteenth century, characterising the first two by considerable limits on contractual freedom and ex-ante product definitions, and the nineteenth century distinguished by contractual freedom and only ex-post definition of goods (in the event of conflict). Contractual freedom was recognised throughout this period, but it was included in wider considerations concerning the social and political order of the market. Similarly, from the eighteenth to the

---

[48] "Chambre des Députés, session of 16 Dec. 1904." *Journal Officiel*, 17 Dec. (1904): 3100–2.

twentieth centuries, goods were assessed before and after trade and this equivalence ensured (or failed to ensure) market coordination.

Of course, differences emerged within this common framework, but they should be viewed less as breaks or oppositions (between freedom and constraint, market and regulation, etc.) than as different doses of instruments that were ultimately complementary (rules and market, contract and regulation) rather than substitutes for each other. Thus, although it is true that guild regulations were abolished at the end of the eighteenth century, they did not cover all goods. In the nineteenth century, rules were introduced by trade associations to define product quality prior to trade, and the definitions in the foodstuff markets often continued to be the result of municipal regulations.

At the turn of the nineteenth century, the definition of the quality of goods for trade was partially reduced by the free will of the parties. These goods, at least certain foodstuffs and products such as phosphates, were the subject of a series of regulations aimed at reducing contractual uncertainty. In contrast to the Ancien Régime, the rules did not concern the majority of products but only certain categories (foodstuffs and beverages). This choice can be explained by the fact that, owing to technical innovation and the globalisation of trade, these products were still particularly associated with the public and political order of the markets, due to the political strength of farmers and consumer-wage earners. Another difference from the Ancien Régime was that the rules were not drawn up by trade associations but were made by ministerial institutions with their agreement and cooperation. In any case, the measures were adopted not in a break from the contractual order of the Civil Code but in continuity with it. Information was supposed to be delivered to the weakest party, that is, the consumer, to preserve the balance between the parties. On this basis, I will now examine the similarities and differences between the system in France and the one used in other countries.

SALES, CONSUMPTION AND MARKET ORDER: A COMPARATIVE PERSPECTIVE

We have just seen that, in France, the evolution of norms to control sales was linked to changes in those regulating consumption, especially food. Consumption law emerged at the turn of the nineteenth and twentieth centuries, calling into question the contractual free will of the parties. At first glance, this would seem to differentiate French (and Belgian) norms from those adopted in Germany and Great Britain, which emphasised *caveat emptor*.[49] In Germany, consumer protection began during the first half of the nineteenth century, through rules (in 1829, in Betherland, a law against additives hazardous to health was approved) and public debates. In this case, too, hygienists considered consumer health to be threatened by the "taste for lucre among dishonest tradesmen."[50]

The Prussian code contained measures to protect the buyer in general (concerning the loss sustained). Even though the measures might benefit consumers, the latter were not the explicit target of these rules. However, unlike the Napoleonic code (which mentioned only the purchase of real estate), the Prussian code extended this protection to buyers of movable property, and thereby to consumer purchases.

The 1871 criminal code took up the Prussian code, seeking above all to unify the different rules applied in the various German states. A general law "On the trade of food, fine foods and practical objects" was approved on 14 March 1879. Like its 1905 counterpart in France, this law did not define products and substances, but limited its scope to falsification and fraud, and left the task of specifying the measures applying to different products and substances to the government and the judges. Yet, in contrast to France, German lobbies succeeded in avoiding strict definitions of products through regulations or special laws.[51] On the contrary, the National Union of Food Producers and Tradesmen (Bund Deutscher Nahrungsmittel-Fabrikanten und Händler) published a reference document in 1905 indicating the

---

[49] Michael French, Jim Phillips, *Cheated not poisoned?* Manchester, Manchester University Press, 2002; Gunnar Trumbull, *Consumer Capitalism*. Ithaca, NY, Cornell University Press, 2006.

[50] Pierre-Marie Vincent, *Le droit de l'alimentation*. Paris, PUF, 1996: 20.

[51] Vera Hielholzer, *Die Regulierung von Nahrungsmittelqualität*. PhD, Max-Planck Institut, Frankfurt, 2004; Uwe Spiekermann, *Basis der Konsumgesellschaft*. München, Beck, 1999; Jean-Louis Halpérin, "Quelle histoire pour le droit des consommateurs." *Zeitschrift für Neuere Rechtsgeschichte*, 1–2 (2001): 62–80; Hans Teuteberg, "Food Adulteration and the Beginnings of Uniform Food Legislation in Late Nineteenth Century Germany." In John Burnett, Derek Oddy (eds.), *The Origins and Development of Food Policies in Europe*. London, New York, Leicester University Press, 1994: 146–60.

standard composition of the main products. This document was to serve as a guide for professionals, scientists and political leaders in charge of revising the standards required by law. This outcome can be explained in large part, as we shall see in Part IV, by the type and level of industrial concentration in Germany. It is also the reason why firms and branches in areas where such concentration was weaker or even rejected were opposed to any institutional definition of production standards.

At the same time, these measures were based on contract rules similar to those in France. They had evolved in much the same way, with increasing limitations on contractual free will, especially where public health was at stake. Some German rules, like other French and English rules during the same period, tried to link the definition of product quality and consumer protection to the control of competition rather than to public health. For example, a civil law passed in May 1896 condemned abuses in advertising and the use of trade names.

In view of these considerations, the contrast usually asserted between French rules regulating consumption and sales on the one hand and German and Anglo-Saxon norms on the other should be qualified. The 1905 law on fraud and falsification, which came under the auspices of criminal law, emphasised labelling and consumer information rather than prohibiting products and substances and brought the French law closer in line with the principle of *caveat emptor* proper to Anglo-Saxon law.

Since the eighteenth century, British law and jurisprudence wished to protect not only property but also, and above all, legal rights and expectations on contractual performances. Protection of promises and fair exchanges became synonymous.[52] Rooted in the seventeenth-century statute on fraud, as well as common law doctrine and case law in the eighteenth and more than half of the nineteenth century, free will in contract with regard to contracts on goods was intended above all to protect small tradesmen against large manufacturers and wholesale traders. This protection of the "weak" from the contractual standpoint was based on the assumption that all the actors were supposed

[52] Atiyah, *The Rise*: 110.

to have equal access to information and the same cognitive ability to process it; if fraud and deceit were eliminated, the competitive market and its legal corollary, contractual freedom, would guarantee a just and efficient equilibrium.[53] Thus, in contrast to France, contractual freedom in Great Britain tended, more than in the United States, to converge with contractual free will. This meant that neither judges nor public authorities could intervene in contractual agreements, except of course when they involved toxic substances or contracts contrary to morality and public order. This did not prevent Britain from passing several statutes to prevent adulteration of tea (1730, 1777), vegetables (1718, 1724, 1803) and bread (1758, 1822, 1836).

However, in the course of the nineteenth century, these provisions and their interpretation were increasingly challenged due to technological progress and fears concerning food. The end of the Napoleonic wars raised fears that processes invented during the continental embargo would be widely adopted. In 1820, Frederick Accum, a German chemist, published his *Treatise on adulterations of food and culinary poisons* in London; wine was mentioned as the most adulterated product, through dilution, addition of artificial colouring, alum, potassium supertartrate, and other methods.[54]

As in France, between 1851 and 1855, English hygienists launched an offensive against product adulteration. A. H. Hassall, a physician, published numerous articles in *The Lancet* testifying to the nature and extent of these processes. He ranked milk as the most highly adulterated product: Dilution, using the milk of diseased animals and the addition of flour and other substances were common practices.[55]

[53] Albert Ven Dicey, *Law and Public Opinion in England during the Nineteenth Century*. London, Macmillan, 1905; Willibald Steinmetz, *Private Law and Social Inequality in the Industrial Age. Comparing Legal Cultures in Britain, France, Germany and the United States*. Oxford, Oxford University Press, 2000; Wolfgang Friedmann, "Changing Functions of Contract in the Common Law." *The University of Toronto Law Journal*, 9, 1 (1951): 15–41; Patrick S. Atiyah, "Contract and Fair Exchange." *The University of Toronto Law Journal*, 35, 1 (1985): 1–24.

[54] Frederick Accum, *Treatise on Adulterations of Food and Culinary Poisons*. Longman, Hurst, Rees, Orme and Brown, 1820; Robert Scheuplein, "History of Food Regulation." In Kees van der Heijden, Maged Younes, Lawrence Fishbein, Sanford Miller, Marcel Dekker (eds.), *International Food Safety Handbook*. New York, Basel, Marcel Dekker, 1999: 647–60; John Burnett, *Liquid Pleasures*. London and New York, Routledge 1999: 148.

[55] A. H. Hassall, *Food and Its Adulterations, Comprising the Report of the Analytical Sanitary Commission of the Lancet*. London, Longman, Brown, Green and Longmans, 1855.

These articles were widely relayed in the press, and the Parliament finally set up a commission to study the issue; its conclusive report declared that there was indeed a considerable amount of adulteration, public health was at risk, public morality was scorned and the entire community was affected from a monetary standpoint. Whatever uncertainties the government still entertained were shattered by the public outcry following "poisoning" due to adulteration. In 1860, The Adulteration of Food and Drink Act was approved, followed by The Adulteration of Food, Drink and Drugs Act (1872) and The Sale of Food and Drugs Act (1875).[56] These food safety rules, like those in France, resulted from the convergence of two different interests: those of hygienists and the consumer movement on the one hand and those of traders on the other. Concentrations of commercial companies were especially common in the food industry. Wholesalers and hygienists maintained that retail tradesmen were responsible for adulteration, and consequently, the controls and policies adopted were aimed primarily at that category.[57] Regulation in this area therefore aroused the hostility of retail tradesmen and their associations,[58] which sought support from local authorities.[59]

Finally, in a process resembling the one we detected in France, legislative innovations in Great Britain also responded to the way the judges met (or did not meet) the expectations of a given pressure group in applying common law or existing norms. For example, The Adulteration of Food, Drinks and Drugs Act of 1872 was replaced only three years later by The Sale of Food and Drugs Act because the judges were unable to decide whether or not retail tradesmen could be considered knowledgeable about technical specifications of the products they sold.[60] As in France during the same period, the relationship between the know-how of "professionals" and innovation was crucial to applying norms and determining liability. This concern

---

[56] Burnett, *Liquid Pleasures*.

[57] French, Phillips, *Cheated*; Ingebord Paulus, *The Search for Pure Food: A Sociology of Legislation in Britain*. London, Robertson, 1974.

[58] John K. Walton, *Fish and Chips and the British Working Class, 1870–1940*. Leicester, Leicester University Press, 1992.

[59] Gary Crossick, Heinz-Gerhard Haupt, *The Petite Bourgeoisie in Europe, 1780–1914: Enterprise, Family and Independence*. London, Methuen, 1984.

[60] Paulus, *The Search*: 32–8, 66–8.

led to the act of 1875, strongly supported by wholesale traders and manufacturers, which emphasised the responsibilities of retail trades-men and recommended a local inspection system. It was only with The Food and Drugs Act of 1899 that retail tradesmen were able to evade the issue and pass the blame for adulteration on to their sup-pliers (and the suppliers in turn on to the manufacturers), provided they had kept proof (the invoices) of their purchases, business cor-respondence and any expertise carried out by approved laboratories testifying to their good faith. A new definition of adulteration resulted; like the one in France, it sought to reconcile the protection of public health with business interests. If, on the one hand, adulteration was a practice that made food injurious to health, on the other hand, "adul-teration alters the nature, substance and quality of the product to the prejudice of the purchaser".[61]

As in France, state regulation of the food trade required a definition of the product's "substantial quality" and not the quality related to contractual will and the "preferences" of the contracting parties. This change testifies to the shift from permissive norms based on *caveat emptor* to prohibitive norms demanded by pressure groups such as but-ter or milk producers and merchants as well as analysts. The Board of Agriculture was thus given new authority in cases where "the general interests of agriculture were affected".[62] The Sale of Milk Regulation of 1901 and The Sale of Butter Regulation of 1902 set minimum lev-els for the main components of these products, reflecting a stronger regulatory tendency than in France where such minimal norms were rejected for milk.[63] With regard to milk, a specific debate arose in Great Britain over condensed and skim milk. The debate was framed in the same terms as in France: It involved setting minimum stan-dards for the amount of cream present in milk and deciding whether or not these "other types" of milk could still be called "milk" and should be sold in different places and for different purposes (especially medical ones) than "ordinary" milk. These health concerns coincided with more strictly commercial ones, especially since English milk

---

[61] Quoted in French, Phillips, *Cheated*: 37.
[62] U.S., "Sale and food drugs act, 1899." *Public General Acts*, Washington, DC, 1899, chapter 51; Board of Agriculture, *Annual Report, 1900*, Washington, DC, 1900: 4–6.
[63] Stanziani, *Histoire de la qualité*.

producer-merchants saw them as a way to eliminate competition from Nestlé, whose products would have to comply with the new English regulations.[64]

This regulatory tendency was even more pressing in the United States where restrictive measures (all the way to embargoes) were adopted beginning in 1870 on European produce considered to be adulterated or corrupted (cattle, meat, wine). In 1880, discriminatory taxes were approved on oleomargarine, imitation cheese and mixed flour. In addition to the interests of lobbies, there was also pressure from consumer leagues, which were already powerful at the time in the United States.[65] In 1879, a General Bill Aimed at Protecting the Purity of Food and Drink was introduced in Congress but failed to pass. At the same time, several states in the Union passed laws against food fraud, which also aimed at specifying the accepted characteristics for the production and sale of a given product (mainly butter, milk and meat). The adoption of these rules immediately created the problem of federal coordination: How could trade be ensured if one and the same product might be accepted in Minnesota but prohibited in Chicago?

These tensions led to the passage of the Federal Food and Drugs Act in 1906. Its basic principle was the same as the one underlying the 1905 law in France – consumers should be given full information on the composition and manufacturing of the product.[66] According to this approach, the circulation of information was the necessary and

---

[64] French, Phillips, *Cheated*: 130–1.

[65] Frank Trentmann (ed.), *Paradoxes of Civil Society: New Perspectives on Modern British and German History*. New York, Berghan Books, 2000; Susan Strasser, Charles McGovern, Matthias Judt (eds.), *Getting and Spending: European and American Societies in the Twentieth Century*. Cambridge, Cambridge University Press, 1998; Peter Gurney, *Co-operative Culture and the Politics of Consumption in England, 1870–1930*. Manchester, Manchester University Press, 1996; Victoria De Grazia, Ellen Furlough (eds.), *The Sex of Things: Gender and Consumption in Historical Perspective*. Berkeley, University of California Press, 1996; Elizabeth Cohen, *A Consumers' Republic: The Politics of Mass Consumption in Postwar America*. New York, A. Knopf, 2003; Marie-Emmanuelle Chessel, "From America to Europe: Educating Consumers". *Contemporary European History*, 11 (2002): 165–75; Ellen Furlough and Carl Strikwerda (eds.), *Consumers against Capitalism? Consumer Cooperation in Europe, North America, and Japan, 1840–1990*. Lanham, Rowman & Littlefield Publishers, 1999.

[66] "When purchasers know where a product is made, when it was made and who made it, and are informed of the true nature and substance of the article offered for consumption, it is almost impossible to impose upon the most ignorant and careless consumer". Quoted in Scheuplein, "History of Food Regulation": 652–4.

sufficient condition to avoid fraud; however, owing to "market imperfections", tradesmen had to be required to display product characteristics because prices were not always a reliable indicator.

This law dealt with both product adulteration and brand counterfeiting; unlike the French law of 1851, there was no reference to product
qualities, followed by a distinction between fraud and falsification;
American law took drugs, which could be standardised, as its reference,
but this conception of products still had to be applicable to others,
such as wine. Here, the relation to brand falsification is obvious.[67]

However, this approach was soon challenged by the Department
of Agriculture, which put the emphasis on pure foods. Unlike
the general law of 1906, adulteration was not associated with the
standardisation of pharmaceutical products, nor was it limited to the
addition of substances of inferior value; this also meant that prices did
not necessarily reflect the "qualities" of a product. Federal laws reveal
that both definitions of adulteration continued to be used as the years
went by and ultimately accounted for the different norms approved
by each state.

The Americans, like the French, had trouble arriving at an institutional definition of product quality insofar as both associations of
economic actors (manufacturers versus farmers) and state administrations defined products and consumer rights differently.[68] This also
means that opposition between French and Anglo-Saxon food regulation was not as clear-cut as some interpretations claim. In particular,
whereas labelling was the primary, if not unique, means of regulating
consumption in the United States, it also played an important role in
France and the rest of Europe.

Similarly, it would be difficult to associate France with regulation
in the sense of prohibition and the Anglo-Saxon countries with the

---

[67] Article 8 stresses that "The term misbrand as used herein, shall apply to all drugs, or
articles of food or articles which enter into the composition of food, the package or
label of which shall bear any statement, design, or device regarding such article, or the
ingredient or substances contained therein which shall be false or misleading in any particular, and to any food or drug product which is falsely branded". "Pure Food and Drug
Bill, 30 June 1906." In the Department of Agriculture, Bureau of Chemistry, Bulletin n.
98, *Drug Legislation in the United States*. Washington, DC, Government Printing Office,
1906: 20–3.

[68] Ibid.

principle of free choice, for free choice was also the basis for the 1905 law in France. Conversely, the United States, like the main countries of Europe, did not hesitate to practice forms of prohibition in the name of food safety both in the domestic market and above all in the international market. Even Britain, where support to the principle of "free will in contract" was the highest among the Western nations, adopted several rules aiming at regulating the food market.

In short, between 1875 and 1914, the rules governing trade and contracts underwent considerable changes throughout the Western capitalist world; technical innovations in the food industry, together with the increasing importance of consumption in public debates (due to the consumer movement as well as the socialist movement) and the major role of international trade supported this normative evolution. The expansion of the press and journalistic scoops also contributed to this result. Everywhere, economic policies in this area sought to reconcile commercial honesty with consumer protection, the demands of trade with the interests of consumers and employees, free trade with market order. The renewed debate over contractual freedom was significant but only partial, and in any case, it reflected previous orientations (equality of the parties before the contract and the law). What had changed was the fact that henceforth, economic actors and political leaders were aware that the market could only ensure imperfect circulation of information. For this reason, at the turn of the nineteenth century, a new chapter was added everywhere to the control of trade: the display of information concerning the product. This marked the institutional introduction of a representation of the market that was not "perfect" but needed only to be nudged towards circulating information to overcome its problems. It was the neo-liberal reformist response (that of "market imperfection") aimed at thwarting radical socialist critiques. The market simply had to be corrected, not eliminated. Nowadays, the theory of information asymmetry and public policies on labelling confirm the force and tenacity of this innovation in the early twentieth century.

Thus, the contrast between contractual freedom and regulation needs to be qualified, both chronologically and geographically. France under the Ancien Régime was not the kingdom of regulation as opposed to the contract, and hence, of ex-ante definition of product qualities as opposed to definition at the time of contract performance. Both of these aspects already existed in the eighteenth century. A similar system in the Germanic countries can be contrasted to the absence of regulatory product definition in Britain, with the relative exception of certain foodstuffs. The first half of the nineteenth century added to the complexity of this panorama; in France, guild regulations disappeared and goods were defined before as well as after contract performance. However, this apparent deregulation was accompanied by still limited, and in any case late, recognition of contractual free will. Freedom of contract was identified with contractual free will insofar as the social order of the market never really ended. The concerns about commercial fraud indicate how fragile this solution was.

This situation was somewhat similar to the one in Britain where the freedom to contract did not prevent the rapid growth of case law increasingly focused on commercial fraud and then on food adulteration. Great Britain was, in fact, the first large European country to adopt a law against food fraud, well before France and the United States.

Naturally, these regulatory policies, which shifted the emphasis away from the liberal principle of freedom to contract, did not suffice in themselves to ensure market coordination, above all at a time when agreements on quality, beliefs and the economic environment in general were changing significantly. Other variables needed to be taken into consideration, starting with the signs used to define product qualities in addition to displaying their contents. Were trademarks basically intended to reduce uncertainty about products? Did quality intervene to reduce information asymmetries? If yes, then how can we explain the general decline of freedom of contract, in particular in sale contracts?

7

TRADEMARK, QUALITY AND REPUTATION

According to mainstream economic theory, the objective of intellectual property protection is to create incentives that maximise the difference between the value of the intellectual property that is created and used and the social cost of its creation, including the cost of administrating the system.[1]

Yet the economic analysis of intellectual property has mostly focused on patents and copyright, whereas brands and trademarks have received far less attention.[2] The reason is probably that trademark protection does not originate as an incentive for innovation but to provide rules for product identification. As such, trademark protection has long been identified with the medieval guild system and with oligopolistic markets.

Recently, however, the protection of trademarks has increasingly been considered as a form of indirect protection of the consumer. A primary benefit of trademark protection is to lower consumer search cost while eliminating the risk that competitors will free-ride upon investments.[3]

Some passages in the following pages have been published in Alessandro Stanziani, "Wine Reputation and Quality Controls: The Origins of the AOC in Nineteenth Century France." *European Journal of Law and Economics*, 18, 2 (2004): 149–67. I express my gratitude to Springer for having granted permission to reproduce them here.

[1] Stanley Besen, Leo Raskind, "An Introduction to the Law and Economics of Intellectual Property." *Journal of Economic Perspective*, 5, 1 (1991): 3–27.

[2] Peter Menell, "Intellectual Property: General Theories." In Boundewijn Bouckaert, Gerrit de Geest (eds.), *Encyclopedia of Law and Economics*. Aldershot, Edward Elgar Bouckaert, 2000, vol. II: 129–88.

[3] William Landes, Richard Posner, "Trademark Law: An Economic Perspective." *Journal of Law and Economics*, 30 (1987): 265–309; George Stigler, "The Economics of Information." *Journal of Political Economy*, 69 (1961): 213–25.

Positive effects on investments and innovation have equally been studied. Producers are discouraged if other producers can easily emulate their product.[4] The free-riding competitor will, at little cost, capture some of the profits associated with a strong trademark. Last but not least, trademark protection has a positive impact on quality. A valuable trademark would be reluctant to lower quality because it would suffer from a capital loss on its investment in the trademark.[5]

To what extent can this analysis be enlarged to collective trademarks (for example, Marseille soap, Bordeaux wine, Cognac) and labels? This question has been thoroughly explored as regards guilds in medieval and modern Europe. In this context, the basic purpose of trademark protection was to make it illegal to pass off the goods of another artisan as those of a guild member. Trademarks took on the function of product identification and differentiation, as well as a source of identification. Protection was thus extended from the trademark to include a trade name, a descriptive word or a collective mark.

In industrial Europe, collective marks were abolished as heirs of a corporative system; nevertheless, two related legal categories had been progressively developed: generic names and collective trademarks. If a trademark becomes a generic name, trademark protection immediately ceases. The original producers' aim will thus be to avoid such an outcome. If this effort is successful, then exclusive rights will reduce the offer, increase net profits and reduce the cost of information for consumers. In other words, labelling is a way a seller can commit to product attributes that are difficult for third parties, such as courts, to verify.[6]

Because of these effects, one would expect that producers in a given area would support the adoption of a law protecting a collective trademark if the costs of negotiating and enforcing this law do not exceed the expected benefit. The question is how do producers' benefits compare to the consumers' well-being. According to several

---

[4] Keith Arrow, "Economic Welfare and the Allocation of Resources for Invention." In National Bureau of Economic Research, *The Rate and Direction of Inventive Activity: Economic and Social Factors*. Princeton, NJ, Princeton University Press, 1962.

[5] Carl Shapiro, "Premiums for High Quality Products as Returns to Reputations." *Quarterly Journal of Economics*, 98 (1983): 659–80.

[6] Landes, Posner, "Trademark Law"; Benjamin Klein, Keith Leiffer, "The Role of Market Forces in Assuring Contractual Performance." *Journal of Political Economy*, 89, 4 (1981): 615–41.

studies, in a strongly asymmetrical information context, a public law quality sign (label or *Appellations d'origine contrôlée* [AOC]) ensures a better product quality than a private sign. This conclusion has been frequently confirmed for wine.[7]

Other authors, however, have supported the opposite conclusion: Public quality signs create a rent to the producer without increasing the consumer information and the quality of the produce.[8] The example of pre-industrial guilds shows that individual producers may ask for a collective quality sign in order to prevent fraud and a consequent negative impact on the reputation of the whole corporation. But the risk with a collective trademark is that it can further stimulate free-riding attitudes which in turn lead to a general reduction in the quality of the concerned product, with a negative impact on the reputation of the whole group. To avoid this, rules have to fix the characteristics of the product, of its techniques and so on, while producers have to be monitored.

But here, standardised industrial products should be distinguished from agro-food produce. In the latter case, standards are difficult to set up because of the influence of environmental (the *terroir*) and atmospheric variables. Presumably, these features have an impact on the link between individual and collective trademark and product quality. Which ones?

In the case of agro-food products, will local producers, willing to escape the banalisation of their product, be encouraged to apply for a collective rather than for an individual trademark? Or will they use the individual trademark to proclaim the banalisation of the collective?

Historically, the question of generic terms in the wine market was raised immediately after the French revolution and the suppression of guilds. Winemakers and traders wished to deal with counterfeiting, especially abroad. The constant argument evoked was that a generic name is conceivable only for standardised products whose identification necessarily passes through its name (for example: eau de Cologne). Wine, as

---

[7] Dennis Smallwood, Joan Conlisk, "Product Quality in Markets Where Consumers Are Imperfectly Informed." *Quarterly Journal of Economics*, 93, 1 (1979): 1–23; Ivan Png, David Reitman, "Why Are Some Products Branded and Others Not?" *Journal of Law and Economics*, 38, 1 (1995): 207–24.

[8] Laurent Linnemer, Anne Perrot, "Une analyse économique des signes de qualité." *Revue économique*, 51, 6 (2000): 1397–418.

a "natural product", could thus not be admitted to this discipline, and people located in Germany or in the United States could not use the word "Bordeaux" or "Champagne" for their products.[9]

The producers' main effort was to avoid a given name becoming a generic name. A number of case law and jurisprudential cases testify to this attempt made by French producers of Bordeaux, Armagnac, Champagne, and others. In these terms, the question was relatively easy to solve, at least in theory, because in practice, it was difficult for a French court to prosecute a foreign trader residing abroad. In this case, a mutual arrangement between the countries involved was the necessary but often insufficient condition to proceed. It was much easier for the courts to stop any attempt made in France to make Bordeaux, Cognac or Champagne a generic name; French producers making this attempt incurred legal penalties.[10]

I now turn to the impact of judicial interpretations on economic behaviours. Landes and Posner's theory predicts that if a generic name is not trademarked, the supply will increase and no monopolistic rent will be earned. We can test this theory by considering the evolution of vineyard surface area in Champagne and in Gironde during the period in which neither the law nor the courts tolerated generic names.

In Aude, the growth was limited during the first half of the nineteenth century and more sustained afterwards. In Gironde, the trend was comparably stable; the growth of production met some obstacles in grapevine disease (years 1850 and 1880) and, in part, in the negative economic trend during the last quarter of the nineteenth century. The thesis of Landes and Posner is therefore confirmed: The supply increased precisely when the law and the judges did not protect generic names.

However, the problem was much more complicated for fixing the "origin" of wine when only French actors were concerned. Two related problems were raised: on the one hand, the relationship between the place where an agent was legally settled and/or registered and that of her product; on the other hand, the practice of "mélanges" (blending). The question was whether not only a producer but also

---

[9] Louis Lacour, *Des fausses indications de provenance*. Paris, A. Rousseau, 1904: 15–17.
[10] AN F 12 6844, decision of Court of Grenoble, 31 December 1852. Also: Ambroise Rendu, *Des marques de fabrique et de commerce et de la concurrence déloyale*. Paris, Imprimerie et librairie générale de jurisprudence, Cosse et Marchal imprimeurs, 1857: 12–15.

TABLE 7.1. *Surface Area of Vineyard in Main Departments, 1788–1919 (Thousands of Hectares)*

Departments	1788	1808	1824	1835	1840	1852	1862	1870–1879	1880–1889	1890–1899	1900–1909	1910–1919
Aude	29.3	32.3	36.0	50.1	52.8	63.5	81.8	98.3	112.3	115.9	127.2	177.0
Marne	20.3	22.8	19.6	18.4	17.8	17.3	16.6	16.6	15.0	15.1	14.8	11.2
Gironde	135	99.2	137.0	138.8	103.5	137.7	126.2	139.6	141.1	139.0	139.4	134.8

Source: Marcel Lachiver, *Vins, vignes et vignerons.* Paris, Fayard, 1988: 594–600.

TABLE 7.2. *Production of Wine in Main French Departments, 1768–1919 (Millions of Hectolitres)*

Departments	1768–1788	1805–1812	1823–1841	1852	1862	1870–1879	1880–1889	1890–1899	1900–1909	1910–1919
Aude	0.3	0.5	1.1	1.1	1.1	2.8	3.5	3.6	5.6	4.6
Marne	0.6	0.7	0.6	0.4	0.5	0.4	0.3	0.3	0.4	0.1
Gironde	2.7	2.4	2.3	2.8	1.8	2.9	1.5	2.5	3.9	3.4

Source: Lachiver, *Vignes,* 594–600.

a trader could benefit from a territorially identified trade name (for example: Bordeaux). A trader could be registered in Bordeaux but have his grapes come from outside the Gironde; conversely, he could work in Montpellier while buying his grapes in Gironde. These cases expressed different situations according to the area. For example, in Champagne, since the beginning of the nineteenth century, *négociants* dominated the market: They manufactured the products and mixed them.

In Gironde, it was much more complicated; if in the eighteenth and early nineteenth centuries traders led the market, by the mid-nineteenth century, the strength of the winegrowers increased. Châteaux and individual brands were increasingly successful. However, this did not prevent traders from exerting increasing control over the producers, in particular at the end of the nineteenth century because of the economic crisis.[11]

For example, in Gironde, unions and professional associations increased during the last quarter of the nineteenth century and in the early twentieth century. This phenomenon leaned on the law of 1884 allowing liberty of association. The economic crisis and the uncertainty dominating the markets encouraged the birth of these associations; however, they strongly opposed each other. For example, the chamber of commerce of Bordeaux was favourable to the imports, to the miscellanies and to the use of new vines and techniques.[12] The *Chambre syndicale* of Bordeaux winegrowers was interested in exporting while preserving quality.[13]

Gironde winegrowers thus opposed miscellanies, which they blamed on traders. At the same time, winegrowers were divided among themselves. Such conflicts reflected the fact that several property transfers had taken place. New owners – often former tradesmen – adopted unacceptable (to the old owners) strategies. Some did not hesitate to follow the traders in selling low-quality mixed wines. The divisions within the unions of Saint-Émilion confirm this trend.

---

[11] Philippe Roudié, *Vignobles et vignerons du Bordelais, 1850–1980*. Paris, CNRS, 1988; Lachiver, *Vins*.

[12] AN BB 18 6024, "Chambre de commerce de Bordeaux au ministre de la Justice, 23 mars 1881".

[13] AN BB 18 6024, "Rapport de Ambaud, Brouardel, Dubrisay, Gallard, rapporteur au Comité consultatif d'Hygiène, séance du 22 novembre 1880".

This conflict did not calm down, but increased even more with the passing of the years. In particular, high-quality wine producers started with the assumption that regional reputation matters to consumers. The label had thus put into evidence "tradition". From the opposite end, those who focussed on quantity gave much less priority to the label than to a quality agreement between the producer and the trader. According to this approach, the consumer's protection would implicitly be guaranteed too.

A third attitude had it that the information given to the consumer on the label is not very relevant insofar as the choice is made on the basis of the taste rather than the origin of the wine.

These orientations leaned on different beliefs producers and traders had on consumers' preferences. As testified by the meetings' reports of professional associations,[14] this largely explained the inability to reach a cooperative agreement. In turn, this issue mostly explains the amount of case law debated in those years about the "origin" of wine. Article 1 of the law of July 1824 on trademarks and intellectual property "totally prohibits and punishes the use on an industrial product of the name of a place other than that of winemaking, or its appearance following any alteration whatsoever". This provision applied to the winemaker but did not protect the tradesman's mark or the collective mark such as "Bordeaux wine". Litigation on these aspects was thus extremely widespread despite their uncertain issue. When the name belonged to a city or a region, for example Gironde or Champagne, the false name could also be pursued. The Court of Cassation repeatedly declared that one had to interpret the name of a place as the place of manufacture for industrial products and as that of the harvest for "natural" produce.[15]

On 28 June 1847, the chamber of appeals of the Court of Cassation ruled that estate owners and winegrowers had the right to have the wines from their harvest protected, and deemed that all estate owners of *grand crus* were entitled to stamp the vessels containing their wines with a picture representing the wine, that is, the place where the grapes were harvested, even though the cellars and vats were not located there. This resolution naturally opened up a breach in the definition

---

[14] AN F 12 6872, AN F 12 7003, AN BB 18 6024, 6030.
[15] Court of Cassation, 16 June 1847, *Sirey* 1847, 1, 521; Court of Cassation, 12 July 1845, *Sirey* 1845, 1, 842.

of the *appellation d'origine*. Indeed, it allowed wine merchants or wine-growers located, for example, outside the Bordeaux region to buy products from that region, locate them elsewhere and sell them under the name of Bordeaux.

It is precisely to face these uncertain judicial court decisions that a new law on trademarks and brands was adopted in 1857. It protected the tradesman's mark whereas, according to the rapporteur, no protection was granted to collective marks.[16] As such, was the regional name protected or not? Following the decisions of the Court of Cassation in 1845 and 1847 on Champagne, several judicial decisions[17] confirmed that the name of a locality belonged to all its inhabitants who had an interest in exploiting it to establish the place of origin or manufacturing of their products.[18]

On 19 July 1887, the Court of Angers asserted that the Champagne appellation would henceforth be exclusively reserved to wines grown and made in the Champagne region.[19] Because of this, several decisions were obliged to specify what was meant by "place of fabrication". The jurisprudence of the appeal courts and the Court of Cassation admitted as a place of manufacture a private domain,[20] a city, a region or even a whole country.[21]

To sum up, during all of the nineteenth century, judicial interpretations guaranteed the protection of individual trademarks and brands but refused to take into consideration collective marks and generic names. At the same time, this position was relatively uncertain insofar as the *terroir* appeared among the arguments assuring the protection of individual marks.

Moreover, product characteristics were hardly mentioned. Quality of wine and protection of the mark were not synonymous. This was

[16] "Rapport fait au nom de la commission chargée d'examiner le projet de loi relatif aux marques de fabrique et de commerce par Busson, député au corps législatif." In Rendu, *Des marques*: 399–589.

[17] Court of Aix, 27 May 1862; Court of Cassation, 15 July 1863; Court of Grenoble, 11 February 1870, *Dalloz* 1871, 2, 120; Court of Bordeaux, 1 June 1887, *Dalloz* 1889, 2, 27; Court of Cassation, 1 May 1889, *Dalloz* 1890, 1, 470.

[18] Lacour, *Des fausses*: 24.

[19] AN F 12 6969.

[20] Law court (tribunal) of Paris, 5 February 1870; Court of Cassation, 26 April 1872, *Dalloz*, 1874, 1, 47. Court of Bordeaux, 11 August 1886; Court of Cassation, 2 July 1888, *Dalloz*, 1889, 1, 11.

[21] Roger Hodez, *Du droit à l'appellation champagne*. Paris, PUF, 1923: 27.

the exact opposite of another tendency during the same period regarding industrial patents, which were identified and protected by their specifications and not at all by the geographical location of the factory or the manufacturer. This disparity confirms the courts' perception of "industrial products" versus "agricultural products". The former were characterised by their mobility and the possibility of transferring production technologies. The latter, on the other hand, were characterised by qualities associated primarily with the location of the estate. The qualities of the soil, the climate and other such aspects would continue to have priority over technical production processes; this was so because, at the very moment when winemaking techniques were evolving, "traditional" techniques were appealed to, to certify the truth of the appellation. For otherwise, one could use chemical means to offset product inadequacies linked to climate or natural conditions.

The impact of these practices on production has been estimated. For example, Gironde produced between 2 million and 3 million hectolitres of wine; about 6 million hectolitres of wine from Bordeaux were put on sale at this time.[22] Indeed, the Gironde *négociants* bought grapes and wine in the south of France (Midi) and then, fully aware of the threat of phylloxera, did not hesitate to mix their wine with wine imported from Italy, Spain and Algeria.

All the same, Champagne traders traditionally stocked up in the Aube, which assured production close to the Marne. With the passing of years, the Seine-Et-Marne was also included in their network. The traders of the Marne also bought in Touraine and in Anjou. As a result, supply increased and conflict among the actors multiplied as well.

Because of these difficulties, more actors increasingly invoked state-controlled regulation of the quality problems. This intervention could be conceived in different ways. It could be limited to litigation in the framework of existing rules; alternatively, a modification of the rules could be necessary to fix the legal qualification of the norm (law, decree, fiscal, administrative, criminal) and its content. In the following pages, I am going to show how these choices were made in France at the turn of the century.

---

[22] Roudié, *Vignobles*: 208.

DECREES AND LAWMAKING

A first solution to these problems would be to let the judges decide. However, judicial decisions taken on the basis of the laws of 1824 and 1857 had expressed different attitudes concerning collective and generic names. Because of this, involved actors had difficulty forming expectations on the outcome of litigation; in turn, this incited speculation.

At the beginning of the century, considering the decrease of the exports and the difficulties on the home market, a majority of actors was favourable to modifying the norms on the marks in order to lower the uncertainty of litigation.[23] Parliamentary proceedings put in evidence that the representatives of big Gironde winegrowers and big Champagne (Marne) companies wished to lower the jurisprudential uncertainty on this topic. They were therefore favourable to modify the existing norms. How? Two related questions had to be solved: the content of the norms and the authority supposed to define them. Let's start with this latter aspect.

The 1905 law on fraud and falsification condemned "anyone who attempts to deceive the contracting party as to the nature, substantial qualities, composition and content of productive principles of any goods, either with regard to their variety or their origin, when, according to conventions or customs, the designation of a falsely attributed variety or origin is to be considered as the main cause for the sale". The law established the appointment of local commissions to fix the regional boundaries and the AOCs. However, these commissions had a merely consultative power and aimed just to lower the political tensions related to the appellations question.[24]

These commissions, composed of elected and local economic actors, failed to resolve the conflicts of the previous years. In the Gironde region, within the commission, the prefect of the Gironde region was surrounded by regional representatives, mayors of towns and *département* councillors, as well as winemakers and wine merchants. However, the work of the commission immediately ran up against two problems: How

---

[23] AN C★I/478.
[24] AN C★ I/478: "Chambre des députés, 14 Juin 1907." *Journal Officiel*, 17 June (1907); "Chambre des députés 9 juillet, 1907." *Journal Officiel*, 10 July (1907): 1807; "Sénat, 4 Juillet 1907." *Journal Officiel*, 10 July (1907): 1798; "Sénat, 7 July, 1908." *Journal Officiel*, 8 July (1908): 912; "Sénat, 9 July 1908." *Journal Officiel*, 10 July (1908): 932.

the "Bordeaux" region should be delimited and how the estates and the wines within it should be classified. As the number of winegrowers' associations increased, a majority of the commission finally chose a strictly administrative solution: The Bordeaux region was thus assimilated to the Gironde department. This solution set off protests by winegrowers from the communities that were excluded.[25] Similar commissions were established in other concerned areas (Armagnac, Champagne, Cognac). In these cases too, no agreement was reached.[26] To break this impasse, two solutions were available: to adopt a centralised decision or to come back to the judges within the existing laws.

POSITIVE LAW VERSUS CASE LAW

Because of the impasse in local commissions, a new law was passed on 5 August 1908. Article 1 stated that "the regions which have exclusive claim to the appellation of product origin ... shall be delimited on the basis of 'established local customs'". New commissions were set up; unlike the previous commissions, the representatives of several trade associations and agricultural associations were excluded; they were replaced by technicians, agronomers and agronomy professors. The hope was that they would be less influenced by local lobbies and would adopt a widely accepted solution. This was not necessarily an indication of change. In the Bordeaux region, the new commission confirmed the solution already adopted by the previous commission: The Bordeaux appellation was to be based on the administrative territorial division.[27]

The order of 17 December 1908 delimited the territories to which the Champagne appellation was to be reserved; that of 1 May 1909 performed the same operation with regard to Cognac. The decree of 4 January 1909 delimited the Champagne region; the order of 25 June 1909 delimited the regions of Armagnac, Bas-Armagnac, Haut-Armagnac and Tenarèze; that of 21 April 1910 determined the regions authorised to produce *clairette de dieu* and finally, on 18 February 1911, the "Bordeaux" appellation was delimited.

[25] AN F 12 6969.
[26] AN C 7392; AN F 12 6969; AN BB 18 6031. On this, also: Roudié, *Vignobles*; Lachiver, *Vins*.
[27] Roudié, *Vignobles*: 222–9.

Not all of these provisions were inspired by the same principles. Whereas the Bordeaux appellation was reserved solely to communities in the Gironde *département*, the Cognac and Armagnac appellations were also granted to products made outside of the administrative territories in question.[28] As a consequence, social unrest grew in all the concerned departments.

For those who were excluded, waging the war was judged to be less costly than being excluded from a delimited region. Indeed, in their view, the producers that were included enjoyed a monopoly. Conversely, no winegrower was prepared to seek a multilateral agreement with the others and thereby escape conflicts. Such an agreement would require, in fact, circulating information relating to the product and its supply and distribution channels. During this period, however, market segmentation operated precisely on the basis of product differentiation excluding any circulation of information on the product or the sales networks.

In the face of increasing social demonstrations and growing dissatisfaction among a large portion of the parties in question, several voices spoke out in the French Parliament in support of suppressing the law concerning delimited regions and transferring exclusive protection of *appellations d'origine* to the courts. On 30 March, a bill was introduced to this end in the Parliament. "No doubt", asserted the rapporteur, "it will be necessary to prosecute counterfeiters, professional cheaters, all those who deceive with regard to the type of goods, who thus sell ordinary wine as Bordeaux or Burgundy. Fraud is not new, it stems from the predilection for certain wines". What was new was the fact that for some time, this type of fraud had reaped the benefits of progress in chemistry; hence, the need for stricter legislation.

Conversely, it was not enough for a vine to be planted in a particular region to yield good wine. With geographical delimitation, the trademark could fall into a slump, for people could plant vines anywhere in the region concerned, only to take advantage of the regional name.

The report concluded that it was necessary to go back to the previous law. It was the job of the courts, and not of the administration, to punish fraud. Trade associations should be granted greater

[28] AN F 12 6969.

legal authority.[29] In other words, the return to the procedures aimed not only to deactivate political tensions but also to reach a definition of quality good enough to fight against counterfeiting and free-riding at the same time.

However, a decision to go back to a judicial solution would have been unsatisfactory without specifying on what basis the judges would decide. On 30 June 1911, Pams, the new Minister of Agriculture, proposed a bill "to set up a method of delimitation by the courts" and no longer by the administration.[30] The first article of the bill stated that judges should take into account the origin of the product, its nature, composition and quality. The reference to quality was the real innovation of the bill. The problem arose, however, as to how to define product quality: by consistent taste or grape variety?

This was the turning point. In July 1911, the Parliament discussed the report presented by Fernand David in the name of the agriculture commission in charge of examining the bill on appellations of origin and regional delimitations. Punishment was proposed for "those who, for commercial purposes, had used a geographical appellation to designate products that were different either by their origin or their type from those to which that appellation applied, by virtue of local, fair, established practices". At the same time, proposed rules did not seek to guarantee the uniform quality of the products but "simply … to prevent the appellation used to designate them from being fraudulently usurped".[31] In other words, regional appellations were not supposed to take into consideration the characteristics of products. Winemakers who were wagering on quality immediately protested against this approach: How could one defend the name of a wine without first defining the characteristics of the product?

The commission's reply was quite clear: Mediocre wines could be sold with a Bordeaux appellation merely because they were produced from the grapes of the region. The commission evoked the difference between manufactured and agricultural goods in respect to trademarks: "When we recognised the property rights of wine merchants

[29] AN F 12 6969, "Chambre des députés, séance du 30 mars 1910".
[30] Roudié, *Vignobles*: 231.
[31] AN F 12 6971, *Chambre des députés*, n. 1136, 7 July 1911.

or winemakers to their trademarks, the personal rights of writers and artists over their works, the exclusive right of the inventor to dispose of his patented invention, we never meant to assert that the trademark, the work or the invention would be of good or bad quality. Their freedom to produce remains full and complete, at their own risk and it is up to the public to assess its value."[32]

Given the considerable influence of atmospheric conditions on wine production and quality, "who would even dream of creating a uniform type, or even an average type for each of the innumerable wines of France?"

"Nevertheless, in addition to the origin of the agricultural product, your commission has been led to specify the type. It is necessary that the *appellation d'origine* be protected only when it is in the presence of products resembling by their nature those to which the appellation is applied according to fair, established, local practices... the *appellation d'origine*, by itself, is meaningless. Indeed, when one speaks of Bordeaux wines, the name of Bordeaux does not designate anything in itself, since the city of Bordeaux has never contained vineyards. It takes on its full meaning, however, when it is a question of products grown on the same soil, under the same climatic conditions, from the same grapes that have always been used to make the type of wine called Bordeaux. The name of origin in this case is a generic name, the appellation of which is determined by the nature of the product."[33]

Hence, the protection of the consumer could no longer be separated from that of the trademark owner: "The law of 1905 considers the damage caused to consumers who are deceived about the origin; we think that the winegrower, who is the legitimate trademark owner, should also be compensated." This was an attempt to mediate between the conflicting interests of winegrowers, merchants and consumers. Unfortunately, during the following months, a number of petitions from employer's federations, Chambers of Commerce, winegrowers' associations and others were addressed to the Ministry of Trade and to Parliament.[34]

---

[32] AN F 12 6971, *Chambre des députés*, n. 1136, 7 July 1911.
[33] AN F 12 6971, *Chambre des députés*, n. 1136, 7 July 1911.
[34] AN F 12 6969, *Chambre des députés*, n. 2564, 27 February 1913.

The First World War forced any solution to the problem into abeyance, but the debate started up again after the war; the law of 6 May 1919 reiterated the principle adopted in 1911, which left the decision about whether or not a wine was entitled to an *appellation d'origine* to the judges. The decision was supposed to be based on fair, unchanging, local customs. However, a review of the case law from 1911 to 1914 reveals that no attempt was made to define these terms more precisely. As a result, disputes multiplied through the years, almost always over what was meant by a fair, unchanging, local custom.

Tensions sharpened with the crisis in 1929, to the point that in July 1931, the government decided to support a bill proposed by winemakers in the south of France to raise taxes on output of more than one hundred hectolitres per hectare while prohibiting the planting of new vineyards by winegrowers that already had more than ten hectares or produced more than five hundred hectolitres.

However, these measures soon proved inadequate to curb the crisis, which was linked to falling income, reduced consumption and increased product imports from the United States. In 1934, a new law gave bonuses to winegrowers who uprooted vine plants and stopped growing hybrids. Although the collapse of prices subsequently ceased, the problem of trademarks remained. Indeed, many producers reacted to the new rules by selling their surplus production under false names and labels. The winegrowers' associations of the Bordeaux region succeeded in passing a decree proposal at the national conference of winegrowers' associations that was sent on to the government and quickly transformed into the Decree of 30 July 1935. This was the famous law that brought into being *Appelations d'Origine Contrôlée* (AOC) as they are known today. The decree not only limited the surface area of origin but also called for a list of accepted techniques and grape varieties for each region. The regulations were concerned with the process rather than the product per se, which to this day continues to be the essential difference between AOC and other labels. The AOC label controls production techniques without referring to the quality of the final product, whereas other labels focus on the quality aspect.

Definition of territory is still central to the French wine appellation. The unity of political identity and production is apparent in all the regions making wine that are eligible for an appellation, where the name of the commune is often synonymous with the name of the wine. This association is particularly marked in Burgundy. The identification of place names with territory begins at a more detailed scale than the commune. Throughout France, fields are often named after attributes of their sites. In Burgundy alone, more than 1,000 *lieux-dits* have been identified. Most of them take their name from the physical characteristics of the site, but others take their name from the human endeavour to raise plants and animals.

Within the AOC's category, a clear hierarchy has been established. Less than 5 per cent of French vineyards with a right to an appellation are classified as *grands crus*, and each level lower in the hierarchy has a larger area than that above it. Each commune has its own *syndicat of vignerons* without which the INAO can do very little. The appellation system is underpinned by a complicated network of organisations which represent different groups in the industry. The industry is supported by a highly professional bureaucracy. These groups and people have to identify and negotiate the main aspects of production subjected to control, namely the varieties of grapes to be grown, cultural practices in the vineyard and yields of grapes or wine. In most regional appellations, the number of authorised varieties is fewer than five, and individual varieties are restricted as to the appellation in which they may be used. Specifying the varieties that the viticulturalist is permitted to grow in any appellation means that innovation in varieties is prohibited in many vineyard regions of France, notably the most successful ones.

THE COLLECTIVE TRADEMARK: INVENTING TRADITION AND NEGOTIATING INNOVATION

A number of conclusions can be drawn regarding the issue of collective trademarks, which was raised immediately after the revolution and continued to generate political debate and legal disputes throughout the nineteenth and twentieth centuries. Those disputes pertained to three interrelated aspects: the recognition of collective trademarks; the protection of a distinctive sign for each producer or for the merchant; and the definition of wine as a natural or a manufactured product. These three aspects referred to one and the same problem, namely the process of agricultural industrialisation and the hierarchies between trade and production. It is untrue that France consistently protected collective trademarks as a heritage of guilds. During the entire nineteenth century, the reverse was true. Justices, legal scholars and an overwhelming majority of political representatives rejected the idea of *appellations régionales* precisely because they were considered a resurgence of guilds, an obstacle to the market, but primarily because they were estimated to be impossible to identify insofar as economic spaces were under constant change.

Towards the middle of the century, the recognition of individual trademarks encouraged the development of vineyards, which fuelled rather than impeded the uncertainties relating to market dynamics and the outcome of disputes. During the last quarter of the nineteenth century, however, the system experienced a major crisis coinciding with market internationalisation and the sudden appearance of synthetic chemicals in agriculture. At that point, the uncertainties became more radical, and new rules were required. Traders seemed to take control of the wine market, the phylloxera blight made the situation more difficult for winegrowers by increasing their dependence on credit, and the international market was quickly changing. Industrial property succeeded in imposing recognition of collective trademarks (regional appellations); however, opinions were divided regarding the geographical limits and technical or other criteria to be taken into consideration. The reason was that winegrowers of a given area were themselves divided about the extension of the concerned region and the techniques and practises to be considered "traditional" and "loyal". The introduction of the AOC label thus required not unanimous agreement on the part of the economic actors, which was impossible to attain, but a consensus of the majority on rules that were acceptable but not necessarily optimal.

The delimitation of the territories entitled to *appellations d'origine* and the list of accepted techniques and grape varieties were the fruit of a painful but necessary agreement among certain actors at the expense of others who until then had been allowed to produce Bordeaux or Champagne wines. In addition to their local, unchanging character defined by the appellation, AOC wines were also to be the result of "fair" customs, in which fairness referred not to spontaneous trade practices but to the way in which they were defined by a group of actors and institutionalised as such. This was a far cry from the AOC as the expression of a *terroir* and its traditions. The set of rules, justified on behalf of consumers and their interests, was in fact aimed at ensuring guaranteed income to a group of producers and an institutional framework in which any innovation would be negotiated. This solution was to become a formidable institutional tool for the economic activity of a group of producers. For decades, the winegrowers and merchants of Bordeaux and Champagne were to be protected not only from foreign counterfeiting but also from the temptations of some among them to make unilateral changes in production techniques or simply to "cheat". Hence, the desire of producers from other regions and of other products to benefit from the same advantages, which led to the multiplication of AOC labels during the second half of the twentieth century.

Contrary to standard theories, trademarks and collective trademarks were used primarily to provide the producer with a guaranteed income while offering a stable normative framework for negotiating innovation, rather than to inform consumers. From this standpoint, the AOC have achieved three complementary goals: first, to ensure fair practises within a group of producers; second, on these grounds, to better protect winegrowers against traders; and, third, to protect them from international competition. Collective trademark protected not only winegrowers against traders, but also helped small winegrowers. Still, between 1990 and 2003, while the total area of vines in the EU fell by 0.7 per cent per year, the average (wine) farm size only rose from 7.6 to 9.2 hectares.[35] Most European wine grapes therefore continue to be produced by thousands of relatively small holdings, each employing few salaried workers.[36]

AOC IN A COMPARATIVE PERSPECTIVE

French AOC rules have enjoyed great success in other European countries, especially in Spain and Italy where, for reasons similar to those in France, wine production played an important role in market

---

[35] Andy Smith, "Globalization Within the European Wine Industry: Commercial Challenges But Producer Domination." Paper presented at UACES annual conference, session 9, 1–3 September 2008.

[36] Alfredo Manuel Jesus Oliveira Coelho, Jean-Louis Rastoin, "Globalisation du marché du vin et stratégies d'entreprise." *Economie rurale*, 245–65 (2001): 16–34.

equilibrium and in the introduction of quality norms. French lobbies and criteria (mainly Bordeaux and Champagne areas) have strongly influenced contemporary European legislation on collective trademarks. The regulations for quality wine in the EU involve much more than identification of a geographic source. They clearly come within the definition of *appellations d'origine* because they include demarcation of the area of production, vine varieties to be grown, cultivation methods, winemaking methods, minimum natural alcoholic strength by volume and yield by hectare. These rules have been strongly supported by French representatives; the list and the eligible criteria are continually re-negotiated (in particular between French and Italian representatives). In France, collective trademarks served to control a group of producers faced with the emergence of innovations on the one hand and with the impact of trade on the other. The invention of traditions aimed precisely at closing the ranks of winegrowers and producers.

On the contrary, collective trademarks (but not trademarks of origin)[37] were not used in Anglo-Saxon countries where product value was mainly indicated by individual trademarks and *terroir* was not an economic and legal asset.[38] This was partially linked to the technical and economic organisation of the U.S. wine market at the moment of its emergence. In contrast to France, the rise of wine production took place after the introduction of organic chemistry and industrial methods of winemaking and conservation. California wines, like those in Argentina, Australia and South Africa, developed in response to an increasing internal and international demand and decreasing production in France, Italy and Spain because of phylloxera.[39]

The first secular winery in California was built near Los Angeles in the 1820s by a Frenchman appropriately named Jean-Louis Vignes.

---

[37] In the United States, some quality signs identify, for example, wines from different areas; however, these labels never refer to a group of producers or to a given technique of production. Michael Maher, "On Vino Veritas? Clarifying the Use of Geographical References on American Wine Labels." *California Law Review*, 89, 6 (2001): 1881–925.

[38] Jim Chen, "Le statut légal des appellations d'origine contrôlée aux Etats-Unis d'Amérique." *Revue de droit rural*, 249 (1997): 37.

[39] Vicente Pinilla, Gema Aparicio, Maria-Isabel Ayuda, "The International Wine Market, 1850–1938: An Opportunity for Export Growth in Southern Europe?" *European Review of Economic History*, 6, 1 (2002): 51–85.

He got his cuttings from South Africa. By 1851, he was producing nearly 1,000 barrels a year, including some premium wines. Thanks to German and Hungarian immigrants, there were more than 400 vineyards in Napa by the late 1800s. Agoston Haraszthy (1812–1862), an Hungarian immigrant, was a leading actor in the raising of California vineyards. Haraszthy's critical contribution to California wine was his trip to Europe in 1861 and the subsequent import of nearly 100,000 vine shoots representing 1,400 European varietals. There was no mass market for Californian wines until the trans-continental railroad was finished in 1869. In 1894, the California Wine Association was created. It controlled a large fraction of the production and was able to stabilise prices and costs. At the 1900 World Exhibition in Paris, Californian wines won forty awards, but few people noticed. By the mid-1890s, California production of raisins surpassed Spain's and a decade later it exceeded Turkey's. By the period 1909 to 1913, California accounted for more than 38 per cent of the volume of commercial output, and by the 1920s for more than 63 per cent of the world's supply.[40] By 1910, the demand for wine was enough to consume 50 million gallons produced by the industry nationally. California's share of the national wine market grew from 50 to 88 per cent.

The profitability in California's new commercial wine industry emanated from wineries of a larger size and with aggressive marketing. For example, the Sainsevain Brothers of the Los Angeles area adopted new vertical integration wine business practices. They quickly expanded production by purchasing bulk wine from their growers, purchasing small local vineyards, opening a store in San Francisco and shipping wine to New York and Philadelphia. Most importantly, federal planning and financing also supported the new industry. This new wine industry also benefited from patterns established by other agricultural and food-processing industries. Sulfur dioxing the must (fermenting juice) and refrigerated fermentation were immediately widely adopted. Mechanisation and standardisation of the product have been at the core of this system since its beginnings. Vertical

---

[40] José Morilla Critz, Alan Olmstead, Paul Rhode, "Horn of Plenty: The Globalization of Mediterranean Horticulture and the Economic Development of Southern Europe, 1880–1930." *Journal of Economic History*, 59, 2 (1999): 316–52.

integration overcame the tensions between winegrowers and traders which had been at the core of the AOC in France. Together with the lack of any established local reputation of a given territory, there was no rationale for collective trademark.

In California, alignment and organisational structure of vineyards were and still are different from that in Burgundy or Bordeaux. In the traditional grape-growing areas of Bordeaux and Burgundy, the narrow spacing of rows (one meter) and of the vines within the row (often less than one meter) restricts the vigor of the vines. The outcome is a narrow hedge of vines and few interior shaded leaves, so that maximum use is made of the available solar energy for photosynthesis. Moreover, the rows are less than one meter high. This low height, combined with the rows running north-south (the common practise) provides little shading of one row by another.

In countries such as Australia, New Zealand and the United States, the spacing of rows has been driven by the desire to use large machines not developed specifically for viticulture; rows are therefore frequently spaced more widely than is necessary. To make maximum use of available solar radiation for photosynthesis and still use standard machines, the trellises can be higher. To this must be added the fact that major vine and wine varieties in these locations are not as localised as in France. For example, Cabernet Sauvignon is overwhelmingly localised in Bordeaux areas while being dispersed across large areas in Napa and Sonoma counties. This also contributed to weaken the economic rationale for collective trademarks. Institutional reasons and path-dependency in U.S. legal institutions were equally important. In particular, rules governing wines as food products were part of an institutional framework that emphasised health quality (hence the connection with drugs), and product quality was viewed solely from this angle. Hence, there was to be a threshold of acceptability and compliance but no criteria of product value beyond individual trademarks.

As we have seen in France, the law of 1905 mentioned the "origin" as a criterion for identifying a "fair product". Collective trademark entered a general regulation of adulteration. In the United States, the Federal Food and Drugs Act of 1906 dealt with both product adulteration and brand counterfeiting; unlike the French law of 1851, there was no reference to product qualities, followed by a distinction between fraud and falsification; American law took drugs, which could be standardised, as its reference, but this conception of products still had to be applicable to others such as wine. Here, the relation to brand falsification is obvious.[41] As long as the product was not injurious to health and competition was fair, anything was lawful and there was no need to control innovation by referring to traditions, *terroir*, and so on.[42] Thus, whereas individual trademarks and labelling were the primary if not unique means of regulating consumption in the United States, they were considered a tool among others in France. As a consequence, if in some French areas, AOCs have strongly protected winegrowers against traders and encouraged small units, in the United States, concentration has never stopped developing, to the point that some viticultural areas, such as Texas Hill Country, are larger than nine individual American states.

To sum up, historical experience of wine markets hardly confirms any simplistic and mechanical link between trademark protection and growth. French wines enjoyed tremendous growth in the nineteenth century, precisely at the time when trademark law was weakest (collective trademarks were not yet recognised). Conversely, the increased legal protection of trademarks in European law has not prevented the decline of this segment in favour of non-European trademarks. This outcome can be partly explained by the fact that current international expansion gives major weight to marketers and distributors at the expense of producers, especially small ones. As a result, standardisation and production stabilisation (as we have shown in the chapter devoted to these issues) are the perfect answer to these economic hierarchies and the criteria for putting products on sale.

Another factor helps to account for product dynamics in addition to their legal protection: the role of innovation. For French and European

---

[41] Article 8 stresses that "The term misbrand as used herein, shall apply to all drugs, or articles of food or articles which enter into the composition of food, the package or label of which shall bear any statement, design, or device regarding such article, or the ingredient or substances contained therein which shall be false or misleading in any particular, and to any food or drug product which is falsely branded". Department of Agriculture, Bureau of Chemistry, "Pure food and drug bill, 30 June 1906". *Bulletin* n. 98, *Drug Legislation in the United States*, Washington, DC, Government Printing Office, 1906: 20–3.

[42] William Derenberg, "The Influence of the French Code Civil on the Modern Law of Unfair Competition." *American Journal of Comparative Law*, 4, 1 (1955): 1–34.

wines, collective trademarks were not intended as a tool to prevent innovation (tradition is a marketing invention), but rather to negotiate it. Any change in the production process had to be approved by the producer associations concerned, as well as the public institutions controlling the wine market. In Anglo-Saxon law, on the contrary, innovation was less subject to these forms of negotiation, insofar as individual trademarks and wine production criteria were only required to meet compliance criteria (techniques and health). The possibility of benefiting from the fruits of an innovation, such as a guaranteed income, was constantly kept in check by the injunction on disturbing market equilibrium. This tension cannot be described as a "contradiction" because it constitutes the very core of the workings of a capitalist economy.

As such, collective trademarks were not only a distinctive feature of Ancien Régime guilds but they are widespread up to our day. In particular, they fully developed in the second half of the nineteenth century much less to inform the final consumer than to guarantee rents to producers and traders. Within this general context, collective trademarks aim to ensure fair practises within a given group, whereas individual brands aim to protect a producer from outside competitors. From this perspective, they do not aim and therefore cannot guarantee a correspondence between price and quality, but only an equilibrium between innovation and market stability. This issue explains why, historically, and despite statements of economic theory, trademark protection has not developed as an alternative to state regulation of contract, but in accordance with it.

From that standpoint, the collective trademark undoubtedly expresses a different form of market regulation in France – and later in the EU – from other wine-producing countries. This leads us to raise further questions, namely: Are not collective trademarks limited to some products and sectors? If so, then, how do markets coordinate in the lack of collective trademarks? And how much do wine and agriculture products matter in both economic and institutional French (and European) dynamics?

To answer these questions, after contracts and brands, we have now to enlarge our perspective and consider, on the one hand, manufactured goods and on the other hand, two other forces for market coordination, that is, expertise and the international market.

8

EXPERTISE AND PRODUCT SPECIFICATION

Is expertise the foundation of a "third wave" of science studies, which seek answers to the question "how do you make decisions based on scientific knowledge before there is an absolute scientific consensus?"[1] The issues at hand are, first, the indeterminacy of standards, and second, the ferocious arguments that erupted around the solidification of standards (agreed or imposed) into the form of regulations and their enforcement through the law. In the period under review, the debate was partly philosophical, about the relationship between food and nature, and partly about the degree to which the practical methods used by the food industry to make a profit were socially and commercially acceptable.

In the following pages, I will discuss some concerns of products expertise; I am not going to go into its history, which we have already discussed elsewhere and which is now documented by a substantial bibliography.[2] I am going to examine a rather neglected aspect, namely, the relationship between the form and organisation of expertise on the one hand and the organisation of production and product quality definition on the other. In particular, I will address three points: first,

---

[1] Harry M. Collins, Robert J. Evans, "The Third Wave of Science Studies: Studies of Expertise and Experience." *Social Studies of Science*, 32 (2002): 235–96.

[2] Alessandro Stanziani, *Histoire de la qualité alimentaire*. Paris, Seuil, 2005; Frédéric Chauvaud, *Experts et expertise judiciaire, XIXe–XXe siècles*. Rennes, PUR, 2003; Louis Dumoulin, *L'expertise comme nouvelle raison politique? Discours, usages et effets de l'expertise judiciaire*. PhD dissertation (University of Grenoble): 2003; *L'expertise dans les principaux systèmes juridiques d'Europe*. Paris, University Paris II, Éditions de l'épargne, 1969. Christelle Rabier (ed.), *Fields of Expertise: Paris and London since 1600*. Cambridge, Cambridge Scholars Press, 2007.

I will explore the designation of experts, the nature of their methods, and the *imprimatur* of their pronouncements. Traders considered themselves as the best qualified people to judge product quality; for example, wine merchants in France stressed that only they had the required know-how to conclude whether a wine has been falsified or not. In contrast, the municipal administration and a part of public opinion were favourable to a recourse to those scientists whose methods were presented as "objective". As such, the organoleptic analysis of traders stood against scientific chemical expertise.

Second, to these conflicts between traders and scientists we must add the question of disputes between the State and the municipalities. Because different municipal laboratories used different methods of analysis, the question arose of how to prevent meat that had, for instance, been rejected in Lyon being accepted in Paris. The French response was to establish an official list of the methods of analysis valid for all municipal laboratories. However, in the early twentieth century, strong centralisation reversed previous policies: Municipalities lost any control over the quality of food products. This was accompanied by a standardisation of the methods of analysis. Third, I will compare major issues for food and beverages to manufactured items.

EXPERTISE ON FOODSTUFFS

When discussing trademarks, we have shown that winegrowers and cattle breeders supported collective trademarks and "tradition" to preserve their strength when facing wholesale traders and manufacturers. In contrast, throughout the nineteenth century, especially from the 1870s onwards, wholesale traders pushed for the standardisation of foodstuffs or to obtain products of "uniform" (unvarying) type, as defined during this period. Thus, in the course of the nineteenth century, for products such as wine and milk, wholesale traders encouraged product standardisation and stabilisation through two main processes: blending wines or milk of different origins; and the use of preservatives, antiseptics and artificial colouring. Their business correspondence reveals the pressure these traders put on producers, arguing that the market and the customers wanted to receive stable products (especially wines) from one year to the next.[3] For food industry products, this phenomenon had existed at least since the eighteenth century in Gironde and Champagne, where merchants adopted the practice of "stabilising" products by blending different wines. This attitude was strengthened by the expansion of international markets in the 1850s and even more by the development of organic chemistry and the possibility of resorting to preservatives and stabilisers.[4]

During the same period, a similar trend can be seen in the milk market where, thanks to the first refrigerated wagons and the development of chemical preservatives, more and more wholesale traders became accustomed to using milk from different herds and blending and processing it before putting it on sale in the cities.[5] This strategy aimed to please the public, who wanted products with stable visual and gustative characteristics, but it also gave traders greater power over producers and cattle breeders.[6] By stabilising products through blending and preservatives, wholesale traders played on competition among producers and imposed their terms and prices on them.

At the same time, this outcome was different in different markets, depending on several variables: the relative power of producers and wholesale traders, the technical features of the concerned product, the attitudes of authorities, consumers' responses and, last but not least, the role of experts and scientific discourse in public debates. Without forgetting this, in the following pages, I will focus on experts and expertise. Nowadays, the introduction of traceability (especially for meat) has led producers to standardise products according to certain characteristics rather than others. This process is not new; in fact, it has been quite common in the history of advanced capitalism, as the history of forms of expertise in France demonstrates. In particular, I wish to show that the centralisation and standardisation of administrative expertise on products was one of the driving forces in the process of production normalisation and standardisation.

---

[3] *Revue vinicole*, years 1880–1890. For Italy: Archivi centrali di Stato (ACS), fond MAIC (Ministero de l'agricultura, industria e commercio), Direz. gen. agric. vers.VI, busta 251; for France and French-Italian relations: AN F 12 6353.

[4] AN F 12 7452, 9183, 6353.

[5] Stanziani, *Histoire*.

[6] AN F 12 7452, AN BB 18 6031.

A general political tendency during the first years of the French Third Republic was to grant municipalities more power. It was in this context that the question of municipal laboratories arose. After the first International Congress of Hygiene and Demography in Brussels in 1876 highlighted the role that the municipal laboratory played in that city, the second Congress in Paris two years later stressed the need to organise similar laboratories in the main French towns. This was achieved in Paris in 1878, Le Havre in 1879, Reims in 1882, Rouen in 1883, Saint-Etienne and Amiens in 1884 and Pau in 1885.[7] In these units, medical doctors acted as statisticians and demographers; they were in charge of hygiene, vaccination and food safety problems. This was not only because of budgetary constraints, but also because, according to the hygienist credo, prevention had to be global, covering food habits, vaccination, housing and general education.

We may ask whether these laboratories were primarily intended to serve traders (for example, wine retail merchants who were suspicious of the composition of the product they bought from wholesalers), consumers (complaining about retailers) or local authorities (the prefecture, the municipality in their campaign against adulterated products). We can also question whether they were supposed to protect public health (and thus the consumer) or to regulate competition (and thus the relationship between traders). In Paris, the organisation of a municipal laboratory was at first conceived as a form of public control of the markets; as such, services of the municipal laboratory would not have been accessible to the public, only the police. This type of laboratory was agreed upon in 1878; however, there were protests from both traders and consumers, and two years later, the municipal laboratory and its activity became a public service. It aimed to solve the problem of increasing information asymmetries on the food market, and to do this, the laboratory was accessible not only to the police and the prefecture, but also to private actors. This hybrid solution testified at the same time to the increasing involvement of both the central state and the municipalities in food matters and in economic activity generally, and to the aim of private economic actors to regulate contractual problems by appealing to a third party.

[7] Stanziani, *Histoire*.

The laboratory's budget quickly increased during the 1880s. In 1881, it made 3,958 analyses free of charge, and 378 were paid for by private customers. To this, one has to add 2,181 samples that municipal inspectors seized – that is, 6,517 analyses in total. In 1882, 5,188 analyses were free of charge, 50 paid for by private customers and 5,238 samples came from inspectors. In 1883, almost 15,000 analyses were made. If we now distinguish by product, wine was the most analysed product. In 1883, almost half of the analyses (7,444) concerned wine, 5,280 of them free of charge (that is, related to watering down), 283 paid for by private customers and 1,581 referred by inspectors. Second was milk: In 1883, there were 4,172 analyses as a whole, including 491 free on the request of private individuals, 14 paying, and 3,667 from inspectors.

The major importance devoted to wine and milk is above all an outcome of the private-public purpose of the laboratory. In fact, while wine inspection and analysis was often required by *cabaretiers* (publicans) and *débitants* (retailers) to protect themselves from litigation, milk analysis was mostly the result of the autonomous action of inspectors. This created indirect political pressure and gave milk and milk adulteration a mediating role in encouraging change.[8] Overall, the probability that a food or drink retailer would be visited was remote, and the incentive to renounce fraud was low, unless his reputation for quality was well established.

This efficiency problem was related to another, broader issue: the rise of a national market and the local nature of rules and their enforcement. Different municipal laboratories used different methods of analysis, and the question arose of how to prevent food rejected in one city being accepted in another. The solution consisted in establishing an official view on methods of analysis valid for all the municipal laboratories; however, this could only be done if these laboratories adhered to state rather than municipal rules. This is to say that the creation of a national market was inseparable from that of national regulatory institutions. On the supply side, economic actors mobilised different definitions of food quality and adulteration to gain a legal-institutional organisation of the market, and thus the legal exclusion

---

[8] Dr. Hogg, "De l'organisation de l'inspection des substances alimentaires." *Revue d'Hygiène et de Police Sanitaire* (1881): 431–50.

of a part of the competition. This is not to say that economic lobbies completely controlled the market rules. The related issues would have been impossible to reach without the role food security played in the public debate of the time. Under the Third Republic, several scientists were elected, which was quite different from the preceding Second Empire, when, often excluded from political activity, scientists mobilised their knowledge as a clear political weapon. This also helps to explain the very complex attitude that scientists had with regard to business. It is commonplace to stress that French scientists criticised capitalism and its prioritisation of profits. This attitude was indeed quite widespread and became particularly evident during the major sanitary crisis (trichinosis, tuberculosis) of that time, as well as in the public debates about wine adulteration. For those holding such opinions, solutions were to be found less in science than in limitations imposed on the new consumer society.[9]

However important, these attitudes were not the only ones, and a majority of scientists (for instance, as a member of a consultative board or as an elected Deputy) considered that science and business had to walk hand in hand to find the most appropriate rules – that is, rules balancing profits with trade transparency and health security. Some of these scientists were also members of economic associations (chambers of commerce, winegrowers' unions, etc.) and because of this they were constantly accused of collusion by their colleagues. Those scientists claimed that science possessed the instruments to deal with public health problems. Safety became synonymous with a "pure", standardised product. This led hygienists to agree with trader circles they had criticised on other occasions. This convergence of initially opposing interests was expressed very clearly at the turn of the nineteenth century.[10]

These orientations prevailed even more when, beginning in 1907, a commission was set up to determine, in compliance with the general law of 1905 on adulteration, a series of decrees defining the accepted characteristics and techniques for the principal products.

[9] AN F 12 42443, 4843. Also *Revue d'hygiène et de police sanitaire*, several years, 1878–1895.
[10] AN F 12 6970, "Lettre du ministre du Commerce au président de la délégation française" without date; "Le congrès des aliments purs." *Le moniteur viticole*, 21 January (1908): 1–5.

In the succeeding discussions and projects, tensions mounted among the various pressure groups: manufacturers, farmers, wholesale traders (each category was often undecided about the criteria to be adopted, depending on the industry and the region concerned), hygienists and administrative managers (who were also divided). Each group wanted to impose a definition of the product involved and tried to get certain techniques approved at the expense of others. Generally speaking, agricultural producers encouraged detailed product specification, whereas wholesale traders and their associations sought wider institutional definitions as well as techniques to stabilise the products in question. The result was usually a compromise between these differing orientations. For example, wine was defined in opposition to "industrial wines". The regulations provided a list of lawful manipulations and therefore confirmed the trends already manifest in the special laws that had prohibited certain practises (dilution, vinage, sweetening); they summarised the observations of the hygienists (e.g., the prohibition of sulphuric acid), of the winemakers of southern France (the prohibition of sweetening) and the Gironde (the prohibition of certain blends).[11]

Scientists' varied attitudes to business are reflected in the debate about methods of analysis. For example, the addition of plaster in wine (beyond two grams per litre) was forbidden in 1880, but because of the protests of Midi winegrowers and traders (those most affected), the application of this rule was delayed. In 1886, the Ministry of Agriculture requested experts to assess the "real impact" of plaster on health. This Commission focused not on this problem, but on the question of how to measure the quantity of plaster in wine.

Two different procedures and instruments were available on the market: one patented by Pasteur, the other by Berthelot and Fleurieu. Unfortunately, these different methods gave different results. If the Pasteur method had been in use, most of the questioned wine would have been considered "legal", whereas the second method would have led to its interdiction.[12] This raised the basic problem (that in our own time still lingers with doping tests) of the measures and the

---

[11] AN BB 18 6055.

[12] [Anon.], "Analyse chimique des vins du département de la Gironde, vins rouges de la récolte de 1888 et vins blancs de la récolte de 1887." *Bulletin du ministère de l'Agriculture*, 6 (1889): 510–30.

instruments of expertise. The scientists developed different measures but were unable to agree upon a means of choosing one method over another. From this point of view, scientific uncertainty and political mediation were constant components of market regulation via expertise.

In other cases, traditional organoleptic analysis (tasting wine, smelling milk) by food professionals was set in opposition to chemical expertise. This mirrored the problem of quality measures for foodstuffs and drink. Food traders stressed that, as these items were not standardised products, it was impossible to conclude the presence of adulteration only by chemical analysis. For example, how could one demonstrate that an excess of water in wine (or in milk) was due to the producer rather than to "nature"? For their part, scientists sought to list the main components and acceptable values for every product. This supposed the possibility of establishing a correspondence between the standardisation of products and of expertise; unfortunately, for most of the period in question, this was more a project than a reality.

Organoleptic expertise was based on the experience and professional skill of food traders and wine merchants. However, such professional skill met increasing difficulties when confronted at the end of the nineteenth century with the wide use of organic chemistry. When they were defendants in a trial, traders maintained they were not scientists and, as such, could not identify artificial substances in wine or other "natural" products. At the same time, however, they argued that "natural" products such as wine should not be evaluated solely by chemical analysis. Scientists might confuse bad vintages with adulterated products. On these grounds, traders and professional associations criticised the stance of the Paris laboratory in identifying upper and lower limits for several components of wine beyond which adulteration was presumed.[13]

Because of such criticisms, the Ministry of the Interior asked the Director of the Paris laboratory, Charles Girard, and the Prefect for a detailed report. In it, Girard denied the fact that the laboratory made use only of chemical analysis for wine, pointing out that tasting

---

[13] AN F 12 7417, "Feuilles d'analyse du laboratoire de Paris" (January 1884).

(*dégustation*) was also used, particularly for the top-ranked wines. His concern was not just with food safety but also with adulteration. He displayed contempt for the profit motive of the capitalist food industry and advocated the disclosure of detailed information about the composition of foods. Here, we need to make a distinction between two different phases in product quality: ex-ante (information on labels or in contracts) and ex-post (laboratory analysis). Girard entered the ex-ante debate, but he and his laboratory were responsible only for ex-post problems of evaluating the already sold products. His position gave traders a solid basis for their complaints and led to the debate on the legal value of expertise. As the Prefect explained in his report, the laboratory was just a simple source of information, and its analyses constituted only indices of presumption, not clear evidence for legal judgements.[14] As to the judges, this did not imply that they had to acquire scientific training or competence. Expertise addressed technical concerns but also contained a conclusion expressed in legal terms: adulterated wine or milk. After that, the judge had to attribute responsibility, and here expert analysis was only one element among many because it could not say anything about who had adulterated the product.

Despite attempts to defuse the debate, criticisms did not stop and even increased, to the extent that some judges in the 1890s raised doubts about using laboratory analyses, even as simple indices.[15] This was so because the chemical analysis of foodstuffs and wine still faced serious difficulties in the accuracy and stability of its observations. For example, the watering down of wine could not be detected if the added water was below 20 per cent of the volume.[16]

In 1896, a special Commission was set up at the Ministry of Finance. It was charged with an attempt to identify standard criteria for analysing wines and alcohol generally. It was not by chance that this Commission was made up only of scientists, with no representative from business associations.[17] This was an attempt made by

[14] AN F 12 7417, "Préfecture de Police au Ministre du Commerce" (9 March 1883).
[15] AN BB 18 6025, "Lettre du Préfet de Paris au Ministre de l'Intérieur" (18 March 1895).
[16] *Ibid.*
[17] AN F 12 7417, "Décret du Président de la République sur la Constitution d'une Commission d'Expert auprès du Ministère des Finances" (25 September 1883).

civil servants both to reduce contestation and to coordinate different branches of the administration (that is, municipal as well as different ministry laboratories). Science was supposed to be the strong unifying and legitimising factor.

The Commission indicated the most appropriate methods of analysis but added that administrative expertise as practised in municipal and fiscal laboratories was only one piece of evidence, among others, in a judicial trial. Guilt could only be attributed on the grounds of several concomitant factors (letters, accounts, testimonies). These suggestions left unsolved the problem of the institutional setting for the standardisation of expertise. Should municipalities be left in charge of these services? How were local and central institutions to be coordinated?

These questions deeply affected not only the economic dynamics but also the institutional equilibrium of the Third Republic and in particular the relationship between municipalities and the central state. The tensions were such that the Commission's recommendations were not translated into rules until, at the beginning of the twentieth century, a new general law on fraud and falsification laid out a basis for expertise. This general law on food adulteration of 1905 was followed in July 1906 by a Ministerial Decree confirming the creation of a new Service for the Repression of Frauds at the Ministry of Agriculture. The decree detailed the organisation of laboratories and their methods of analysis. Still, the relationship between these new central laboratories and the previous municipal laboratories had to be clarified: Should the municipal laboratories be curtailed, and if not, should they be dependant on the Ministry of Agriculture?

A circular issued by this Ministry stated that municipal laboratories could survive only by agreement and then under the control of the Minister of Agriculture.[18] This meant that, unlike in the first years of the Third Republic, now the balance of power had shifted from municipalities towards the central government. The reform was not without its problems; the Paris laboratory, in particular, refused to submit to the Service of Repression of Fraud and contested the value of its

---

[18] AN BB 18 6055, "Note interne du Ministère de la Justice" (no date).

selected methods of analysis. The result was that the Ministry denied the laboratory official status and the courts refused to take its analyses into consideration.[19]

Of course, this issue only concerned administrative law expertise. Other forms of expertise were available in different contexts. In particular, judicial counter-expertise in law courts could not be standardised nor practised by officials but only by *assermentés* experts who were free to choose their methods. This was so because officials were considered as "involved parties" and also because, since the experts could not be chosen from among state officials, they could not impose any methods.

Private product expertise was also developed to satisfy the increasing needs of business to control product or semi-product quality to avoid litigation. This development also responded to the evolution of contractual responsibilities. At the turn of the century, the legal invention of the consumer went along with that of the "professional". The rights of the former were protected when challenging the quality of a product or even when the purchase of an adulterated product was the result of ignorance. In both cases, it was the responsibility of the professional to take care to evaluate the product, applying expertise where necessary. Here, analyses mostly acted as a check on negligence rather than as proof of a guilty action, because for that, further official expertise was required.

To sum up, throughout the nineteenth century, and in particular during the second half of it, administrative and health inspections of produce and foodstuffs, which had already been in place for several centuries (market inspections), were at the core of public debate. There were a number of reasons for this: the extension of market intermediation networks and thus the lengthening of the chain from producer to end consumer raised the problem of product qualities from the point of view of consumer health protection as well as fair trade. The increasing authority of scientists and their arguments in public debate was also a factor. More and more scientists became

---

[19] Décrets du 19 mars 1907 (*Journal Officiel*, 7 avril 1907) et du 13 juin 1907 (*Journal Officiel* du 20 juin 1907); AN BB 18 6031, "Rapport du Procureur Général de la Cour de Cassation au Ministre de la Justice" (27 April 1909).

elected representatives or took part indirectly in the political debate and scientific argument became a full-fledged component of political rhetoric.[20]

In this context, two issues arose: the technique of expertise and the spatial organisation of laboratories. On the first point, the representatives of the business world were opposed to administrative officials; as such, debate over the form of expertise was the one between business self-regulation and external regulation. The latter prevailed because the business world itself was divided insofar as many traders opposed producers precisely on the grounds of standardised products and expertise.

Debates on the form of expertise crossed with those on who was in charge of them, whether municipal or state laboratories. There were considerable problems involved in the territorial and institutional organisation of administrative analysis laboratories. Firstly, the relationship between municipal governments and central authority; and secondly, the possibility of the same product circulating throughout the national territory, namely the formation of a genuine national market. These two knots dissolved in the early twentieth century when republican elites reversed the trends of the previous decades. In particular, when the service for the repression of frauds was set up, municipal laboratories were closed or subordinated to the new institution. This reform was coupled with another, aimed at standardising analytical procedures within laboratories.

The use of standardised methods was a key factor in forming a genuine national market. Indeed, along with transport and changing production techniques, the possibility of having relatively uniform rules for defining product qualities and authorising their sale encouraged the production of comparable or even standardised products and the development of prices conditioned exclusively by transport costs (at equal quality).[21] With the decrees defining product characteristics, these measures fostered the implementation of a real national market

---

[20] Alessandro Stanziani, "La mesure de la qualité du vin en France, 1871–1914." *Food and History*, 2, 1 (2004): 191–226.

[21] AN BB 18 6055, "Arrêté du 13 août 1907"; "Chambre des députés, séance du 9 mars 1911, rapport de Fernand David au nom de la commission." *Bulletin international de la répression des fraudes*, 37 (November 1911): 453–62 ; A. Métin, "La répression des fraudes en France, extrait du rapport sur le budget du ministère de l'Agriculture." *Bulletin international de la répression des fraudes*, 47 (September 1912): 273–89.

of relatively homogeneous products. Indeed, given the cost of legal challenges and the frequency of inspections, it became increasingly advantageous for economic actors to produce and sell products with relatively stable characteristics that were likely to pass administrative inspection easily. From this point of view, standardised expertise was therefore less the result than the cause of product standardisation. The case of ordinary wines, milk and pasta confirms this argument. Their development followed rather than anticipated the introduction of public administration rules concerning them, which provided an institutional definition of their characteristics.[22]

This process was not specific to France. Generally speaking, beginning in the second half of the nineteenth century, the entire capitalist world was confronted by the same circumstance, namely agricultural industrialisation and the development of national and international markets. Within this scope, product expertise was central, from the point of view of both hygiene and competition policies. However, the details of implementing expertise and its institutional organisation differed. In Germany, as in France, recourse to scientific expertise increased during the last quarter of the nineteenth century. At the same time, in contrast to France, standardised methods originated less from state authorities than from the association of chemists. This solution was based on the existence of more highly consolidated trade associations than in France at the time, particularly in the liberal professions, as well as on the fact that German rules regarding food fraud and falsification did not include detailed definitions or production techniques.[23]

Finally, whereas in France and Germany the centralisation of the analysis system corresponded to the standardisation of methods, in Great Britain, this process did not really take place until the Second World War. Until that point, laboratories were run by municipalities, and their criteria of analysis differed from one city to another. This outcome corresponded to the main English liberal principles and the belief in the market's ability to overcome the problems of product information and quality definition. At the same time, the fragmentation of institutions and methods of expertise also reflected the

---

[22] Stanziani, *Histoire*; Françoise Sabban, Silvano Serventi, *Les pâtes*. Paris, Actes sud, 2000.
[23] Stanziani, *Histoire*.

technical and historical characteristics of the British agribusiness sector which depended heavily on imports and hence was less interested than France in aligning regional disparities with uniform criteria for product acceptance in the market. In other words, municipal autonomy in the area of expertise did not call into question the principle of examining products at the time they were imported.

In the United States, the case was again different; the demands of international trade (this time oriented towards exporting agricultural products) had to be reconciled with those of local markets and the national market, but within a federal framework. In particular, standardised forms of expertise were soon suggested and achieved in the area of exports, due to pressure from importing countries (mainly in Europe) and trade lobbies that had every reason to demand standardised products from farmers.

Similar coordination was required at the federal level. However, in this case, the need to arrive at single product assessment and classification criteria collided with the interests of local producers and wholesale traders who were reluctant to standardise their products because it would entail considerable cost and imply greater dependence on large traders. The problem was solved by requiring twofold expertise. Trade between the states was subject to the same rules as export, that is, the same offices and identical types of expertise. For local trade within the state, other laboratories and expertise criteria, and hence product classification, could be used. This double system had the advantage of reconciling stability with flexible rules, but at the same time, there were major loopholes. Thus, once wheat or other products were accepted in a state with several ports or large cities, they could be transferred from one port to another or from one city to another in compliance solely with the norms of that state. This posed the problem of reconciling domestic trade with foreign trade in the event of their subsequent export, leading to major disputes with European importing countries that complained delivered products did not comply with orders, and with American farmers who accused officials of playing favourites and showing preferences in product assessment.[24]

[24] J.C.F. Merrill, "Classification of Grains into Grades." *Annals of the American Academy of Political and Social Science*, 38, 2 (1911): 58–77; Henry Crosby Emery, "Futures in the Grain Market." *Economic Journal*, 9, 33 (1899): 45–67.

As a result, whereas in France and Germany the standardisation and centralisation of expertise accompanied and supported that of products to the advantage of wholesale traders and at the expense of farmers, in Great Britain the process was much less strict (as the difficulties of regulating the milk market testify). Finally, in the United States, there was considerable standardisation of agricultural production, but its extent should not be overestimated because it applied above all to export products and less to products intended for the domestic market.

To sum up, expertise in the regulatory situations under scrutiny constituted a set of constructions of goal-orientated knowledge deployed in laboratories, in courts and in the corridors of power to achieve the insertion of rational ordering and standardisation of the food supply. From this standpoint, the normalisation of foodstuffs was a process that grew out of the converging interests and actions of different groups: wholesale traders who wanted to take control of the food industry; hygienists eager to have healthy, cheap products available for the "working classes"; and the central administrations which aimed to regain control over expertise for tax, commercial and health reasons. From this point of view, the stabilisation of foodstuffs, the birth of a nationwide market and the form of market regulation went together. Tensions arose between the two criteria of product evaluation, two notions of the law (one close to administrative-police rules, the second to judicial law) and, last but not least, two different ways by which the law was supposed to orient the economy.

At the same time, the issue of the specificities of these products arose in market regulation operations. Were foodstuffs in fact the privileged sector of regulation and for the very long term? To verify this hypothesis, I am going to study the process of expertise and the definition of specifications for manufactured products.

MULTIPLE SPECIFICATIONS FOR MANUFACTURED PRODUCTS

We have seen that expertise as a tool for product identification and market coordination plays a crucial role for foodstuff and produce. In those cases, expertise lies at the crossroads of health, business and private and public interests. We now have to understand whether it plays a similar or different role in markets for manufactured items. This analysis is obviously linked to the history of patents and brands in industry, yet I do not intend to engage such a broad topic for which a huge bibliography is available. I will limit my investigation to a more modest aim, that is, the problem of product specification on markets where, in principle, since the early nineteenth century at least, standardisation is supposed to be much more widespread and accepted than for produce and foodstuffs. Yet, this clear-cut contrast between agriculture and foodstuffs on the one hand and manufactured products on the other is misleading. This is so, first of all, because as we have seen the link between agriculture, food and "natural" products as such is an invention of the late nineteenth century, precisely at the moment when those products and industries were confronted with the rise of organic chemistry and their overall process of industrialisation. Agri-food business was far from being un-standardised; quite the contrary, it was its increasing industrialisation that gave rise to methods of production and marketing stressing the uniqueness and "natural" features of products.

Standard qualities for manufactured items have not been "spontaneously" selected by market forces alone. Counterfeiting has been an issue persistently at the forefront of manufacturing since early modern times. On this topic, during the past two decades, traditional views facing regulated French manufactures from the time of the Ancien Régime to capitalistic free markets have been deeply challenged. Rules of eighteenth-century factories are now said to not so much stop innovation as to aim at stabilising certain product characteristics while allowing for increased varieties and shared inspection criteria.[25] In part because of the rapid development of the rural putting-out system, and in part because of the out-of-guilds activity in towns, guild regulation concerned a small percentage of the overall production and productive units. Even in those cases, they expressed an odd combination of rigidity and flexibility.

---

[25] Philippe Minard, "Réputation, normes et qualité dans l'industrie textile française au XVIIIe siècle." In Alessandro Stanziani (ed.), *La qualité des produits en France (XVIIIe–XXe siècles)*. Paris, Belin, 2003: 69–92.

In this context, brands and labels were not always regulated (most of them actually were not) and they conveyed much information on the product origin, its making, the producer or the trader, and so on. Those different kinds of information were not necessarily present all the time; a label could mention only the place of production without any explicit or implicit reference to quality.[26] In this last case, innovation and adaptation to market constraints did not meet any obstacles in label rules; however, this was partially true also in cases when quality standards were mentioned. In textiles as in iron making, label rules aimed much less at stopping innovation than putting it in a stable context for negotiation between the main involved actors. Negotiations on product characteristics occurred before as well as after production and exchange. Before the exchange, several institutions and rules attempted to regulate production and circulation of items; certificates of conformity were required.[27]

However, because of the multiplication of institutions and rules (guilds, municipalities, state, etc.), and also because of quickly advancing technical progress, regulation and ex-ante expertise did not suffice to provide perfectly transparent markets with perfect information on products. Main economic actors thus considered that the identification of products and their qualities before the exchange had to be completed with expertise after the exchange. Necker's reform of 1779 made explicit this system: Anyone worried about fraud could find the item he was accustomed to buying still produced, inspected, and marked in the usual way. All others were free to follow the system of *caveat emptor*.[28] In both cases, ex-post expertise was important. This could be made either by the purchaser himself or by third-party institutions. The first solution explains the wide success of handbooks for traders, such as the well-known *Dictionnaire universel du commerce*

---

[26] Corine Maitte, "Labels, Brands, and Market Integration in the Modern Era." *Business and Economic History on Line*, 7 (2009); Corine Maitte, *Les chemins de verre*. Rennes, PUR, 2009; Gabriel Glavez-Béhar, "Brevet d'invention." In Alessandro Stanziani (ed.), *Dictionnaire historique de l'économie-droit, XVIIIe–XXe siècles*. Paris, LGDJ, 2007: 35–48.

[27] Liliane Hilaire-Perez, *L'invention technique au siècle des lumières*. Paris, Albin Michel, 2000; Minard, *La fortune*.

[28] William Reddy, "The Structure of a Cultural Crisis: Thinking About Cloth in France Before and After the Revolution." In Arjun Appadurai, *The Social Life of Things*. Cambridge, Cambridge University Press, 1988: 261–84.

by Savary de Bruslon first published between 1720 and 1730 and re-
issued and translated at least six times between 1741 and 1784.[29]

Articles on products such as linen cloth, for example, included a list
of points to check when buying a piece of cloth. The threads had to be
of uniform twist, the cloth had to be of the same tightness and fineness
at both ends as in the middle, and so forth. In practise, purchasers were
required to be familiar with techniques of production and finishing,
as well as with the seals of the various towns and the regulations associated with them. Because of the increasing complexity of rules and
products, third-party expertise was welcome. Expertise was provided
at the request of main guilds, municipal and central authorities. In
sum, expert bodies intervened under their own or third-party initiative, and there was no clear-cut distinction between private and public,
business and administrative rules and powers of inspection.

Precisely because of this complexity, and despite the disappearance
of guild regulations, ensuring equivalent characteristics continued
to play an important role in the nineteenth century. As the eighteenth century was not the epoch of state and guild regulation, the
nineteenth century was not that of the "free market". Business actors
invoked the necessity of forms of product specification in manufacture.[30] Producers wished for this to protect their market and traders
were led to the same issue in order to avoid fraud and counterfeiting. The length and width of a given cloth, the intensity of the red
colour, as well as the size of bricks, wires, and so on in buildings[31] – all
these elements entered into sales, preliminary agreements and contract

---

[29] Reddy, "The Structure": 275; Also: Claude Reynard, "Manufacturing Quality in
the Pre-Industrial Age: Finding Value in Diversity." *Economic History Review*, LII, 3
(2000): 493–516.

[30] Serge Chassagne, *Le coton et ses patrons*. Paris, EHESS, 1991; Gérard Gayot, *Les draps de
Sédan*. Paris, EHESS, 1997; Jean-Pierre Hirsch, *Les deux rêves du commerce*. Paris, EHESS,
1991; Alain Cottereau, "The Fate of Collective Manufactures in the Industrial World: The
Silk Industries of Lyons and London, 1800–1850." In Charles Sabel, Jonathan Zeitlin,
World of Possibilities. Flexibility and Mass Production in Western Industrialization. Cambridge,
Cambridge University Press, 1997: 75–152.

[31] Robert Carvais, "Comment la technique devient une science? De l'usage des classifications de normes techniques: l'exemple de l'ordonnancement raisonné des règles de l'art
de bâtir au XVIIIe siècle." In Jérôme Bourdieu, Martin Bruegel, Alessandro Stanziani
(eds.), *Nomenclatures et classifications: approches historiques, enjeux économiques*. Paris, Inra,
2004: 273–302.

performance. On the ground of what texts were comparisons and evaluation supposed to be made?

With the lack of guilds and official municipal rules, local customs provided the main reference for contractual negotiations and disputes that arose.[32] However, as I previously indicated, trade customs were increasingly challenged during the course of the nineteenth century, to the point where, pushed by one or another business association, the ministries in charge during the Second Empire and again under the Third Republic launched major investigations in order to codify customs in a given industry. The main aim of both administrative elites and some business groups was to settle by law the deeply changing business customs and thus to stabilise markets.

The new fact was not technical progress in itself insofar as the question of making innovation compatible with economic and social stability had been constantly evoked since the eighteenth century. The new fact was that now, under the post-revolutionary regime, the convergence of innovation and social stability was supposed to be accomplished not only by informal agreements (as in the model of pure competition) or by state law (as in the model of regulated economy), but also and above all by the integration of business rules into state law. This process was supposed to be achieved through the cooperation of state, judicial and business institutions.[33] However, the variety of responses confirmed rather than solved the problems of product specification. Answers to questionnaires were so scattered, even in the same area, that no "customary rule" could be identified and incorporated into a state rule.

Confronted by this issue, state and interested business associations agreed that, alongside trade associations, merchant and civil courts, state expertise bodies had to solve product quality disputes. These institutions had varying authority; sometimes they were merely consultative (the Consultative Committee of Arts and Manufactures, Technical Office), whereas other times they came under executive authority (various ministries and cabinets). The Consultative Committee on Arts and Manufactures, for example, was called upon to decide on

---

[32] Claire Lemercier, *Un si discret pouvoir. Aux origines de la chambre de commerce de Paris, 1803–1853.* Paris, La Découverte, 2003.

[33] Lemercier, *Un si discret.*

innumerable manufacturing and marketing techniques. This committee intervened at the request of the Ministry of Commerce and Industry, which relayed requests from other ministries and departments (Customs, Indirect Taxation, Agriculture) or by various trade associations. As during the eighteenth century, private and public institutions and administrative, civil and commercial law intersected.

A detailed history of those institutions and their evaluations would probably shed new light on the evolution of innovation, its eventual bifurcation and its diffusion. For example, in 1894 the question came up about how to differentiate the various types of velvet due to new manufacturing techniques enabling wool modifications and fabric blends. French manufacturers did not always view these innovations favourably, mainly because most of the new varieties were imported. The Consultative Committee started from the distinction, accepted both by professionals and the customs office, between smooth velvet, known as "silk-like", and "other" velvets. The former were taxed without taking fabric weight into consideration, whereas the latter paid different taxes according to whether their warp contained more or less than 26 yarns per centimetre. Smooth velvet was distinguished by a "cut or velvety surface with a smooth back, i.e. showing the weave of the cloth or the calico (wool yarns perpendicular to the warp)".

On the contrary, "other velvets" had a fabric-blend back, and the surface velvet was not cut. "Other cut velvets are differentiated from silk-type smooth velvet by the contexture of the back". The novelty lay in seeking to introduce such fabrics under the name of satin, which theoretically belonged in the first category. However, in the Committee's view, these kinds of fabrics were different: "[V]elvets intended to be cut contain *duites de fond* (weft yarns) that serve as the base for the cutting operation. Satins should not undergo this operation and therefore they do not contain *duites de fond*".[34]

The organisation of labour entered into definitions of quality and items. Thus, again in 1894, cotton fabrics appeared which, through a new technical process, "imitates *aliciennes*, but the dark parts are obtained by using a cylinder filled with a chemical solution". At the time, the customs and indirect taxation offices asked the Committee if this new

---

[34] AN F 12 7001: "Avis du Comité du 11 avril 1894."

product should be classified among solid fabrics made using an ordinary manufacturing process or as *façonné* fabrics which were naturally more expensive. The Committee based its assessment not on the final product's characteristics but on the definition of the labour involved in producing it: "The labour is in fact finishing and hence cannot be assimilated to *façonnage* which results from the weaving method. On the other hand, the Committee thinks it is impossible to apply the embossing surtax to *aliciennes*-type fabrics. Therefore, they should be classified as solid fabrics".[35]

These examples could be multiplied over and over for all products and their varieties. Issues differed according to the concerned product, the technical specificity under examination, the involved interests and their equilibriums and, of course, the main actors and institutions. In many cases, disputes were solved in an informal way; in some others, the fiscal offices found a solution and a compromise with business associations without the intermediation of the ministry of commerce and its evaluation committees. Despite this complexity, the most interesting fact for our discussion is that market coordination on the qualities of product was never spontaneous, but constantly negotiated at the interplay of different institutions (fiscal, trade, international, local business, etc.). This overwhelming importance of institutions in market assessment testifies to the fact that, in the view of a vast majority of the involved actors, market conveyors of information, such as label and prices, were insufficient to guarantee market performances. This outcome was not specific to food and agriculture produce, but was at hand also for manufactured goods. Rather than expressing a "market failure", this phenomenon reflected the very way the market operated.

This finds confirmation in the major importance of expertise in countries other than France. In the nineteenth century, government-sponsored committees as well as expertise performed by trade associations were widely found in other countries, following a pattern similar to the one in France. Chambers of commerce and trade associations developed benchmark standards for the main products; these

---

[35] Comité consultatif des arts et manufactures, Decision of 27 June 1894, copy in *Custom circular*, 3 August 1894 in AN F 12 7001.

standards were used to obtain quality certificates and also served as a standard for judges in the event of disputes. Thus, in the United States, the leading trade associations introduced classification criteria for wheat, cotton, cooking oil and raw materials for industry to facilitate domestic and international trade and reduce the risk of disputes. The same occurred with the final manufactured product, including toys, textiles, and others. These associations and their inspectors delivered compliance certificates on this basis.[36] Similar services were offered by English commercial and professional associations which provided certificates for imported as well as colonial and domestic items.[37]

Quality certificates were said to facilitate transactions and reduce the risk of litigation. However, disputes were widespread and concerned both invention and the patent law and contractual performances. In the case of the former, the judge had to decide whether the defendant had illegally imitated an item, whereas in the case of the latter the judge had to compare promised to delivered products. In both situations, most decisions reveal the difficulties judges had in the identification of product. Lack of specification was often mentioned and, contrary to widespread argument, protection of private property (as in patent and trade law) was weak.[38] Yet, these issues not only did not undermine the industrial revolution but even stimulated it through wider access to product and increasing technical progress. Imitation was one of the key routes of transmission of material culture.[39]

In short, in the nineteenth century, for most of the products and countries studied here, the definition of product qualities at the time of trade was never left solely to the subjective assessment of the actors. Nor was it solved by market conveyors of information, such as price and label. This was so because rapid technical improvement and spatial

---

[36] Merrill, "Classification"; Emery, "Futures"; William Becker, "American Wholesale Trade Associations, 1870–1900." *The Business History Review*, 45, 2 (1971): 179–200.

[37] Eugene Ridings, "Chambers of Commerce and Business Elites in Great Britain and Brazil in the Nineteenth Century: Some Comparisons." *Business History Review*, 75, 4 (2001): 739–73; Alain Wolfe, "Commercial Organizations in the United Kingdom." *Department of Commerce Special Agent Series*, Washington, DC, 102 (1915).

[38] Christine Macleod, "The Paradoxes of Patenting: Invention and Diffusion in Eighteenth and Nineteenth Century Britain, France, and North America." *Technology and Culture*, 32, 4 (1991): 885–910.

[39] Maxine Berg, "From Imitation to Invention: Creating Commodities in Eighteenth-Century Britain." *Economic History Review*, LV, 1 (2002): 1–30.

expansion of markets increased the number of intermediaries and technical skills required for exchange. All this made evaluation difficult to achieve, the more so because standardisation was far from being achieved. Thus, certifying institutions were in place to reduce uncertainty over product characteristics. Public certification and inspection institutions arose, initially at a faster pace for agricultural and food products, which was extended later on to include manufactured products. In other words, in a dynamic world in which technical progress, spatial market dynamics, unequal distribution of information and individual perceptions of it counted, the evaluation of products required institutions that contributed to coordinate the marketplace. Rather than expressing market pathology, expertise reflects its real functioning.

In this context, standardisation aimed at reducing the contractual problems by guaranteeing products with certain unvarying characteristics over time, consequently reducing the cost of negotiations and inspections. Still, standardisation never was a definitive process; nor did it concern all the characteristics of a given product, even in manufactures. Standardisation was less a national than a sector-based process.[40] For example, in Great Britain the association of major firms with product standardisation and capitalism was closely tied to the case of cotton, and it was difficult to extend it to the entire English economy.[41] Generally speaking, standardisation in Great Britain took place only in a few sectors in the nineteenth century, rather late for industry in general (the second half of the twentieth century) and for agriculture, which was less subject to pressure from wholesale traders and administrative departments than in France. The normalisation of agriculture was to be partly linked to the special role of milk (with a direct connection between normalisation and health issues) and partly to the territorial structure of English production, which had little connection

---

[40] Michael Storper, Robert Salais, *Les mondes de production*. Paris, EHESS, 1993; Patrick Verley, *La révolution industrielle*. Paris, Gallimard, 1997; Michael J. Piore, Charles F. Sabel, *Les chemins de la prospérité. De la production de masse à la spécialisation souple*. Paris, Hachette 1989; Sabel, Zeitlin, "Historical Alternatives"; Reddy, *The Rise*.

[41] Maxine Berg, *The Age of Manufactures: Industry, Innovation and Work in Britain, 1700–1820*. London, Routledge, 1984; Maxine Berg (ed.), *Markets and Manufacture in Early Industrial Europe*. London, Routledge, 1991; Patrick Verley, *L'échelle du monde*. Paris, Gallimard, 1997.

to *terroirs* and was highly dependent on imports.[42] This problem spread
to the food industry, especially with the development of tinned foods
and the success of "exotic" cuisines from the colonies.[43]

The United States is usually associated with the early and widespread expansion of standardised mass production. The explanation for
this supposedly originates in lack of a labour force, abundant natural
resources and capital and the scope of the domestic market.[44] Recent
studies have shown, however, that in fact even in the United States, the
process of product standardisation and concentration took place later
(it began in the early twentieth century but did not take off until the
Second World War) and was limited to certain industries and regions
of the country.[45]

On the contrary, it was in the agricultural area that the United
States showed a tendency towards normalisation or even standardisation of products much earlier and more extensively than in Europe.
The examples not only of wheat but also of American meat and wine
are well known. The size of the domestic market and the strength
of wholesale traders compared with producers contributed significantly to these dynamics. The rules governing product quality definition and inspection were also important. In the United States the
rules for product compliance to certain safety regulations played a far

[42] Michael French, Jim Phillips, *Cheated not Poisoned? Food Regulation in the United Kingdom, 1875–1938*. Manchester, Manchester University Press, 2000; E.J.T. Collins, "Food Adulteration and Food Safety in Britain in the Nineteenth and Early Twentieth Centuries." *Food Policy*, April (1993): 95–109.

[43] Derek Oddy, Lidya Petranova, *The Diffusion of Food Culture in Europe from the Late Eighteenth Century to the Present Day*. Prague, Academia, 2005; Marc Jacobs, Peter Scholliers (eds.), *Eating Out in Europe*. Oxford, Berg, 2003.

[44] Alfred Chandler, *The Visible Hand*. Cambridge, Mass., Harvard University Press, 1977; Alfred Chandler, *Scale and Scope. The Dynamics of Industrial Capitalism*, Cambridge, Mass., Harvard University Press, 1990; Stephen N. Broadberry, "Technological Leadership and Productivity Leadership in Manufacturing Since the Industrial Revolution: Implications for the Convergence Debate." *Economic Journal*, 104, 423 (1994): 291–302; William Lazonick, "Industrial Organization and Technological Change: The Decline of the British Cotton Industry." *Business History Review*, 57, 2 (1985): 195–236.

[45] Gavin Wright, "The Origin of American Industrial Success, 1879–1940." *American Economic Review*, 80, 4 (1990): 651–68; Steven Fraser, "Combined and Uneven Development in the Men's Clothing Industry." *Business History Review*, 57, 4 (1983): 522–47; Gordon Winder, "Before the Corporation and Mass Production: The Licensing Regime in the Manufacture of North American Harvesting Machines, 1830–1910." *Annals of the Association of American Geographers*, 85, 3 (1995): 521–52.

more important role than in Europe, even though products were less frequently enhanced by associating them with a given territory, as we have seen in our discussion of AOCs.[46]

It is therefore possible to confirm that, at least until towards the end of the nineteenth century, within capitalist economies the standardisation of production was a rather limited process; it concerned only certain sectors at a given moment and in specific regions. Product standardisation became a dominant process in Western economies only after the First World War. If this is true, how are we to understand the functioning and role of international markets in the eighteenth and nineteenth centuries? Ahead of multiple product specifications and increasing national rules defining products, how was the exchange practised on international markets? Did the international market operate on the grounds of specific rules and forms of coordination? And if so, how did these rules intersect with national institutions and individual industry specifications?

---

[46] Michael Maher, "On Vino Veritas? Clarifying the Use of Geographical References on American Wine Labels." *California Law Review*, 89, 6 (2001): 1881–925; José Morilla Critz, Alan Olmstead, Paul Rhode, "Horn of Plenty: The Globalization of Mediterranean Horticulture and the Economic Development of Southern Europe, 1880–1930." *Journal of Economic History*, 59, 2 (1999): 316–52; Carol F. Nuckton, *Demand Relationships for California Tree Fruits, Grapes and Nuts: A Review of Past Studies.* Berkeley, University of California Press, 1978; Michael Tracy, *Agriculture in Western Europe: Challenge and Response, 1880–1980*, 2nd ed. London, Granada, 1982.

9

RULES OF INTERNATIONAL TRADE

It is not my intention to develop a full analysis of international trade; the evolution of tariff barriers and trade policies in the nineteenth and early twentieth century is well known. Protectionism dominated the first half of the nineteenth century, liberal policies held the upper hand between the 1850s and the 1870s, while protectionism regained priority between the 1870s and the First World War. During this last period, in Europe protection concerned at first agriculture, then (especially in latecomer countries) industry. Most of the debates in economic history have focused on the impact of tariffs on growth.[1] I am not entering this debate, but instead will focus on a related and partly preceding question, that is of the role of non-tariff forms of protectionism and the general rules of international exchange. Analyses of international trade mainly have stressed the role of other tools of coordination – *lex mercatoria*, contracts, networks, circulation of information, product qualification and identification.[2] My aim is to explain the historical hierarchy of these tools for coordination; in particular, the decline of *lex mercatoria* and the way networks and contracts were

---

[1] Paul Bairoch, *Commerce extérieur et développement économique de l'Europe au XIXe siècle*. Paris, Mouton, 1976; Forrest Capie, *Tariffs and Growth: Some Insights from the World Economy, 1850–1940*. Manchester, Manchester University Press, 1994; Maurice Lévy-Leboyer, François Bourguignon, *L'économie française au XIXe siècle*. Paris, Economica, 1985; Kevin O'Rourke, Geoffrey Williamson, *Globalization and History: The Evolution of Nineteenth Century Atlantic Economy*. Cambridge, Mass., MIT Press, 1999; Kevin O'Rourke, "Tariffs and Growth in Late Nineteenth Century." *Economic Journal*, 110, 463 (2000): 456–83.

[2] Marina Wes, "International Trade, Bargaining and Efficiency: The Holdup Problem." *The Scandinavian Journal of Economics*, 102, 1 (2000): 151–62; James Rauch, "Business and Social Networks in International Trade." *Journal of Economic Literature*, 39, 4 (2001): 1177–1203.

able to substitute for it. We have already seen that customary rules of trade had been habitually included into municipal and later into state rules. This issue did not prevent tensions over the identification of specific customs at one moment or another, but it gave them a legal framework for negotiation between the involved parties. At the international level, this outcome was much more difficult to reach, insofar as international official agreements were undermined by protectionist interests; even today, international trade organisations have difficulties imposing common rules. To study the historical coordination on international markets, I will at first briefly evoke *lex mercatoria* and its fate; I shall then explore networks and economic information and, finally, product standardisation and qualification as tools for market coordination.

LEX MERCATORIA

Medieval merchant law did not spring from a void; a considerable part of it was based on Roman commercial law; however, over centuries, this last had received different interpretations in different places and countries. This means that legal coordination at the international level relied upon merchants themselves. As international trade developed, the benefits of uniform rules and uniform application of those rules superseded the benefits of discriminatory rules that might favour a few local individuals.[3] From this standpoint, the universality of merchant law was at the same time a result of and a prerequisite for the rapid development of trade. Commercial rules were intended to be the language of interaction rather than a list of compulsory practises. Merchant court judges were able to solve disputes on the grounds of their technical knowledge. In the same light, rules of evidence and procedures were kept simple and informal. All this did not prevent the accumulation of decisions and rules in "merchant codes" that could set a precedent at both the local and international levels.[4]

---

[3] Bruce Benson, "The Spontaneous Evolution of Commercial Law." *Southern Economic Journal*, 55, 3 (1989): 644–61.

[4] Roberto Sabatino Lopez, *The Commercial Revolution of the Middle Ages, 950–1350*. Englewood Cliffs, NJ, Prentice-Hall, 1971; Armando Sapori, *The Italian Merchants in the Middle Ages*. New York, Norton, 1970.

Since the seventeenth century, the incorporation of merchant law into state rules and/or common law led to more difficulties in trade coordination at the international level. This means that contract enforcement in international trade was considered weak, if not altogether nonexistent; information on products, actors and techniques therefore had to play a crucial role.[5] Given the lack and/or weakness of legal protection, economic theory would suggest that networks and repeated contacts might overcome these difficulties.[6] Indeed, trust is linked to reputation; if one merchant cheats and he is rational, he will foresee that the loss due to cheating is more important than profit.

However, for this mechanism to work, several conditions are required. First, individuals must have some memory of previous experiences[7] and assume that past behaviour is indicative of future behaviour.[8] Second, a network (often identified with a merchant diaspora) must exist. Third, information affecting reputation must circulate; this enables a merchant community to adopt sanctions against a cheating member. However, this last solution is efficient only when a clear contract is stipulated between a merchant and his community. Incomplete contracts undermine the operation of a coalition among merchants.[9] Common values, ethics and informal control can intervene there;[10] however, their action cannot be taken for granted. Discussions have flourished on this point, some stressing that ethics, trust and values precede trade and formal rules (making them enforceable), others maintaining that calculativeness (research of profit) is the only ground for trust and

[5] Wes "International Trade"; Rauch, "Business and Social Networks".

[6] Oliver Williamson, "Calculativeness, Trust, and Economic Organization." *Journal of Law and Economics*, 36, 1 (1993): 453–86; Avner Greif, "Contract Enforceability and Economic Institutions in Early Trade: The Maghribi Traders' Coalition." *American Economic Review*, 83, 3 (1993): 525–48; Avner Greif, Paul Milgrom, Barry Weingast, "Coordination, Commitment, and Enforcement: The Case of the Merchant Guild." *Journal of Political Economy*, 102, 4 (1994): 745–76.

[7] Partha Dasgupta, "Trust as Commodity." In Diego Gambetta (ed.), *Trust*. London, Basil Blackwell, 1990: 49–72.

[8] Peter Kollock, "The Emergence of Exchange Structures: An Experimental Study of Uncertainty, Commitment, and Trust." *American Journal of Sociology*, 100, 2 (1994): 313–45.

[9] Greif, "Contract Enforceability".

[10] James Coleman, "Social Theory, Social Research, and a Theory of Action." *The American Journal of Sociology*, 91, 6 (1986): 1309–35.

cooperation.[11] An intermediate position consists of saying that regulation can infuse trading confidence into otherwise problematic trading relations.[12] Still, the impact of regulation is not the same on calculative trust, personal trust and institutional trust. One can predict behaviour of a commercial partner and expect a given reliability of, say, judicial institutions. Of course, these different levels of trust are mutually linked.

In the following pages, I am going to question these assumptions; in particular, I am going to explore a particular context in which, for a number of reasons, networks were still to be built, memory of the past was weak (if not lost) and thus past behaviours could not be taken as indicators of future behaviours. In this case, trust and international market were mostly linked to learning and therefore to the acquisition and elaboration of information.

INFORMATION AND TRUST ON INTERNATIONAL MARKETS

Scholarship on the history of international trade chiefly accentuates trade politics (tariff and non-tariff tools), markets (supply and demand, transportation), price dynamics and, to some extent, commercial networks.[13] Quite surprisingly, the "oil of business", *information* on both products and actors, has been neglected. Yet the acquisition and interpretation of information is crucial to the formation of expectations and behaviour, and therefore for market dynamics. This is all the more true because, in comparison to local and domestic markets, contract enforcement in international trade is weak.[14] These considerations

---

[11] Among the others: Williamson, "Calculativeness"; Gambetta, *Trust*; Nathalie Lazaric, Edward Lorenz, *Trust and Economic Learning*. Cheltenham, Edward Elgar, 1998; Marc Granovetter, "Economic Action and Social Structure: The Problem of Embeddedness." *American Journal of Sociology*, 91, 3 (1985): 481–510.

[12] Victor Goldberg, "Toward and Expanded Economic Theory of Contract." In Warren Samuels (ed.), *The Chicago School of Political Economy*. New Brunswick, Transaction Publishers, 1976: 259–76.

[13] The following pages are a version of my article "Economic Information on International Markets: French Strategies in the Italian Mirror (Nineteenth–Early Twentieth Centuries)." *Enterprise and Society*, 11, 1 (2010): 26–64. I express my gratitude to Oxford University Press for having permitted me to reproduce it.

[14] Wes, "International Trade"; Rauch, "Business".

appear to be particularly relevant for the years from the last quarter of the nineteenth century through 1914. This period is usually regarded as one of increasing protectionism and of a consequent strong contraction of international trade. However, despite that view, this same period also represents the "first wave of globalisation",[15] the two phenomena being hardly compatible at first sight. Economic information may help us find a solution to this puzzle. In fact, during this period, urbanisation, the growing internationalisation of the economy, and social instability (the advance of new industrial classes and commercial groups at the expense of traditional commercial and landed elites) in most advanced countries led traders to deal with relatively unknown correspondents involved in short-term contracts and profits rather than in long-term relationships.

Business actors were therefore concerned about increasing uncertainty and occasional cheating in commercial relationships. In this situation, microeconomic strategies and macroeconomic dynamics depended on two major forces: attitude to risk and access to information. When uncertainty is high, risk grows, and, all other conditions being equal, the attitude economic actors have towards risk is the crucial variable. At the same time, economic actors seek to improve the information they have so as to benefit from strong comparative advantages over their competitors. This provides a rationale for acquiring and exchanging information, which can be done either through a market or by exchange of information between organisations, that is, between firms, trade associations and official institutions. In the following pages, I analyse the acquisition and circulation of information and the actors and rules involved between 1870 and 1914, using a comparative approach (France and Italy). As for actors, I shall consider individual trading firms, professional associations, information-intermediating agencies and state offices.

Competition and complementarities among these actors are important determinants of how the market for information functions. I argue that these agencies (and therefore markets and institutions) acted much less as rivals than as complements in this era. This was so for two main reasons: Economic information was not a homogenous

---

[15] O'Rourke, Williamson, *Globalization*.

good, and it was unequally distributed. Indeed, product information is different from information on the reputation of economic actors, the latter generating further distinctions between reputation for payment, respect of deadlines and fidelity to the terms and objects of the contract. In turn, such kinds of situated micro-information differ from general statistics on market evolution and prices. I shall show that most economic actors were much more interested in the former (specifics) than in the latter kinds of information. I explain this by arguing that in a highly uncertain economic environment, in which social and financial instability are high and technical progress increases difficulties in identifying goods, economic strategies and hierarchies are more affected by information and expectations concerning correspondents than by data on general market trends.

To demonstrate this point, we will compare the way traders, their associations, and private and state agencies intervened in the gathering, circulation and interpretation of economic information in two countries, Italy and France, between 1870 and 1914. The choice of these countries is easy to explain. According to the dominant historiography, during the last quarter of the nineteenth century, both France and Italy confronted agricultural crisis, social instability and the general problem of "catching up" with Britain and, to some extent, Germany and the United States.[16] In this context, international trade played a crucial role. The usual arguments advanced in the historiography maintain that France lost important international market shares due to both the character of its products (mostly luxury goods, difficult to export amid depressing economic trends) and the attitude of its actors (risk averse).[17] Protectionism thus helped compensate for these attitudes.

Quite to the contrary, Italy is taken for an example of quick integration into the international market (along with Spain); this was partially linked to its mixed policies (alternating protectionism and free

[16] Kevin O'Rourke, Geoffrey Williamson, "Factor Price Convergence in the Late Nineteenth Century." *International Economic Review*, 37, 3 (1996): 499–530.

[17] Bairoch, *Economics and World History*; Capie, *Tariffs and Growth*; Levy-Leboyer, Bourguignon, *L'économie française*; Vincent Nye, "The Myth of Free-Trade Britain and Fortress France: Tariffs and Trade in the Nineteenth Century." *Journal of Economic History*, 51, 1 (1991): 23–46; Patrick O'Brien, Keydar Caglar, *Economic Growth in Britain and France, 1780–1914*. London, Allen and Unwin, 1976; Brian Mitchell, *European Historical Statistics, 1750–1970*. New York, Palgrave-Macmillan, 1975.

trade according to the economic trend and the sector concerned) and the more aggressive attitudes of its economic actors compared to the French.[18] For sure, Italy was not alone in pursuing aggressive strategies and was not the unique concern of French officials and economic actors. The example of Germany was also constantly advanced at the time; I will also evoke it when speaking of general trends on the international market and the overall French attitudes to them. At the same time, as we will mostly focus on the wine market, Italy appears to be a far more direct competitor for France than Germany. Moreover, when discussing the general politics and strategies on international markets, most French actors of that time considered Germany yet another example of strong state support for private business, like Italy.

However, if we consider the way economic actors formed their expectations, we may have a different picture of French and Italian performances. We shall argue that these opposite outcomes were not simply the result of different "mentalities" or attitudes to risk (as exogenously given), but rather can be traced to the different institutional settings and economic segmentation of the market for information in these two countries. In fact, unlike the Italian government, French ministries refused to provide their traders with micro-information on potential overseas correspondents and product characteristics. This was so for both institutional reasons (administrative rules, strong opposition from the ministry of foreign affairs) and organisational reasons (conflicts between ministries and within each department). That is to say that "attitude to risk" and "animal spirits" are not exogenous and cannot be studied outside a given historical and institutional context.

One outcome of this approach is that stressing the traditional opposition between liberalism and protectionism proves misleading in several ways. First, demand for a strong state supply of economic information came from both liberal and protectionist circles. Second, the presumed protectionist French state gave far less support to business than did the "liberal" Italian government. Last but not least, in both France and Italy, using public resources for private purposes and the development of state interventions took place much less during

---

[18] Giovanni Federico, Antonio Tena, "Was Italy a Protectionist Country?" *European Review of Economic History*, 2, 1 (1998): 73–97.

the traditionally recognised protectionist wave (that is, during the 1870s and the 1890s) than during the later Belle Époque.

After recalling the main economic and political rationales behind protectionism in Italy and France and evoking the dynamics of wine markets domestically and internationally, I am going to explore the way information structured expectations and market dynamics. First, I will describe the importance of cheating on the international market between 1870 and 1914, in transactions in which French firms and actors were involved. The ensuing section analyses solutions developed to overcome this problem during the 1880s, that is, information provided by state and the (weak) development of information networks of firms. Explanations of the failure of these solutions will be provided. We will then consider private agencies for information and how French firms and French public institutions overcame the earlier impasse. The second part of this chapter explores these same questions for Italian traders. The conclusion will draw together comparative and general views on the link between information, market and institutions.

INTERNATIONAL MARKETS AND TRADE POLICIES

Unlike classical and neoclassical economic theory, usually linking protectionism to reduced growth and consumers' well-being, recent economic analysis advances more nuanced positions on this matter. Protection can either increase or reduce long-term growth rates and consumers' well-being.[19] These new theoretical issues have surfaced during a revision of historical analyses. Indeed, traditional historiography's chronology runs as follows: Protectionism dominated the first half of the nineteenth century, liberal policies between the 1850s and the 1870s, and protectionism regained priority between the 1870s and the First World War. During this last period, in Europe, protection concerned first agriculture, then (especially in latecomer countries) industry.

This scheme has been the subject of increased scrutiny. Most debates have focused on the evaluation of tariffs and their impact on

[19] Sebastian Edwards, "Openness, Trade Liberalization, and Growth in Developing Countries." *Journal of Economic Literature*, 31 (1993): 1358–93; Henry Bruton, "A Reconsideration of Import Substitution." *Journal of Economic Literature*, 34 (1998): 903–36.

growth and income distribution. Paul Bairoch[20] was one of the first to criticise the long-standing negative evaluation of French protectionism during the "long depression"[21] and showed that it actually enhanced economic growth. After that, Capie[22] and then O'Rourke and Williamson[23] strongly criticised his argument and maintained that Bairoch did not have sufficient empirical evidence to support his claims; these authors returned to the previous view, according to which protectionist tariffs reduced market integration, growth and well-being. Still, they admitted that the impact of protectionism depended on the evaluation of tariffs and on the sectors and countries concerned. For example, according to O'Rourke, Italy and France were among those countries adopting the highest protectionist rates in Europe, even if the average rate of protection was consistently higher in Italy than in France, particularly after 1896. However, when disaggregating the national economy, in manufacturing the rate of protectionism was lower in Italy than in France, whereas the reverse was true for agriculture.[24]

The underlying question has been whether the differentiated and somewhat surprising impact of tariffs on growth and income distribution was due to the inadequacy of standard economic models to explain complex realities, or rather to an inaccurate statistical measurement of tariff levels. In the latter case, once correctly evaluated, tariff and trade policies perfectly fit standard models. Lévy-Leboyer and Bourguignon,[25] Nye[26] and Verley[27] have maintained that French

[20] Paul Bairoch, "European Trade Policy, 1815–1914." In Peter Mathias, Sidney Pollard, *The Cambridge Economic History of Europe*. Cambridge, Cambridge University Press, 1989, vol. 8: 1–160.

[21] Charles Kindleberger, "The Rise of Free Trade in Western Europe, 1820–1875." *The Journal of Economic History*, 35, 1 (1975): 20–55; Gabriel Désert, Robert Specklin, "Les réactions face à la crise." In Georges Duby, André Wallon (eds.), *Histoire de la France rurale*. Paris, Seuil, 1976, vol. 3: 383–428.

[22] Capie, *Protectionism*.

[23] O'Rourke, Williamson, *Globalization*.

[24] Kevin O'Rourke, "Tariffs and Growth in Late Nineteenth Century." *Economic Journal*, 110, 463 (2000): 456–83.

[25] Lévy-Leboyer, Bourguignon, *L'économie française*.

[26] Nye, "The Myth"; John Vincent Nye, *War, Wine and Taxes: The Political Economy of Anglo-French Trade, 1689–1900*. Princeton, NJ, Princeton University Press, 2007.

[27] Patrick Verley, *Nouvelle histoire économique de la France contemporaine*. Paris, La découverte, 1995.

tariffs, when correctly evaluated (i.e., averaged, deflated and weighted) were lower than usually stated and in some cases even lower than the British.

O' Rourke and Williamson have evidence supporting the opposite view.[28] Given these premises, the first orientation leads to the conclusion that tariffs were not so important, and that France's limits to growth were mostly due to the lack of "entrepreneurial spirit" among French traders. The second interpretation has conversely stressed the role of the state as a source of blockage. Federico has reached similar conclusions for Italy: Real tariffs were much less important than usually stated, in particular if one considers the whole nineteenth century and makes clear distinctions between sectors.[29] However important, by itself, the evaluation of tariffs and their impact on growth and income distribution does not provide a satisfactory solution to the problem of identifying the rationale behind trade policies. The rate of protection may be linked to the importance of a given sector and to its path of development.[30] Italy and France were more protectionist than Britain because industry was less developed and agrarian structure and lobbies were more important. In other words, politics mattered, but the weight of lobbies reflected the real structure of the economy.[31]

An alternative hypothesis consists of assigning politics relatively greater independence from economic rationale. In particular, in France as in Italy, the adoption of tariffs was sustained by agrarian lobbies against the interests of industry and consumers and those of the economy as a whole.[32] Indeed, archival sources hardly confirm the

---

[28] O'Rourke, Williamson, *Globalization*.

[29] Giovanni Federico, "Il valore aggiunto nell'agricoltura". In Giovanni Rey, *I conti economici nell'Italia. Una stima del valore aggiunto per il 1891, 1938, 1951*. Bari, Laterza, 2000: 3–112; Giovanni Federico, "Per una revisione critica delle statistiche della produzione agricola italiana dopo l'Unità." *Società e storia*, 15 (1982): 87–130; Giovanni Federico, *Feeding the World*. Princeton, NJ, Princeton University Press, 2005.

[30] O' Rourke, "The European"; Federico, *Feeding the World*.

[31] Douglas Irwin, "Political Economy and Peel's Repeal of the Corn Laws." *Economics and Politics*, I, I (1989): 954–85; for Italy: Giovanni Toniolo, *Storia economica dell'italia liberale*. Bologna, Il Mulino, 1988; Gino Luzzatto, *L'economia italiana dal 1861 al 1914, vol. 1, 1861–1894*. Milano, Banca Commerciale Italiana, 1963.

[32] For France: Hudson Meadwell, "The Political Economy of Tariffs in Late Nineteenth-Century Europe: Reconsidering Republican France." *Theory and Society*, 31, 5 (2002): 623–51. For Italy: Giorgio Giorgietti, *Contadini e proprietari nell'italia moderna*. Torino: Einaudi, 1974; Salvatore Lupo, *Il giardino degli aranci*. Venezia, Marsilio, 1990.

existence of solid lobbies behind trade policies. In the "commercial war" between the two countries (from 1886 to the mid-1890s), in Italy as well as in France, most of the decisions the governments adopted in the 1880s and the 1890s were reached despite strong divisions within the government and against the opposition of several deputies (in some cases, even against a majority of them).[33]

Broader geopolitical considerations played a major role; "left" governments in Italy progressively maintained some distance from France (which had been its closest political and commercial ally since the Italian unification) and moved closer to Austria and Prussia. From this perspective, maritime trade and wine market considerations, although important, offered an equal degree of a political pretext for breaking relations with France.[34]

As a whole, several interlinked factors intervened in the adoption of commercial policies during the last quarter of the nineteenth century: institutional change (such as the Third Republic in France, the "republican crisis" of 1887–1889, the passage from the right to the left in Italy's politics);[35] the tensions related to an increasing urbanisation, although of different intensities in Italy and France; price evolution (notably, falling agriculture prices); the important reduction in transportation costs;[36] the increasing world supply of agricultural products[37] and the re-affirmation of the gold standard.[38] Such a complex set of variables provides a good foundation for explaining trade policies; yet, the variables do not by themselves provide a satisfactory solution to the following question: If real tariffs were lower than usually believed, then how can we explain traders' attitudes towards, and capacities for, integrating international markets?

[33] AN F 12 6551, 6552, 6556, 6558.
[34] AN F 12 6455.
[35] Charles Kindleberger, "The Rise of Free Trade in Western Europe, 1820, 1875." *The Journal of Economic History*, 35, 1 (1975): 20–55; Daniel Verdier, *Democracy and International Trade: Britain, France, and the United States, 1860–1900*. Princeton, NJ, Princeton University Press, 1994.
[36] Nick Harley, "Transportation, the World Wheat Trade, and the Kuznets Cycle, 1850–1913." *Explorations in Economic History*, 17, 3 (1980): 218–50.
[37] Federico, *Feeding the World*.
[38] Antony Estevadeordal, Brian Frantz, Alan Taylor, "The Rise and Fall of World Trade, 1870–1939." *Quarterly Journal of Economics*, CXVIII, 2 (2003): 359–407.

If we trust contemporary sources, one key concern is systematically evoked to explain success (or failure) in international trade: access to economic information. Indeed, developing new markets required, from a purchaser's view, information on products and sellers, whereas the sellers needed information on foreign correspondents and markets. Now this issue was far from being resolved in advance, insofar as information was not readily available. This problem was familiar to the international wine market;[39] what was relatively new during the last quarter of the nineteenth century was the convergence of increasing uncertainty on both product qualities (because of new techniques and the entry of organic chemistry in the agro-food and wine industry) and commercial correspondents (because of increasing social instability in Europe, emigration to the New World and the quick entry on the market of new, relatively unknown "houses" and traders on both sides of the Atlantic). The following sections detail this process and explain its significance.

GENERALISED CHEATING?

New commercial partners linked to changing domestic hierarchies and to new international equilibria; new techniques in the production of the principal products – namely, the advent of organic chemistry into the agro-food business[40] and difficulties in securing reliable information on both products and commercial partners – all these factors served to create a feeling of increasing uncertainty in business circles. These perceptions seemed well founded in that the press and business associations denounced more and more cases of cheating. In part, this was a strategic argument business actors raised in order to win government support for the acquisition of information in service of expanding exports. At the same time, commercial correspondence between 1875 and 1900 especially emphasised cheating and fraud. To understand, we must specify the form of cheating and the manner in which it was addressed.

---

[39] David Hancock, "L'émergence d'une économie de réseaux (1640–1815). Le vin de Madère." *Annales HSC*, 58, 3 (2003): 649–74; James Simpson, "Cooperation and Conflicts: Institutional Innovation in France's Wine Markets, 1870–1911." *Business History Review*, 79 (2005): 527–58.

[40] Stanziani, *Histoire*.

Cheating can affect the parties themselves (their solvency, reliability, etc.), the products they deliver or both at the same time. Because I have already published elsewhere about fraud in wine and other foodstuffs,[41] I will focus here on commercial cheating involving the qualities of trading partners themselves. In this situation, economic theory would suggest that networks and repeated contacts might overcome these difficulties.[42] Historians, in particular wine industry historians, have contested this approach, showing the conditions under which networks do well. Networks succeeded when they led to profitable sharing of information, goods and services for many parties, but they failed when individuals were unable to get networks to function in their interests.[43] I am going to push this approach further and consider the situation in which, because of high social and economic instability (the "long depression") and due to the establishment of new markets and techniques, traders' main concern was to enter existing networks. To a given extent, the story here is that of the creation/expansion of networks in a highly uncertain economic and social environment.

In December 1872, the Third Republic's Ministry of Agriculture sent the presidents of the chambers of commerce a report concerning cheating "performed by so-called firms", in particular damaging French producers and distributors of foodstuffs and wines. These swindlers sent fraudulent payment drafts several months in advance, "with seals and all", but which finally would not be honoured to settle debts and clear accounts. In this case, the Ministry envisaged a law that would assure the restitution of the goods. However, usage deadlines often were such that the products delivered would be out of date before ownership could be restored.[44] Many such cases were recorded during the 1870s. In September 1880, the Consul of France

---

[41] Alessandro Stanziani, "Negotiating Innovation in a Market Economy: Foodstuffs and Beverages Adulteration in Nineteenth Century France." *Enterprise and Society*, 8, 2 (2007): 375–412.

[42] Williamson "Calculativeness"; Greif, "Contract".

[43] David Hancock, "The Trouble with Networks: Managing the Scots' Early-Modern Madeira Trade." *Business History Review*, 79, 3 (2005): 467–91.

[44] AN F 12 (Ministry of Trade and Industry), 7452 (commercial frauds), the Minister of Agriculture to the Presidents of the chambers of commerce, December 1872.

in Rotterdam noted additional instances of cheating affecting French dealers in the wine and cooking oil trades. Consular reports of this type became more and more frequent, particularly in non-European areas (Egypt, India, Lebanon, United States, Latin America, the Cape Verde Islands, etc.).[45]

To some extent, reducing the probability of being victimised was a matter of experience and of resources available to overcome uncertainty. As a French consul explained, unscrupulous cheaters especially welcomed new representatives from French houses – still young, inexperienced, impatient, aiming to widen their sphere of action and to make known their products in Germany (in this case):

Not being able to deal either with the clients who buy at the places of production or with those supplied via commission actors, travellers for these houses could only create relationships with this third category of buyers [the swindlers]. These individuals make initially a small order that they discharge perfectly; a second exchange is also regulated without trouble. Then a great order comes. There they play the fraud; the French, not knowing German commercial legislation well, prefer a loss to a long lawsuit.[46]

This report clearly shows the link between cheating, experience and reputation. The most likely victims of cheating were inexperienced and/or emerging firms. They could not (or did not seek to) benefit from established networks that included highly reputable foreign firms. This was also the case because French professional associations sought to limit new firms' access to these markets.[47] From this perspective, trade associations and networks operated as barriers to entry rather than as tools to overcome protectionism, as it was usually stated.[48]

Of course, despite what some reports suggested, French firms were not only the victims of cheating; they also widely practised it. The Ministry of Commerce complained several times about the negative impact that certain firms had on French producers' reputations as a

---

[45] AN F 12 7452, several files, years 1874–1882.

[46] AN F 12 7452, "Rapport du vice-consul de France à Cologne, 17 June 1876."

[47] AN F 12 9183, 9303 several files on the strategies abroad of French trade houses.

[48] James Rauch, "Business and Social Networks in International Trade." *Journal of Economic Literature*, 39, 4 (2001): 1177–203; Hancock, "The Trouble".

whole. These firms exploited the "ignorance" of buyers in foreign and colonial markets.[49] Local producers' associations once had exerted strong control and punishment on cheating producers and traders accused of damaging the reputation of a whole area or sector of production.[50] However, technical progress and economic and social fragmentation weakened this mechanism. Accelerating technical advances, particularly in chemistry and its application in the food industry, dramatically complicated the question of identifying what quality was for most agricultural products. For example, a good wine could be identified with having some organoleptic[51] characteristics or by possessing stable and standard characteristics, or perhaps as a product created through "traditional techniques". This multiplicity occurred at a moment when business associations fragmented precisely because of disagreements over techniques of production and commercial attitudes. For example, in Bordeaux, winegrowers and wine merchant associations multiplied between 1884 and 1914. These associations accused each other of producing blended wines, if not clearly adulterated products, thus damaging the reputation of the whole area.[52] Indeed, as we have shown in previous chapters, this problem did not find any clear solution until the formal, official definition of *appellations* (AOC) in 1935.

This issue demonstrates that market structure and cheating influenced each other. In the wine market (Bordeaux as well as the Midi), the multiplication and fragmentation of business associations occurred in a context marked by falling prices (despite the phylloxera crisis), reduced vineyard areas and increasing polarisation of estates and firms (the crisis concerned primarily middle-sized units).[53] Researching new markets and new techniques were vintners' most widespread reactions;

[49] AN F 12 7452, several circulars from the Minister of Commerce to the chambers of commerce, 1876–1882.
[50] AN BB 18 (Ministry of Justice, criminal division) 6024 (salt wines), "Syndicat général des chambres syndicales du commerce en gros des vins et spiritueux de France au ministre de la Justice, 30 June 1882."
[51] Referring to the sensuous qualities of a product – taste, smell, texture, etc.
[52] AN BB 18 6026 (dry raisin wines), "Chambre de commerce de Bordeaux au ministre du Commerce, 22 April 1885."
[53] Marcel Lachiver, *Vins, vignes et vignerons.* Paris, Fayard, 1988: 410, 464; Rémy Pech, *Entreprise viticole et capitalisme en Languedoc Roussillon.* Toulouse, Université le Mirail, 1975; Ministère du commerce, *Annuaire Statistique,* several years.

however, they were undertaken in a non-cooperative environment in which adulteration and cheating were at the same time practised and feared.

Beyond foodstuffs and beverage, textiles were also much affected by cheating and quality identification, insofar as artificial fibres began developing in this period and were mixed with so-called "natural" fibres.[54] Quick innovation and rapid product differentiation contributed to weakening collective sanctions and moral solidarity within fabric merchant communities. From the 1880s, in Lyon and in the north of France, enterprises developed new mixtures, first of silk and other natural fibres and then of natural and artificial fibres.[55] Uncertainty about quality increased, which led to litigation both within trade associations and in the courts. This process went hand in hand with the multiplication of professional unions and associations between 1884 and 1914. As in Bordeaux and the Midi, these textile unions were highly unequal in their composition and the wealth of their members, with social and professional origins being the main distinguishing factors. Thus, in the public sphere, shared attitudes linked to belonging to a territory and/or an industry (e.g., the silk industry in the Lyon district) were increasingly rare, whereas litigation about the definition of local trade customs, accepted techniques and the like sharpened.[56]

As a whole, the commercial correspondence, newspapers and ministerial archives we have consulted confirm that during the last quarter of the nineteenth century, a large majority of economic actors shared the opinion that uncertainty and "cheating" dominated the markets. We may consider this description as being fundamentally strategic, insofar as it sought to secure strong institutional support by reducing uncertainty to cheating. In part it was so; still, this argument must be taken seriously, for it was constantly evoked at the time and, to some extent, it did much to influence many traders' and producers' attitudes

---

[54] On adulteration concerning food and beverages: Stanziani, "Negotiating innovation"; on textiles, AN F 12 7001 (wines and alcohols, customs), several documents; AN F 12 4929 (General direction of customs), several documents.

[55] Charles Sabel, Jonathan Zeitlin, "Historical Alternatives to Mass Production: Politics, Markets and Technology in Nineteenth Century Industrialization." *Past and Present*, 108 (1985): 133–76.

[56] AN F 12 7452 (commercial fraud), F 12 7602 (industrial property).

and expectations. This attitude derived primarily from the modification of the economic landscape at both the national scale (redefinition of regional balance) and, more particularly, at the international scale, which presented economic actors with previously unknown conditions and behaviours. The economic depression, urbanisation and expanding international markets brought important changes among firms and traders. Such changes expelled from the market several old "maisons", whom new actors replaced. In domestic as well as international markets, uncertainty increased, concerning both the reputation of these new actors and their practises.

Uncertainty became *radical* when it focused not only on economic trends and counter-parties' strategies, but also on the "economic environment" itself (institutions, mentalities, product characteristics and rules). In this situation, except for a minority of economic actors who were particularly risk-oriented, most actors worked towards reducing uncertainty, seeking to regain market stability. But to achieve this aim, they needed more detailed information.

ECONOMIC INFORMATION FROM PUBLIC INSTITUTIONS: MARKET AND GENERAL TREND STATISTICS

Although the acquisition of information is indispensable to any response to cheating and rising uncertainty, it presents costs which must be compared to benefits. Costs of information depend primarily on who is in charge of collecting it and secondarily on the rules for its circulation. In the 1870s and 1880s, large firms and important commercial houses had their own information on foreign markets and overseas correspondents; they were not willing to share this proprietary information without compensation. For example, the chamber of commerce of Grenoble, in a letter to the Ministry of Commerce, strongly criticised the idea of sharing information, because some firms invested considerably in this, and urged instead the reduction of fees and expenses for exports.[57] Cheating and increasing market uncertainty also raised the cost of collecting information for large enterprises. However, this

---

[57] AN F 12 6353, "Letter, 8 November 1884." Several other examples of this in this same file.

situation was much more dramatic for smaller traders.[58] In this context, different solutions were available: Traders could form a coalition and share the costs and benefits of securing information, or traders could appeal to the state to collect it. Both solutions depended on whether "information" was a homogenous or a differentiated good. I will now discuss each of these points.

To share the costs and results of research, individual parties needed to reach a cooperative agreement.[59] Achieving this required that the costs of acquiring information and the opportunity cost of non-competition be outweighed by the benefits the information provided. However, such an outcome could not be taken for granted. Until the end of the 1880s, French firms experienced great difficulty in reaching cooperative agreements for the circulation and sharing of information on foreign correspondents and markets. This difficulty reflected inexperience and a high level of mistrust due to the markets' haphazard nature, supplemented by the uncertainties regarding legislation on associations, contracts and counterfeiting. Associations were legalised only in 1884; before that date they had no legitimate existence in France and thus could hardly impose rules on their members. Even so, chambers had different strengths and influence; and, within each association, there often was an unequal circulation of economic information to members.[60] In fact, chambers of commerce systematically gathered information concerning prices, production, and market dynamics, notably in their regions. This data was at the disposal of individual parties, was published in the chambers' bulletins and, from the 1860s, was also sent to the Ministry of Commerce and the valuation commission for Customs and Excise. Trade associations and syndicates also reported information, as did official goods brokers in the tribunal of commerce.[61]

---

[58] AN F 1 6872, "Rapport du vice-consul à Köln au minister du commerce, 17 June 1876."

[59] AN F 12 6353, 6365, 7297 are full of letters of consuls, official representatives complaining of this attitude and also complaints made by individual firms on this same subject.

[60] AN F 12 9135, "Ministre des affaires étrangères au ministre du commerce, 11 December 1894"; "Ministère du commerce, 3e bureau, rapport, Janvier 1896."

[61] AN F 12 7497 (National office on industrial property), for example: vice-president of the official goods brokers of the tribunal of commerce of the Seine to the Minister of Commerce, October 1888.

However, such general information was insufficient when trying to decide which country to invest in, which foreign representatives to address, and the like. Of course, each chamber tried to acquire such specifics elsewhere, a difficult task because other chambers were not necessarily predisposed to help, sometimes because they themselves did not have adequate details at their disposal.[62] In some cases, precise information on overseas traders and markets was gathered, but only selected members could secure access. The *Bulletin des halles* observed that "Large firms send a special representative to each region and they study the market situation. This is without doubt the best way. Nevertheless, firms with more restricted resources cannot take these risks. They estimate that the costs are too high and the success too uncertain. The only alternative they have is to rely on the work of diplomatic actors and consulates."[63] These conditions stimulated opportunistic (free-rider) behaviour and encouraged cheating. A vicious cycle ensued: The lack of coordination between parties was translated into an incentive to act individually, which in turn encouraged opportunistic behaviour.

As a result, during the 1870s and the 1880s, the most common reaction among French economic actors (mostly small traders) was to call for assistance from the state. However, business groups complained about the low quality of the economic information state agencies provided. Their first concern was the timing of state statistics. For example, in 1874, the chamber of commerce in Vosges (Epinal) expressed the desire to see as soon as possible the publication of statistical documents of French Customs. In Britain and in the United States, such a publication appears regularly and not long after the period it covers. "The Customs office in France compiles monthly the information it receives on imports and exports. The resulting dossier is only available nearly two months after the operations have taken place. This delay means that a large part of the information is useless for commerce."[64]

---

[62] AN F 12 7416 (correspondence between the Ministry of Trade and chambers of commerce on international trade), various documents.
[63] *Bulletin des halles*, 11 October (1894).
[64] AN F 12 7416, chamber of commerce of Vosges, minutes of session of 5 January 1879.

This is why *Le journal des tarifs et traités de commerce* proposed to "centralise at the Ministry all the information obtained."[65] The problem was not only a question of timing; even if those statistics had been rapidly published, their usefulness was doubtful. Businessmen criticised consuls' reports because they did not focus on the relevant information, namely the existing market structure and the product characteristics required in particular countries, but only offered general considerations about economic trends.[66] Enterprises considered consuls and *attachés commerciaux* incompetent regarding business information and suggested replacing them with knowledgeable businessmen. This argument gained support from the Ministry of Trade, although installing this new kind of attaché would have required a joint selection and appointment process (ministries of Trade and Foreign Affairs).[67] Business associations addressed similar criticisms of state statistics, which offered only general data on market trends for generic products (wine, clothes, etc.); such information was judged as having very limited usefulness for business.

What then did business require from both consuls and statistical bureaus? As business associations' records and economic ministries' correspondence clearly show, French economic actors were mostly interested, on the one hand, in timely information concerning product characteristics required for a given market (and not the general demand for, say, "wine" or "clothes"), and on the other hand, reports on the reputations of potential correspondents and local actors.[68] In other words, businessmen were not so much interested in getting macro-statistics on market trends for general products, needing instead detailed information on both correspondents' reputations and product demand.

It is worth noting that this demand for state-generated information was general and by-passed the well-known opposition between

---

[65] "Les attachés commerciaux", *Le journal des tarifs et traités de commerce*, 27 September (1894): 2147–8.

[66] AN F 12 6353, 6369.

[67] AN F 12 6353 (Bureau of commercial information), Minister of Foreign Affairs to the Minister of Commerce, 3 December 1883; L. Chapalaym to the Minister of Commerce, June 1883.

[68] AN F 12 6353, M. Barbe to the Minister of Commerce, 1884; Jules Bernhim to the Minister of Commerce, 17 January 1885; the Blondeau company to the Minister of Commerce, 26 September 1884.

liberals and regulationists, free-traders and protectionists. For example, H. Weiss, in *La réforme économique* stressed that "the demand for State support, although rather widespread, is not unanimous. In commercial matters nothing is better than private initiative and we are not compliant with state interference in issues for which it is clearly incompetent. The State cannot be a commercial party, no more than it can be a manufacturer, and those who want the State to install trading posts in foreign countries will only be disappointed..."

Nevertheless, we must not conclude that the State must be disinterested in these issues. "The government must facilitate enterprises, encourage their efforts, but not by subventions or privileges which favour individual businesses to the detriment of general business as a whole. To create commerce the first requirement is to be well informed. For this reason, the consul is not sufficient. Attachés are what are required.... Nor can the State depend on the good will of companies which, despite the subventions they receive, are completely autonomous; the State must be able to order and not ask for service."[69]

This argument was typical of the liberal economic debate of the end of the nineteenth century; state intervention, in principle excluded, was advocated when confronted with economic uncertainty and the power of lobbies. The previous passage clearly shows that in the eyes of some contemporary economic actors and commentators, economic information constituted a highly valuable asset and, as such, its market needed to be regulated and managed by the state.

In other words, French traders, facing high market uncertainty and unequal access to information, appealed to the state in order to overcome dependence upon big trade houses and foreign correspondents. The heterogeneity of information as a good made this request more urgent. This was a clear appeal for using public resources for private purposes, aiming towards a redistributive effect in favour of "small units".

How did French state officials react to these requests? Despite these pressures, public institutions refused to provide information on

---

[69] Henri Weiss, "Attachés commerciaux." *Réforme économique*, 30 September (1894): 1001–2; AN F 12 9183 (attachés commerciaux).

particular firms and traders to other firms and traders; and the reform of the diplomatic body never occurred. Several French representatives still considered that consuls and *attachés commerciaux* needed to have a general "political science" background and should not be traders themselves. As a sort of compensation for this refusal, in April 1883, the Minister of Commerce decided to create a bureau of commercial information "charged with centralisation for the purposes of delivering to our businessmen and firms the information available from the different services of my department. This information will be published in a weekly journal."[70] However, this new institution did not necessarily respond to private requests for economic information. In fact, many economic actors and firms reiterated their interest in information on the reliability and reputation of their potential correspondents.[71] These demands were once again dismissed. "The bureau of commercial information provides only information of general interest to those interested parties, either by correspondence or by an official journal of commerce."[72]

In the eyes of French officialdom, economic information on particular actors and markets had to be collected by private enterprise. To those who maintained that small firms could have difficulty getting this kind of information, the minister of commerce Lucien Dautresme replied that they had to enter associations or make coalitions and share information. "Our competitors show the advantages of working together."[73] Such an attitude could not but irritate the business community. *Le nouvelliste de Rouen* judged that:

Collective action is impossible because large firms, which are the only ones able to export, operate unilaterally and competitively [with smaller enterprises]. The true collective representative is the [commerce] commissioner. Finally, the French chambers of commerce abroad are an anomaly, because

---

[70] AN F 12 6369 (consular reports and correspondence with the chambers of commerce), circular of the Minister of Commerce to the presidents of the chambers of commerce, 3 April 1883.

[71] AN F 12 6353, M. Barbe to the Minister of Commerce, 1884; Jules Bernhim to the Minister of Commerce, 17 January 1885; the Blondeau company to the Minister of Commerce, 26 September 1884.

[72] AN F 12 6353, E. Chandelet to the Minister of Commerce, 2 July 1883; reply by the latter, 10 July 1883.

[73] AN F 12 9183, circular of 26 December 1885.

the most influential French firms established abroad have specialised in the fabrication of products which are similar to that of the homeland.[74]

Given this asymmetry, why did the French state refuse to provide the required information, and what were the consequences of its attitude on business organisation and market dynamics? Several considerations underlay French representatives' refusal to collect information on private firms; some of them were sincere supporters of free trade and pure competition and, as such, considered state interference as constraining economic growth and liberal ideals. A second reason was that the French foreign office had traditionally benefited from a particular status, that is, the secrecy of its actors' activity and a strong independence vis-à-vis other ministries. Delivering information collected by consuls and their actors was considered a first step towards a considerable restriction of the Ministry of Foreign Affairs' autonomy and a prelude to a second, even more dangerous step – the transformation of consuls into business representatives, chosen and appointed in collaboration with the ministries of Agriculture, Industry and Trade.[75]

To these "old" reasons, a new one has to be added. During the last quarter of the nineteenth century, French administrative law was subject to considerable reforms;[76] in particular, the immunity of administrative personnel from the public's demands was undermined, and contemporary administrative law was being elaborated and adopted. It would thus have been against this trend to allow consuls and employees of economic ministries to collect information on private business and deliver it to other private actors. A further reason for this was that large firms contested the state's provision of information on private foreign traders. They considered this "intrusion" as an attack on their freedom of trade and on their "well-gained" superiority in this field over other French enterprises. Several French officials supported this view.[77]

Nevertheless, it would be misleading to attribute the behaviour of public authorities only to economic, legal or political constraints.

---

[74] AN F 12 9183, Une circulaire de M. Dautresme, *Le nouvelliste de Rouen*, 5 January 1886.
[75] AN F 12 6353, several dossiers.
[76] François Burdeau *Histoire du droit administratif*. Paris, PUF, 1955.
[77] AN F 12 6353, several documents.

Actually, their reticence in delivering information on individual parties also reflected substantial internal organisational difficulties in getting this kind of information. Conflicts between ministers, "experts" and bureaucrats were quite widespread. For example, when in January 1884, the *Union des syndicats viticoles* asked for information on different auction conditions for wine (prices and rules) in different countries, the Minister of Trade replied that a list was difficult to establish.[78] In other words, the French state's refusal to provide detailed business information to individual actors was limited not only by legal considerations but also by real organisational difficulties within the state administration.

To sum up, in late-nineteenth-century France, a considerable gap opened between the demand for and the supply of business information. The state delivered only "macro" information on prices, demand, supply and general market tendencies, whereas private business required detailed information on firms, traders and product characteristics locally sought. This gap confirms that information is not a homogenous product. Information concerning markets differs from information on individuals and firms' reputations; equally, statistics on generic products are not equivalent to those on actual, particular products. Hence, this impasse was all the more detrimental to the French economy because private businesses still had great difficulty co-operating. In this context, space opened for developing private information agencies.

PRIVATE AGENCIES FOR INFORMATION

The question of who is in charge of the circulation of information matters. If not the group or the guild (as in Greif's model), intermediaries, information agencies and state agencies may provide the required services. Mostly studied for labour and financial markets, in information markets, intermediary agencies have strong redistributive effects. Indeed, agencies may reveal just enough information to solve the allocative distortion and then appropriate for themselves a part

---

[78] AN F 12 6353, 30 January 1884, reply by the Minister of Commerce to the *Union des syndicats viticoles.*

of the surplus. This is why sellers have preferred imperfect markets with no intermediaries.[79] This is all the more true when the reliability of intermediaries is hard to evaluate.[80] Strong contractual problems therefore arise for both intermediaries and their clients.[81] Historically, it is difficult to evaluate the number and size of these agencies; in ministerial archives and in correspondence, demands for financial support or simply institutional acknowledgements make it possible to identify several dozen of these agencies, appearing from the early 1880s through the end of the century. This development was relatively weak, insofar as large firms (or those already experienced in the international market) had their own networks of correspondents. Most other firms considered private agencies too expensive and/or unreliable. Low-value information (when not actually false) was often quoted in business journals; lawsuits were frequent. Indeed, defendant agencies sometimes threatened to give private information to competitors if a firm would not renew its contract or did not pay fees. Judges usually gave satisfaction to the plaintiff.[82]

In order to overcome these difficulties, officials devised a system of references for these agencies; chambers of commerce and the Ministry of Trade provided lists of "reliable" agencies. However, this solution fell short, for the chambers sought to create their own information offices and/or international trade agencies.[83] Some agencies therefore contacted the ministry of commerce and the foreign office, seeking either a monopoly of foreign trade information in a given place or some financial support. Usually administrators refused both sorts of requests.[84] At the same time, state officials did not hesitate to contact the same agencies in order to acquire information on a given market, a trader or a list of traders. This was done, not only to inform economic and diplomatic policies under consideration, but also in response to private (individual and/or chambers of commerce) requests.[85] This

[79] Alessandro Lizzeri, "Information Revelation and Certification Intermediaries." *The RAND Journal of Economics*, 30, 2 (1999): 214–31.
[80] Rauch, "Business".
[81] Dixit Avinash, "On Modes of Economic Governance." *Econometric*, 71, 2 (2003): 449–81.
[82] *La revue vinicole*, 25 February (1892): 31; 6 April (1893): 55; AN F 12 6353, several documents.
[83] AN F 12 6353, "Sur les agences de renseignement." *Bulletin des halles*, 11 October (1894).
[84] AN F 12 6353, dossier Eckel.
[85] AN F 12 6353, dossier "La confidence".

last attitude contradicted the general refusal of public officials to provide private information to other private businessmen, and confirmed
that this refusal was not only the result of voluntary politics, but also
flowed from and highlighted organisational difficulties within public
administration units. This issue sharpened the tension between public
expenditures for providing economic information and private allocation of it; strong debates occurred on this topic, enhancing both
cooperative agreements between traders and the production of a new
kind of state information.

COMMERCIAL ASSOCIATIONS VERSUS CARTELS

As is evident, during the 1880s, most French firms were unable or
unwilling to share information and co-operate in international markets. This circle was broken at the turn of the 1890s for two main
reasons: the declining international significance of French firms and
traders, and the new institutional support given to business associations. In consequence, as the benefit of gathering information
within an association increased, the costs of collecting it fell.[86] About
1890, generalised cheating and uncertainty started to show signs of
decreasing; first French exporters started to lose markets to German,
English, American and Italian parties.[87] The coveted urban market also
shifted – prices of meat and standard wines underwent their first slip-
pages after years of increase.[88] The drop in French exports alerted not
only firms. During the first half of the 1890s, initiatives by the Minister
of Commerce and the Minister of Foreign Affairs to promote international commerce in particular increased. In this context, exhibitions and
commercial museums gained importance as instruments to promote
French exports. With public support, many French towns founded
commercial museums; others were opened abroad.[89] Thereafter, consuls were authorised to deliver information about individual parties to

---

[86] AN F 12 6353, "J. B. Bonnefoy to the Minister of Commerce", August 1884.
[87] Direction générale des douanes, *Tableau décennal, 1887–1896*. Paris, 1897.
[88] Ministère du commerce, *Annuaire statistique*, several years, 1885–1895; Ministère de
l'agriculture, *Statistique agricole*, 1897.
[89] AN F 12 9135, various documents.

other individual parties.[90] The Minister of Foreign Affairs organised conferences, held by former consuls or consuls on sabbatical, to discuss commercial matters and help traders know better the countries where they had served.[91]

However, it would be misleading to interpret the rise in state production of business information as documenting an inability of individual parties to get information themselves. Of course, some firms, and in particular the most well established internationally and the largest ones, remained reluctant to rely on government efforts. For example, for the Bordeaux Region, Delors showed no hesitation in setting up a branch in Buenos Aires in 1892; they were followed shortly after by Calvet. On the side of importers, several large firms from the Gironde had their own network of correspondents, in particular in Spain and Algeria.[92] But this strategy was more and more difficult to practice successfully because of the changing conditions of the international market, particularly for wine. Falling prices and increasing information asymmetries made it difficult for a single firm to rely only on its own network.[93] Because of this, the increasing production of state information paralleled a strong development of commercial associations. Chambers of commerce and business unions devoted greater attention to the collection and circulation of economic information for their members.[94]

Falling prices and increasing costs for privately collecting information were not the only reason for pushing well-established traders and a vast majority of French exporters to play a cooperative game with other firms. Indeed, this new orientation took place in a situation in which new forms of trade cartels (*comptoirs*) were being established.

[90] AN F 12 9057 to 9105 (renseignements commerciaux fournis à des particuliers par les actors diplomatiques et consulaires, commercial information supplied by diplomats to individual parties, 1889–1898).

[91] AN F 12 7414 (renseignements commerciaux) and Weiss, "Les attachés." The chambers of commerce of Reims and Bordeaux were particularly dynamic in this connection, especially towards consuls who used to be posted in the United States and in Latin America.

[92] Roudié, *Vignobles*: 180.

[93] Roudié, *Vignobles*: 209.

[94] AN F 12 7497, for example: "Vice-President of the official goods brokers of the tribunal of commerce of the Seine to the Minister of Commerce, October 1888."

These initiatives aroused a great deal of interest among firms and traders. In September 1884, the firm René Blondeau, *orfèvrerie et couverts argentés*, in Paris, wrote the Ministry of Commerce about an article published in *Le moniteur officiel* on the constitution of a syndicate of firms in Lyons formed to support exports of local products.[95]

From the 1890s on, *comptoirs* opened in most foreign countries, benefiting from the financial and information support of both professional institutions and French officials.[96] French embassies provided legal help and resources, selected personnel to take charge of the *comptoir* and, last but not least, offered information on local traders and firms' reputations. *Comptoirs* were an institutional answer to the fragmentation of French associations and French business circles and to the ensuing lack of co-operation and reputation effects. They operated as a coalition dictating and enforcing rules to members while providing them with reliable information on markets and local correspondents. *Comptoirs* often organised as partnerships for a limited number of years; they assigned customers' orders to be filled by members according to their quota. Fixing the quotas was the subject of careful negotiations, of course.[97] Large trade units controlled them and gave other firms information about markets and reliable correspondents; they guaranteed standard quality, that is, a uniform organisation of production in the industries concerned, and in exchange took control over the export market while profiting not only from private firms' fees but also from state contributions.[98]

Because of this, not every business association and individual actor was ready to accept the *comptoir* discipline. An alternative solution, openly declared in opposition to *comptoirs*, was founding cooperatives, especially in the wine market. In the Midi and southwest of France, vineyard owners created the first cooperatives to finance investments in winemaking and storage, aiming to stabilise wine characteristics thereby. In turn, this technical shift aimed at two further goals. On the national market, cooperatives wished to reduce small winegrowers'

---

[95] AN F 12 6353, "René Blondeau to the Minister of Commerce, 26 September 1884."
[96] AN F 12 9183.
[97] Charles Freedman, "Cartels and the Law in France before 1914." *French Historical Studies*, 15, 3 (1988): 462–78.
[98] AN F 12 9183, "Les syndicats français." *L'industrie française*, 28 January (1886).

dependence upon traders; on the international market, they wished to meet criteria set by international traders and *comptoirs* while increasing their members' bargaining power. As such, cooperatives were not necessarily synonymous with a greater independence of local winegrowers from big traders.[99]

To sum up, the activity and timing of agencies dealing with business information show that private and public institutions were much less substitutes for one another than complementary to one another. Traders and their associations played a minor role in the information market when (in the 1870s and 1880s) the state refused to provide detailed economic information. Conversely, associations developed at the very moment when (from the 1890s) different ministries gave financial, logistic and information support to private business. This was so because information was not a homogenous good and because it was unequally distributed. French state actors did not openly contest these hierarchies, due to lobbies' influence, administrative rules and organisational difficulties. However, after an initial refusal to provide private information on business, the state accepted the task of disseminating it to previously selected firms. This accompanied indirect support to export cartels that confirmed previous hierarchies despite a changing economic environment. The initial reluctance of the French state to develop the required information had its cost; French exports met with significant difficulties on the international market during the last quarter of the nineteenth century. These difficulties have been usually explained by the drop in luxury consumption (the bulk of French exports) as a result of economic crisis and by a general attitude of French actors, supposedly risk-averse. This attitude would have negatively influenced their insertion in an increasingly aggressive and international economic environment.

I have countered these arguments by showing that attitude towards risk was mostly influenced by the access to economic information (particularly limited for French export houses); there was not a specific, "natural" attitude hostile to risk, but rather difficulty in getting information. This last was all the more necessary given that risk and uncertainty had risen considerably during the previous quarter

---

[99] Pech, *Entreprise.*

century. To confirm this conclusion, in the following pages I shall analyse the way the Italian state and Italians actors faced the same historical problems.

ECONOMIC INFORMATION AND INTERNATIONAL MARKETS: THE ITALIAN PERSPECTIVE

I have shown that in France, business units and state functionaries did not agree about what constituted relevant economic information. Even when their views overlapped, state officials judged that it was not their responsibility to provide private information to private businesses. On this topic, the Italian case proves particularly interesting, for the basic conditions in Italy resembled the situation in France – commercial actors faced the "long depression" in a different position than in Britain (trying to protect its advance) or in Germany (pushing new sectors with the help of the state). Links between commercial, civil and administrative rules were quite similar in Italy and France and because of that, private actors and the state should have had a similar attitude towards the production and circulation of economic information. Was that the case? And if not, why not?

In Italy, as in France, from the 1870s on, most economic actors involved in international trade experienced increasing economic uncertainty and encountered cheating as one result of economic progress and the development of new international markets. Italian chambers of commerce often warned their members about fraud in such markets.[100] As in France, these institutions appealed to the state to get confidential information on their commercial counterparts. Italian representatives were initially extremely interested in the French solution. In 1883, the Italian minister for public finance, Luzzatti, visited the newly created bureau of commercial information at the French Ministry of Trade.[101] The Italian government immediately decided to set up a similar bureau. Unlike its French counterpart, however, the Italian information office at the Ministry of Trade, in close collaboration with the Ministry of Foreign Affairs, was from the start allowed to provide firms

---

[100] Archivi centrali di stato, henceforth ACS, Fondo MAIC (Ministero de l'agricultura, industria e commercio, divisione industria e commercio), fascio 303, several documents.
[101] AN F 12 6353.

and traders with private information on their potential counterparts abroad. The archives are rich with requests and supply of this type of information all over the world.[102] Still, two important distinctions have to be made. Unlike the French, Italian traders willing to enter a new market abroad were primarily in search of Italian correspondents. The sizeable presence of Italian emigrants (far greater than the French community abroad) encouraged this approach. The importance of the overseas Italian community in commercial relations made it easier for the Italian foreign office to get timely information for homeland companies and traders seeking to enter a particular market.

Emigration also assisted the establishment of commercial networks. Family networks usually followed patterns of emigration; family members (in the broad sense) gave commercial support to their relatives' homeland trade or productive unit. They provided information about their local market, helped to find correspondents (when they themselves did not play this role) and promoted the family or local product. Village-based or regional out-migration equally sustained this kind of networking. Exporters of wines from Puglia, Piedmont, Calabria and Sicily made wide use of this solution.[103] Yet the importance of family and emigration networks must not be overestimated. Indeed, family and local networks ran into problems when they confronted powerful (state or chamber of commerce) associations, or when information and networks were scarce and financial risk was high.[104] Even if the Italian diaspora was far more widespread than the French one, it assured only a limited solution to the problem of cheating, insofar as loyalty and moral engagement within emigrant communities was relatively weak.[105]

Moreover, the strong support the Italian government gave traders in collecting business information was confined to the international

---

[102] ACS, MAIC, fasci 303, 304, 305.

[103] ACS, MAIC, direz. gen. agric., vers. V, fascio 325.

[104] "Fonctionnement de l'agence italienne de commerce à Liverpool pendant le deuxième semestre 1894." *Moniteur officiel du commerce*, 21 February (1895) n. 698; ACS, MAIC, direz. gen. agric., vers. V, fascio 323, 325, on export trade.

[105] On the role of diasporas in commercial networks: Abner Cohen, *Customs and Politics in Urban Africa: A Study of Hausa Migrants in Yoruba Towns*. Berkeley, University of California Press, 1969; Rauch "Business"; Francesca Trivellato, "Juifs de Livourne, italiens de Lisbonne, hindous de Goa: Réseaux marchands et échanges interculturels à l'époque modern." *Annales HSc*, 58, 3 (2003): 581–603; Philip Curtin, *Cross-Cultural Trade in World history*. Cambridge, Cambridge University Press, 1984.

market. The Ministry of Trade information office systematically refused to share information on domestic companies or merchants with other national actors. They were told to address their inquiries to the Ministry of Finance.[106] In other words, the Italian government engaged public resources to support Italian firms in international competition, whereas such action was taken much more selectively in the national market. Official refusal to provide information did not prevent its selective circulation, due to personal ties or even corruption. This general attitude of the Italian government was pushed so far that, unlike France, ministries devoted minimal effort to producing massive and detailed macro statistics which private economic actors found irrelevant.[107] Italian national economic data lacked precision, resources and more, as most Italian statisticians of the time complained, and played no important role before the First World War and the 1920s. One may justify this attitude by referencing Italy's more "liberal" orientation compared with France.[108] This judgement requires closer scrutiny. Actually, the Italian government strongly intervened in the economy, but its instruments and sometimes its goals were different from those in France. In particular, support for Italian trade abroad involved using public resources for private purposes. Also Italian consuls and commercial attachés came from business circles more frequently than their French colleagues and had commercial rather than diplomatic backgrounds. The foreign office worked in collaboration with the ministries of Trade, Agriculture and Industry. Consuls thus strongly promoted Italian products abroad and devoted considerable funds and energy to this.[109]

At the same time, some analogies with the French case can be detected. In particular, Italian authorities, too, spent considerable

---

[106] ACS, MAIC, direz. gen. agric., vers.V, 304.

[107] ACS, MAIC vers.V, 304.

[108] For an historical analysis of the role of official statistics and bureaus in Italy and France: Giovanni Favero, "La statistica comunale dall'Unità alla Repubblica." *Rivista Usci Notizie*, 13, 3 (2007): 50–4; Jean-Pierre Béaud, Jean-Guy Prevost (eds.), *L'ère du chiffre. Systèmes statistiques et traditions nationales.* Sainte-Foy (Québec), Presses de l'Université du Québec, 2000; Eric Brian, *La mesure de l'Etat.* Paris, Albin Michel, 1996; Silvana Patriarca, *Number and Nationhood. Writing Statistics in Nineteenth Century Italy,* Cambridge, Cambridge University Press, 2003.

[109] AN F 12 9183; ACS, MAIC, divisione industria e commercio, fascio 303; *Bollettino del ministero degli esteri* (July 1902): circulaire du 31 July 1902, "Appui que les actors à l'étranger doivent prêter au commerce national."

energy determining the qualities different products should have in order to enter a given market. Consuls and commercial attachés detailed characteristics of wine for markets in Argentina, Turkey, Uruguay, the United States, and other places.[110] A debate on optimal strategy took place along the same lines as in France; for example, as regards wine, some official representatives and Italian traders supported the idea that both local and international markets in general required stable wines. In consequence, mixtures were not viewed negatively, and the role of wholesalers became crucial. By contrast, other official representatives and winegrowers' associations stressed the idea that "typical" rather than uniform standardised wines should be promoted.[111] Italian officials also backed plans for setting up oenological units abroad to analyse both local products and Italian exports, mostly wines. Surveying the competition and Italian offerings, they forwarded suggestions to producers, winegrowers and traders for better processing and storing of their products.[112] Several units of this kind were opened in the 1880s and 1890s in the main European and American cities.[113]

Similarly, the Italian government decided to help Italian traders and producers in finding local correspondents in a more direct way than by providing information on potential associates. Firms and traders that fulfilled certain requirements listed by both Italian officials and economic associations could secure exclusive licenses for the export of Italian goods.[114] This issue sometimes took a specific and effective form when an official Italian trading post was established abroad. In this case, the public organisation (in the twofold sense that it was authorised and controlled by both chambers of commerce and the government) had exclusivity for Italian imports. French representatives and traders were often quite impressed by the efficiency of these units.[115]

---

[110] ACS, MAIC divisione industria e commercio, fascio 303.

[111] ACS, MAIC, vers. VI, busta 250.

[112] ACS, MAIC, direz. gen. agric., vers. IV, busta 463, fasc. 2497. On the selection of wine specialists for these units: ACS, MAIC, vers. VI, busta 250.

[113] ACS, MAIC, direz. gen. agric., vers. IV, busta 463, fasc. 2497.

[114] ACS, MAIC direz. gen. agric., vers. V, fascio 327.

[115] AN F 12 9135; "Ouverture en 1893 de l'agence commerciale italienne à Amsterdam." *Moniteur officiel*, 592, 1 July (1894) and 579, 2 August (1894); ACS, MAIC, direz. gen. agric., vers. IV, busta 463, fasc. 2497.

To sum up, the Italian market for business information expressed a clear convergence of (private) demand and (public) supply, reached by using public resources for private purposes, thereby adapting economic policies to business needs. Of course, this outcome did not prevent conflicts; in particular, the traders and firms already having a strong network abroad were hostile to the possibility of establishing public trading posts available to most Italian producers and traders. Others expressed doubts about these public organisations' efficiency, preferring to trust personal networking.[116] This is also why the rise of public institutions for collecting information and promoting products did not prevent the emergence of a private market for business information. In Italy, the incidence of paid actors gathering business information was even more widespread than in France.[117]

Yet unlike France during the 1880s, these agencies developed not so much due to the lack of information public institutions provided than as a complement to it (as in France in the 1890s).[118] This left room for various forms of cooperation among firms and traders. We may distinguish two main patterns of organisation: family and cooperative. Together with the search for reliable correspondents, the increasing role of cooperatives responded to wholesale traders' accumulating power and the monopoly they enjoyed through official representatives. Cooperatives aimed to stabilise wine and/or to improve its quality while assisting their members in penetrating foreign markets.[119] The Ministry of Agriculture strongly supported (politically and financially) these initiatives.[120]

We may try to evaluate the impact of these different market structures on business information in Italy and in France. Data on the international wine market show that between the 1880s and 1914, Italian wine deprived French rivals of substantial market share, particularly

---

[116] ACS MAIC, direz. gen. agric., vers. V, fascio 325. Réunion à la chambre de commerce de Paris, 25 July 1888.
[117] ACS, MAIC, divisione industria e commercio, fascio 306.
[118] ACS, MAIC, divisione industria e commercio, fascio 303.
[119] ACS, MAIC, direz. gen. agric., vers. VII, busta 5, fasc. 51: cantine sociali après 1900; ACS MAIC, direz. gen. agric., vers. VI, busta 250, 251, 323, 323A.
[120] ACS, MAIC, vers. VI, busta 250; ACS, MAIC, direz. gen. agric., vers. VII, busta 5, fasc. 51.

in Latin America.[121] Commercial and diplomatic correspondents on both sides of the Alps agreed on the cause of this: What made the difference was not phylloxera (which spread in France as well as in Italy), and not the quality of wine (ordinary quality was better suited to the taste of Italian emigrants), but the commercial attitudes of Italian traders and producers and the support of the Italian government.

INFORMATION AND ECONOMIC DYNAMICS

Historical analyses of international trade fail to take into account the varieties of economic information, the fragmentation of markets, and the common lack of transparency and competition. The market for information was highly segmented and strongly hierarchical. Economic relationships, hierarchies and market dynamics strongly responded to these features. During the last quarter of the nineteenth century, these features acquired a particular relevance insofar as world trade extended, thanks to quick and low-cost transport, new communication tools, better storage and an increasing standardisation of products. At the same time, these trade-favourable features contrasted with a return to protectionism, social and political instability, anxieties about cheating and finally quick technical progress. These latter forces contributed to rising uncertainty and risk and thus to market integration.

The wine market is paradigmatic for this phenomenon: new systems of storage, new techniques for keeping wine safe and the quick development of new urban and transcontinental markets went along with commercial "wars", cheating, the arrival of organic chemistry and other innovations, plus important changes in the main actors involved. Such a rapidly shifting world weakened the value of reputation as a tool for market coordination. The main alternative, law, was traditionally difficult to enforce in international markets – more so at this time because of increasing geopolitical conflicts between countries. Hence reliable information on both products and actors acquired a crucial role. Still, information was not a homogenous good, nor was

---

[121] Direction général des douanes, *Tableau*, 1890–1902; Ministère du commerce, *Annuaire statistique de la France*, several years.

it available to everyone. It is precisely because information was not homogenous that the state could either offer a type of information that was not otherwise accessible to private parties or supply macro-information of no interest to them, but which state policy makers nevertheless considered valuable for policy or prestige reasons.

For a long time, the French state adopted the latter approach before converting to the former near the century's end, while in Italy the state immediately answered business needs. The convergence between demand and supply of information was based on a common defini-tion of relevant information, that is, not general statistics, but detailed materials on local economic actors and on product characteristics. The state collected information, but afterwards officials selectively dissem-inated it. This strengthened producers and traders directly linked to officials and encouraged corruption, but on the whole, it gave Italian traders and producers a consistent advantage over their rivals, primar-ily the French. Private use of public resources seemed to have benefi-cial effects on their economic dynamics.

One implication of this story is that it would be misleading to inter-pret the dynamics of international markets simply in terms of supply and demand or of liberal against protectionist economic policies. In fact, the Italian government neglected massive statistical projects, not because it was against intervening in the economy but rather because it preferred other forms of intervention, namely sustaining exports through financial aid while providing detailed business informa-tion. All the same, in France, officials' refusal to share detailed micro-information with business units was dictated much less by liberal considerations than by institutional equilibriums between ministries and the idea that political-diplomatic action took precedence over economic intervention. The chronology of this intervention is equally significant: The French did not give support to business requests before the middle of the 1890s, that is, when the economic and political cycle reversed, and growth and liberalism were again at the forefront.

A further implication of our analysis is that precisely because of this lack of attention to information, historians have evaluated the attitudes of economic actors towards risk according to an ahistorical, perfectly competitive and unrealistic market for information, and thus, in reference to an abstract notion of "risk". French traders were not necessarily averse to risk; they simply lacked information their rivals had. In turn, this handicap was only partially due to a weak cooperative attitude among French firms (although this was a real problem); the attitude of public officials towards the circulation of information also played a major role. The impact of these features on economic dynamics can be easily summarised. In the short run, Italians took substantial shares of the international market away from France due to the fact that Italians benefited from more detailed information for at least a decade. But once the attitude of the French state changed, this comparative advantage in information about the reputations of firms and traders vanished.

At the same time, this story also shows that it would be misleading to discount the two leading and hardly compatible interpretations of international trade at that time, that is, protectionism and globalisation. First, our conclusions will not be the same if we consider intra-European or trans-Atlantic trade, the former being constrained by tariffs, the latter being enhanced by them. Second, even though the real importance of tariffs should not be over-estimated, non-tariff forms of protectionism (quality rules on products, among others) and economic information must be acknowledged as playing an important role. In particular, "globalisation" is somewhat a misleading notion for that time. If it is true that increasing standardisation of products (increasing wine and agro-food production) undoubtedly helped prices to converge; at the same time the importance actors and markets gave to detailed information on quality of products and reliability of commercial partners shows that standard and non-standard products were far from being in opposition to a "global market", but, quite the contrary, supported each other. It is not by chance that the French AOCs (collective trademark) for wine were invented in response to this process and linked individual products to standard rules for evaluating them.

However, if information on both actors and products is essential to reduce risk and make international markets possible, then product standardisation and international expertise are also supposed to play a crucial role in reducing uncertainty. In the following pages, I am going to test this proposition and consider the agreements on product definitions at the international level. I will begin with foodstuffs and agriculture produce before passing to manufactured goods.

DEFINING PRODUCT QUALITIES IN
INTERNATIONAL TRADE

Product qualification and classification influence duties and/or general barriers for security and health reasons. In fact, international trade and competition were not regulated solely by prices; upstream product classification and labelling played as important a role in devising and implementing trade policies. There were two, interrelated steps in this process: the definition of each product and the arborescence of the products and their variants. The first form of classification involving product definitions reasoned in terms of exclusion and hence applied, above all but not only, to agricultural products (e.g., what is wine?). I have already discussed this. The second form of classification, based more on product variety and resulting in a far more dense arborescence than the first, was applied primarily to manufactured products (varieties of velvet or cotton). These forms of classification were not extended to agricultural products until late in the twentieth century, when the calibre, size, colour, and other attributes of different varieties of the same fruit or vegetable were identified and stabilised. Let us attempt to examine these methods of product classification and quality definition in greater detail.

At the turn of the nineteenth century, the rise of institutional definitions of products in the various countries made it difficult to reach trade agreements. Ultimately, these institutional definitions of products aimed at stabilising the hierarchies within national industries as well as to protect them from international competition. For example, when deciding on which substances and processes should be prohibited in winemaking, each country obviously took into account those that were widely used elsewhere and often ended up prohibiting them. Rules defining typical products differed from one country to another according to the history and economic equilibrium of the market concerned. For example, in France, the institutional definition of wine was mostly connected to the interests of Bordeaux winegrowers and traders, despite the necessity of taking into account the interests of Midi winegrowers and traders. The definition of wine summarised the history of wine adulteration in France.

In Belgium, where wine traders faced much less hostility from winegrowers than from other groups of traders and merchants of alcoholic beverages, wine was defined as "the product of alcoholic fermentation of the juice or must of fresh grapes".[122] Adding substances was prohibited, except for "mechanically acting clarifiers (albumin, gelatine)" and ordinary salt, provided the chloride and lime content did not exceed 2 grams per litre.

In the United States, Standards of Purity for Food Products defined wine as the product obtained by normal alcoholic fermentation of the juice of healthy grapes and by ordinary winemaking processes. As in France, wine was not to contain more than 2 grams of potassium sulphate or one gram of sodium chloride per litre.

In Italy, wine was defined as an alcoholic beverage obtained by the alcoholic fermentation of grape must or sugar with no addition of foreign substances. The addition of water, glycerine, colouring, artificial sweeteners, free mineral acids, salts, strontium and barium were prohibited and considered to be falsifications (laws of 3 August 1890 and 25 March 1900). As in France, these outcomes were linked to the difficult equilibrium between winegrowers and merchants from central and northern Italy (mostly interested in fine wines) and producers of southern Italy, where wines were mostly used to "cut" the weak vintages from the North.[123]

Once adopted, these heterogeneous rules obviously posed a coordination problem, for although there was unanimous agreement on the general definition of wine and the limitation or even prohibition of certain practices, numerous processes were accepted in one country but prohibited in another. Given the rapid growth of the international market, this phenomenon caused considerable legal and economic problems. Whereas it was impossible for a French judge to convict a wholesale trader or winemaker for producing a product using techniques prohibited in France but accepted in his country, but what about a French trader who imported, for example, plastered wine from Spain. For several years, judges were divided

---

[122] AN F 12 6925, dossier législations étrangères.
[123] AN F 12 6925, dossier législations étrangères.

concerning the possibility for the importer to "correct" the initial flaw without being prosecuted.

Governments and economic actors were aware of the fact that these classifications masked significant commercial stakes. For example, the French rules pertaining to wine falsification and the prohibition of plastering were immediately criticised in Spain and Italy as a form of hidden protectionism.[124]

Similarly, The Pure Food Act adopted in the United States drew protests from French winemakers and wholesale traders who asked the government to support their request to the American authorities that their products be exempt from analysis by American laboratories. They argued that such a procedure would reveal their winemaking secrets to competitors.[125]

The problem of coordinating norms was discussed in diplomatic meetings and in conferences organised on the topic by professionals and hygienists. Thus, in September 1907 in Berlin, the conference of the White Cross called for an international commission to be set up for the purpose of unifying the laws and methods of analysis regarding beverages and foodstuffs.[126] The first international conference on protection against food and pharmaceutical fraud, which took place in Geneva on 8–12 September 1908 under the auspices of the White Cross, was supposed to put this resolution into practice. However, during the sessions, significant divergence emerged among hygienists, representatives of business associations (in turn divided between agrarian producers, traders and manufacturers) and government officials not only within each country but also among the different countries. These differences can be explained first of all by the varying interest each group had in the definitions; the hygienists proposed "purely scientific" norms to be imposed on professionals and governments. The governments replied that such norms were aimed at stabilising relations between the countries and hence they should take into account the commercial interests of all.[127] At the same time,

---

[124] AN BB 18 6023.

[125] AN F 12 6858, "Rapport de la part du syndicat des produits alimentaires en gros, Paris, 22 April 1914."

[126] AN F 12 6970, *Congrès international de la Croix Blanche*, 1907.

[127] AN F 12 6970, "Président du conseil par intérim et ministre des affaires étrangères au ministre du Commerce, 25 July 1908."

both government officials and hygienists had to face business organisations, themselves divided. In particular, the demands of agricultural
producers conflicted with those of wholesale traders who were pushing for normalisation of products and international trade. These conflicts prevented the participants from reaching genuine agreements
on the products because the mere acceptance or prohibition of a
technique or a substance would change the international position of
the producers in one country in relation to the others. Thus, the conference succeeded only in adopting rather general product definitions.
Consequently, bilateral agreements between countries were required
for the trade of a given product to take place.

As was seen in the discussion of produce exchanges, the development of these markets was accompanied by the introduction of
typical products. This operation was a prerequisite for future transactions. At the same time, since similar operations were introduced in
each country, coordination was required to ensure that, for example, the types of cotton or wheat listed for export in New York
and Chicago would be the same as those in London and Paris. This
coordination took place at multiple levels, namely of trade associations, the exchanges concerned and the respective governments. In
certain cases, import exchanges refused to accept deliveries that did
not comply with their standards. In several instances, the exchanges
in Le Havre and Paris refused American wheat and cotton.[128] This
refusal brought disputes back to the wholesale traders, who in turn
challenged their suppliers on the other side of the Atlantic. However,
the outcome of these disputes depended on the presence of several
import and export transactions. Thus, the same cotton refused in Le
Havre could be accepted in Liverpool, which tipped the scales in
favour of the exporting country and the wholesale trader. Conversely,
the presence of several export ports in the United States enabled
European importers to call upon different commission actors.[129] This
explains the tendency in the United States to reach a swift agreement between the exchanges and the exporters in order to deliver

[128] F 12 979A, 979D, 980; J.C.F. Merrill, "Classification of Grains into Grades." *Annals of the
American Academy of Political and Social Science*, 38, 2 (1911): 58–77.

[129] Henry Crosby Emery, "Futures in the Grain Market." *The Economic Journal*, 9, 33
(1899): 45–67.

uniform products. From this point of view, the arrival of standard wheat in a city immediately increased the export of products passing in transit through the city and led other cities and exchanges to adopt similar measures. Coordination of the various product classification criteria took place in response first to European requests, and second to aid from the federal government which imposed its own classification criteria and its own experts in the name of American interests.[130]

Of course, this process led to a certain amount of friction. American farmers were often opposed to the exporters' requests which also constituted a way for wholesale traders to take control of the industry. However, those who were interested primarily in exports gave in sooner or later. This concession was especially easy to put into practise because the wheat intended for the domestic market was not subject to the same inspections or the same demand for standardisation as the wheat intended for export.[131]

Finally, tensions also emerged between exporting and importing countries. American trade associations turned to their government when cotton and wheat were increasingly refused in Europe. At this stage, negotiations took place predominantly at the diplomatic level. For standardisation to be accepted at the international level, the governments involved had to tactfully handle the interests of farmers, which were usually opposed to those of manufacturers and wholesale traders.[132] The success of these agreements testifies to the success of this effort, precisely when European farmers were demanding and obtaining protectionist tariffs. This confirms the fact that the history of public policies in international trade is more complex than is usually recognised, as customs tariffs were supplemented by other measures (product standardisation, health regulations) which also contributed to the opening and closing of markets. This issue, and thus the complex interaction between the involved actors, is confirmed by the process of identification of products, substances and their values in the custom tables and regulation.

---

[130] Merrill, "Classification."
[131] Emery, "Futures"; John Williams, "The Origin of Futures Markets." *Agricultural History*, 56, 1 (1982): 306–16.
[132] AN F 12 6313–6337; F 12 6355, F 12 6368, 6918, 6931.

PRODUCT IDENTIFICATION AND THE LOCATION OF VALUE: THE COMMISSION OF VALUES AT THE CUSTOM DEPARTMENT

Historians, economists, social scientists and politicians are too often led to use custom tables as sources for studying the evolution of international markets and the impact of tariffs on it. Extremely complex statistical re-elaborations of international trade data have been provided.[133] Our evaluations of past and current performances of international markets rely upon them. Oppositions or convergences of interests between countries, business actors and their associations are mostly interpreted on the basis of these same tables. In the following pages, I will consider this question from a different perspective: Rather than correcting data according to one or another model and questioning the impact of tariff on growth, I wish to reason backwards and investigate the elaboration of primary sources as made at the time under investigation. In doing so, I wish to complete the approach adopted in previous pages and understand how economic information was created, by whom and to what aim. Indeed, trade associations, politicians and administrative officials took pains systematically to classify the different varieties of a given product and list their technical and manufacturing specifications in order to elucidate their qualities and ultimately establish a correspondence between these characteristics and prices or customs tariffs.[134]

The archives of the commission on customs tariffs reveal the complexity and persistence of these questions. The commission was officially set up in 1857, but the original debates that gave rise to it began in the mid-1830s and became more intense in the mid 1840s. Indeed, in the face of increasingly volatile international prices (a drop towards the end of the 1840s, followed by a rise) and what was perceived to be an acceleration of innovation and commercial fraud, numerous actors and ministerial officials wondered if customs tariffs should

---

[133] Among the others: O'Rourke, "Tariffs and Growth"; Bairoch, "European Trade"; Federico, Tena, "Was Italy"; Giovanni Federico, "Per una revisione critica delle statistiche della produzione agricola italiana dopo l'Unità." *Società e storia*, 15 (1982): 87–130.

[134] Michel Alcan, *Fabrication des étoffes*. Paris, Lièges, Noblet et Baudry, 1866. Archives of the commission on the custom values and duties in: AN F 12 7452, AN F 12 4929.

be constantly adjusted to these phenomena to take into account the demands of the tax office and of private actors. French industrialists were among the most outspoken in demanding tariff adjustments and a more detailed arborescence of products. Admittedly, this demand was supported by protectionist aims; however, those interested in importing new products or substances also followed these approaches with keen interest because they wanted the customs office to make a clear-cut distinction among the varieties of the same product so they might benefit from reduced tariffs on the new varieties that would not be available in France. In other words, as the correspondence among individual actors, their trade associations and the commission on customs tariffs shows, their aim was to arrive at an agreement on the definition of product qualities relating to both taxation and the control of innovation. Thus, in 1907, a group of manufacturers was ready to substitute methyl alcohol used in producing carburised alcohols by merely denaturing alcohol. However, before adopting this solution, the manufacturers asked if it would entitle them to tax deductions provided for the use of alcohol for industrial purposes.

Similarly, in 1909, a producer of artificial silk asked for a franchise on the crystallised sugar used for its production; a farmer also asked to be exempt from taxes on the sugar used in cattle feed; the same solution was requested for salts used in making artificial ice.[135] Depending on the administration's response, the actors would decide whether or not to undertake these innovations; in this case, a refusal from the ministry stopped the use of sugar in silk manufacturing but at the same time brought renewed pressure from several producers, not only in textiles, for reduced taxation on manufactured sugar used for non-food purposes. However, we should keep in mind that such decisions were often accompanied by pressure exerted on top-ranking customs officials by elected representatives or ministries, for example, commerce. Judging from the archive files, these pressures indeed influenced the evolution of customs nomenclatures and with them, the taxation of the products and substances concerned. In this operation, given the tariffs, the way in which these new elements were classified was of great importance. Thus, a circular

---

[135] AN F 12 6934.

from the Central Customs Office in May 1874 ordered wool yarns for weaving and tapestry, which were formerly distinct, to be unified.[136]

Another circular on 15 December 1874 explained that "the new edition of tariffs reproduced the chapter on stone, soil and mineral fuels, native barium carbonate, native barium sulphate and natural phosphates, which had previously been listed under chemical products. It also classified in this chapter rectified cooking oil and petrol and schist spirits."[137] These classifications affected the tariff applied, the final price and hence the economic decisions of the firms concerned.

However, it was not a question of reconciling the interests of the customs office with those of individuals. The government's most general economic policies also influenced the activity of the commission on customs tariffs which regularly sent out questionnaires to trade associations to find out about changes in their products, the techniques they employed and production inputs and supply networks. For example, the questionnaire that the commission sent in 1894 to the St. Etienne Chamber was designed in this way:

- What is the total production figure in 1894 of the St. Etienne factory, dividing the production by fabric categories? What is the value in francs of the quantities exported in 1894? What is the value in francs of domestic consumption?
- What is the average value per kg of these fabrics according to the classification adopted by customs?
- What were the quantities in 1894 compared with 1893 of silk and cotton yarns used to manufacture ribbon?
- What were the changes in the prices of silk and cotton yarns?
- What were the variations in wage rates?
- Do you know any other reasons besides consumer taste for inexpensive articles that accounts for the constant increase in sales of blended articles at the expense of pure silk articles?[138]

This questionnaire reflects the economic theories used by the commission members. Profitability was linked to production inputs; the

---

[136] AN F 12 4929, "Direction générale des douanes, circulaire du 10 mai 1874."
[137] AN F 12 4929, "Direction générale des douanes, dossier autour de la circulaire du 15 décembre 1874."
[138] AN F 12 7004, Commission aux valeurs des douanes, *Questionnaires envoyés aux chambres de commerce, syndicales, etc.*

firm was supposed to adopt the same classification criteria as customs. The last question above all shows how the commission conceived of the relationship between the consumer and the producer and the role of technical progress: It was demand that determined supply. However, in its reply, the Chamber of Commerce called this approach into question: Contrary to what was presumed in the questionnaire, it was asserted that the year 1894 posted a rise in the production of pure silk articles at the expense of mixed articles.[139]

The commission therefore had to try to reconcile the diverging opinions of its members, pressure from administrators and the demands of private individuals. How did it respond to these conflicting demands? The meetings and reports of the commission on customs tariffs and those of the Central Customs Office show that during the 1870s, the problem of product classification arose with particular intensity in three market segments: energy, chemistry and textiles (the latter concerned the arrival of hessian cloth and new fabrics). Thus, the circular from the Central Customs Office dated 27 December 1873 pertained mainly to fabrics and gold and silver plating:

Circular of 27 December 1873. Modification of classifications, by the Central Customs Office

Current Nomenclature	Modifications to Be Made by Hand
solid ecru canvas	solid ecru canvas for packaging
	solid ecru canvas for any other use
waxed solid canvas	waxed solid canvas pour packaging
painted solid canvas on coating for tapestry	waxed solid canvas for upholstery, wall hangings or other
ribbons of pure silk: other velvets	ribbons of pure or blended silk
other ribbons of blended silk: other velvets	
all varieties of rugs	rugs
	tapestries
a) cashmeres and other blended, milled and draped fabrics	a+b
b) draped	
c) sackcloth and crepe de Zurich	abolished

(continued)

---

[139] Ibid.

Current Nomenclature	Modifications to Be Made by Hand
canvas, percale and calico	canvas, percale, calico and drill
oilcloth and tar cloth	the same, but distinguished into: for packaging and for upholstery, wall hangings or other
blended fabrics, dimity, piqué and others	façonné, piqué, dimity, damask and shiny
engravings, lithographs, etchings, photographs and drawings on paper	three entries distinguished for: engravings, lithographs and photographs
plated and jewellery in metals other than gold, platinum and silver	jewellery in metals other than gold, platinum and silver
plated with gold, platinum and silver or other metals	plated with gold, platinum and silver or other metals

One year later (15 December 1874), another circular put out by the Central Customs Office applied modifications that took into account the development of chemistry:

[T]he new edition of tariffs includes in the chapter on stone, clay earth pigments and mineral fuels native barium carbonate, native barium sulphate and natural phosphates which were formerly listed among chemical products. It classified corrected oils and petrol and schist spirits under the same heading.

The tariffs commission also demanded the following modifications: ochre is apparently never sold raw. It is sold only after being washed and pulverised to make it suitable for painting and for this reason it was classified among colours.

Keep a separate account for clay earth pigments from Cologne, Cassel, Italy, Sienna and Umber which have a much higher value than ochre.

The tariff commission also suggested keeping an account of the different varieties of washing soda which also had varying value: Natural soda should be distinguished from artificial soda; kelp soda; caustic soda; soda salts.

"Fine pigments for painting, due to their high price, will form two distinct accounts". Derivatives of coal will be products made from coal tar and distinguished from: benzene, aniline, phenol acid, etc.

Finally, in relation to silk, "the distinction between fine or fake gold or silver braid and that of silk mixed with gold or silver will be abolished". According to the commission, it was one and the same product.[140]

[140] AN F 12 4929.

In the wake of this last provision, the circular dated 10 May 1874 ordered wool yarns for weaving and tapestry, which were "currently distinct", to be unified.

Of course, the many forms of definitions of manufactured products were not specific to France. In the nineteenth and twentieth centuries, customs offices in Italy, Germany, Great Britain and the United States devoted significant attention to nomenclatures and the criteria for product classification. Although the fiscal and financial stakes were crucial for this activity, they were not the only ones; the interests of the customs office had to be negotiated firstly with those of the various lobbies and secondly with those of other countries.[141] In international trade, the criteria for product quality definition from the standpoint of trade (e.g., how to classify a given fabric) or health (compliance with national laws, presence of prohibited substances, particularly colouring, lead, etc.) were a powerful tool for negotiation and non-tariff protectionism. Tinned foods, toys, wallpaper and chemical colouring for fabrics were among the main topics discussed at the international level towards the end of the nineteenth century. The international competitive order required such forms of classification, as the trade associations and "economic" ministries of the various countries testify.

In Great Britain, the United States, Italy and Germany, customs nomenclatures and classifications were negotiated with the ministries involved in coordination with the main trade associations. It was a cumulative, interactive process involving the various market scales (local, national and international). Thus, the criteria for standardising the thickness of cotton yarn were negotiated at all three levels. Manufacturers in Lille and Lyon sought to impose standardised criteria in this area, but in order to succeed, it was necessary for local customs to be accepted and unvarying. However, we have shown that these objectives were not achieved a priori, and that customs in this area underwent increasingly drastic changes in the course of the century. These local interactions added to those between cotton producers and importers. The quality definition and standardisation of cotton in Le Havre and Paris came in response to these concerns.

---

[141] AN F 12 6455, Documents on the commercial relations between France and Britain; between France and Germany: AN F 12 6555, 6970; between France and Italy: AN F 12 8963.

Finally, at the international level, the demands of French wholesale traders and producers (which were not always the same) had to be reconciled with those of American producers and exporters, which also diverged on this subject. International negotiations then intervened, not on the basis of a stable foundation of quality agreements, but on the contrary, on a shaky foundation and through ongoing negotiation among the actors. International agreements sometimes succeeded in reducing instability, but not always. The worldwide cotton market was a fine example of success in this area, whereas that of wine showed, on the contrary, the fragmentation of quality agreements and the success of national or even regional quality standards (at least until the end of the twentieth century, when the standardisation of wine and its classifications and nomenclature rapidly developed).

To sum up, the international market challenges one of the conclusions reached here for local and national markets, namely that legal rules are weak and difficult to enforce without business community intervention. However, merchants' and state regulation are much less substitutes than complementary items. With the increasing specialisation and differentiation of markets, institutions and economic actors, customs, values, trust and networks cannot survive without the support of state agencies. Circulation of information and product identification contributes to reduce uncertainty and make markets possible. At the same time, during the period under investigation, the production and circulation of information and the process of evaluation and standardisation of products were not only a matter for business communities but also required state support. Modalities and strength of this action considerably influenced the economic performance of different countries.

CONCLUSION OF PART III

The notion of information asymmetries can explain some peculiar cases of market failure, such as when economic actors share the same notion of product quality and one wishes to trigger it. In other cases, people can share uncertainty insofar as product characteristics are not exclusively determined by the production process. Exchange equally contributes to product qualification. Exchange generates information, value and utility.

From this perspective, the economic theory of contracts cannot fully capture the fact that contract incompleteness is not always a limit for efficient exchange, but it can equally enhance it, for economic actors need a mix of certainty and uncertainty to adapt their arrangements to a quickly evolving economic environment.

On this ground, contracts, brands and labels do not compensate "incomplete markets" (neo–institutionalist approach), nor do they hamper markets (neoclassical argument), but they are constitutive of the capitalist exchange. This means that we cannot contrast the Ancien Régime's (regulated) economies with capitalistic (self-regulated) systems: Both mobilise micro- and macro-regulation of the exchange. Neither can we oppose manufactured (standardised) products to agricultural (non-standardised) produce, insofar as industrial products are never fully standardised whereas by contrast, agricultural produce can be standardised on the basis of the period, the product varieties and the concerned country.

In a word, specialisation and product standardisation, which comprise the views of both Adam Smith and Alfred Chandler, fail to represent the economic dynamics of the eighteenth- and nineteenth-century Western world. Specialisation and concentration dominated and became the distinctive feature of capitalism only with the second industrial revolution. This process gave rise to a structural shock sweeping away the world of proto-industry and the first industrial revolution. New rules and new market institutions were consequently adopted.

At the international level, the advent of the eighteenth and nineteenth centuries put the old merchant order in a difficult situation (networks and personal ties lost much of their coordinating power), whereas product standardisation and the market for information were still too weak to compensate for this trend. This means that the convergence of economic systems was sharply limited up through the end of the nineteenth century.

Still, we have to understand the way micro-regulation and trade activity could coordinate in the broader market mechanism. The ensuing third part of this study will examine the general competition principle in a global and comparative historical approach.

PART IV

GENERAL RULES OF COMPETITION: SPECULATION, TRUSTS AND FAIR COMPETITION

Thus far, I have studied the institutional construction of the market at the micro-economic level. In particular, I have shown how the law was used to control first physical markets and then trade. It is now time to analyse the third market level, namely the market as a regulating principle, that is, the market as synonymous with competition. As we saw in the first chapter, for more than half of the nineteenth century, both socialist and liberal economic thought paid scant attention to correcting competition. Like Ricardo and Malthus, Marx studied competition firstly in relation to his analysis of crises and secondly to determine the relationship between prices and values. Following this approach, many solutions were recommended. Ricardo thought that free trade would limit the decline in agricultural productivity and hence enable an increase in wages at the expense of profits. Marx confined himself to discussing the presence of crises within capitalism, without proposing any solution aside from abandoning the capitalist system altogether.

Indeed, during the first half of the nineteenth century, liberal and utilitarian economic theory opposed monopoly to competition; the latter was said to enable more products to be obtained at a lower price than monopoly. Starting from this assumption, it was possible to conclude that competition guaranteed greater well-being and efficiency than monopoly. Consequently, for these currents of thought as well as for classical English theory and Marx, there was little reason to study ways of correcting competition.

It was only in a context marked by socialism and the welfare state, large industrial complexes and railways, as well as industrial pollution and consumer protection that economic theory questioned the imperfections of the market (monopolies, negative external factors and imperfect circulation of information). These imperfections prevented the market from achieving the equilibrium foreseen by the theory of pure, perfect competition. Overall well-being as well as the efficient use of resources (scarce) were below the levels which would be attained in the case of perfect competition. With this premise in mind, a series of measures was put forth to bring the real (imperfect) world as closely in line as possible with pure, perfect competition, which was supposed to be fair and efficient at the same time.

The stakes were considerable: It was a question of deciding whether trusts and monopolies should be prohibited. If the answer was yes – as is the case for European policies nowadays – the question then became at what point of concentration public authorities should intervene.

If, on the contrary, these radical measures of prohibition were ruled out, then it would be necessary to introduce incentives and constraints to make firms comply with a certain threshold of concentration and monopolistic power. The debate then turned to the most appropriate instruments for this task and their efficiency; strictly economic criteria (efficiency) were compared with social criteria (e.g., employment policy) as well as political criteria (the impact of lobbies on the government, international relations, etc.). For example, the theoretical efficiency of competition from the standpoint of growth and investments was not always compatible with maximising employment rates nor, by the way, with the interests of one or another industrial group in having their own market "niche".

To understand these debates more fully, they must be viewed in their proper historical contexts, not only because there was only limited industrial and financial concentration during much of the nineteenth and even twentieth centuries, but also because the words themselves, their meaning and use in economic policies and in the strategies of the actors did not always correspond to those we know today. In particular, in the nineteenth century, monopoly was still often associated with hoarding goods, which had been prohibited in the eighteenth century. Therefore, we must first understand the reasons for this institutional legacy to assess if and how these norms could be adapted to the new phenomena of industrial concentration as they appeared at the turn of the nineteenth century.

I am going to study the various aspects of the construction of the principle of competition, starting with hoarding and speculation on foodstuffs and then the stock exchange. I will then study antitrust regulations and will end with the notion of fair competition. As usual, we will develop these analyses in detail starting firstly with the case of France, followed by a comparative analysis. We will show that, while economic, ethical, political and legal aspects influenced competition policies in all the countries studied, at the same time differences stand out in the content of these policies and the timing of their introduction.

10

HOARDING AND SPECULATION

INTRODUCTION

The word speculation is most often associated with the stock market; however, even today, the word is also used, with a rather negative connotation, to account for the scarcity and increased prices of certain products.[1] From the historian's point of view, this definition seems to be a legacy of pre-industrial economies[2] in which there was a threat of scarcity and "speculators", in the sense of hoarders.[3] It is widely held that the problems of scarcity gradually disappeared with industrialisation and the agricultural revolution, and with them speculation in the sense of hoarding. The progressive liberalisation and development of commodity markets is presented as a confirmation of this argument. French historical experience, however, does not confirm these statements. We are going to see that in France, speculation in the negative sense of hoarding scarce resources (particularly foodstuffs and commodities) never quite disappeared but on the contrary increased

---

Translated by Susan Taponier. Part of this chapter was published in *Law and Social Enquiry*. I acknowledge my gratitude to Wiley for permission to use it here.

[1] Among others, cf. Lynn Stout, "Why the Law Hates Speculators: Regulation and Private Ordering in the Market for OTC Derivatives." *Duke Law Journal*, 701, 48 (1999): 777–83; Commodity Futures Trading Commission, *Annual Report*. Washington, DC, 2003.

[2] Georges Duby, Armand Wallon (eds.), *Histoire de la France rurale*, 3. *De 1789 à 1914*. Paris, Seuil, 1976; Fernand Braudel, Ernest Labrousse, *Histoire économique et sociale de la France*. Volumes 3 and 4, Paris, PUF, 1976 and 1979; Maurice Levy-Leboyer, François Bourguignon, *L'économie française au XIXe siècle*. Paris, Economica, 1985. For a critique: Nicolas Bourguignat, *Les grains du désordre. L'Etat face aux violences frumentaires dans la première moitié du XIXe siècle*. Paris, EHESS, 2002.

[3] Steve L. Kaplan, *Le complot de famine. Histoire d'une rumeur au XVIIIe siècle*. Paris, Colin, 1982.

in the nineteenth century and at moments in the twentieth century. Article 419 pertaining to hoarding in the French Criminal Code was inherited from the Old Regime and lasted throughout the nineteenth century and, with few changes, until the 1960s. It is interesting to study the gradual judicial application of this article first to foodstuffs and then to services, the commodities exchange, the stock exchange and ultimately to coalitions and trusts. Indeed, what stands out in the French case is that no genuine antitrust laws were adopted like in the United States. What were the legal reasons and more broadly the perceptions of the actors, the ethical principles and social influences that gave rise to this very specific way of handling these questions?

One may wonder whether the hostility towards speculation and concentration did not express a broader negative attitude of French society towards "capitalism".[4] We are going to question this interpretation and show that French regulation of future trades and speculation aimed to stabilise and enhance markets. From this standpoint, it is true that the history of Article 419 of the French Criminal Code and its enforcement express the *longue durée* of rules institutions, but not in the sense that pre-capitalistic institutions and regulation continued under (supposedly deregulated) capitalism. Quite the contrary, we argue that this strong continuity expresses the compatibility between capitalism and regulation over the long run. The long life of Article 419 was not the result of anti-capitalist judges or regulatory bureaucrats, but of various lobbying actions and, in the courts of law, of the struggle between economic players. This also implies that market institutions have not emerged out of a narrow concern for promoting efficiency but instead are a product of political struggles.

Bibliography on this topic is limited: I would recall the pioneering work of Hirsch who revealed the use of law by economic actors in the Lille region in the eighteenth and nineteenth centuries.[5] Unfortunately, this work mostly focused on family economics and trade and did not

---

4 Steve L. Kaplan, Philippe Minard (eds.), *La France, malade du corporatisme?* Paris, Belin, 2004; Douglass North, *Structure and Change in Economic History.* New York, Norton, 1981; William Landes, Richard Posner, "Adjudication as a Private Good." *Journal of Legal Studies*, 3 (1979): 235–84; Anthony Ogus, "Self-regulation." *Encyclopedia of Law and Economics.* Cheltman, Edward Elgar, 2000, vol. 5: 587–660.
5 Jean-Pierre Hirsch, *Les deux rêves du commerce.* Paris, EHESS, 1991.

concern hoarding and speculation as such. Steve Kaplan has devoted much energy to market regulation under the Ancien Régime but not into the nineteenth century; however, our main approach and issues are sympathetic to his work, not only because of the link between institutional and market dynamics, but also because we find many more similarities than discrepancies between eighteenth- and nine-teenth-century regulations.[6]

In the same vein, Nicolas Bourguignat has recently argued that the Ancien Régime's subsistence crises and their political and social role did not disappear with the revolution but continued in the nine-teenth century (until 1848). My argument incorporates this issue by seeing a strong judicial and institutional component up until 1914. Some studies on French trusts and cartels at the turn of the nine-teenth and twentieth centuries also provide useful insights: They set the economic-historical context but they barely mention the rules and ignore their judicial implementation.[7] In this case also, I will include judicial archive research. However, it is not only a question of sources. By putting a finger on the interaction between law in action, institutions and markets, I wish to revisit some broader issues regard-ing French capitalism. Indeed, speculation and business concentration enter into the debate on the specificity (if any) of economic regula-tion in France. Traditional historiography has stressed the persistence of regulation in France as proof of French hostility to capitalism.[8] A few researchers have expressed the opposite view and maintained the peculiar "French way to capitalism". Regulation did not aim to stop

---

[6] Steve L. Kaplan, *Le meilleur pain du monde. Les boulangers à Paris au XVIIIe siècle*. Paris, Fayard, 1996.

[7] Marc Gillet, *Les charbonnages du Nord de la France au 19e siècle*. Paris, Mouton, 1973; Marc Rust, *Business and Politics: The Comité des Forges and the French Steel Industry, 1896–1914*. Ann Arbor, unpublished Ph.D. dissertation, 1974; Charles Freedman, "Cartels and the Law in France before 1914." *French Historical Studies*, 15, 3 (1988): 462–78; Michael Smith, "Putting France in the Chandlerian Framwork: France's 100 largest firms in 1913." *Business History Review*, 72, 1 (1998): 46–85; Jean-Pierre Daviet, "Some features of concentration in France (end of the nineteenth/twentieth century)." In Hans Pohl (ed.), *The Concentration Process in the Entrepreneurial Economy since the Late Nineteenth Century*. Stuttgart, Franz Steiner Verlag, 1988: 67–89, reproduced in François Crouzet (ed.), *The Economic Development in France since 1870*. Aldershot, Edward Elgar, 1993, vol. II: 501–53.

[8] Alain Plessis (ed.), *Naissance des libertés économiques, le décret d'Allarde et la loi Le Chapelier*. Paris, Institut d'histoire de l'industrie, 1993. Patrick Fridenson, André Straus (eds.), *Le capi-talisme français, XIXe–XXe siècles, blocages et dynamique d'une croissance*. Paris, Fayard, 1987.

capitalism but to enhance it while trying to reconcile growth and inequalities, technical progress and family businesses.[9] We would like to push this last view further and argue that control of speculation and regulation in general responded to ethical, political and economic influences, and that beyond administrative action, jurisprudence and the use of the law made by different economic and institutional actors have shaped French capitalism.

RULES ON SPECULATION IN POST-REVOLUTIONARY FRANCE

Revolutionary law, and then the Criminal Code (Article 419) inherited from the Ancien Régime the offence of hoarding goods, especially when the goods were considered "essential"; the text runs as follows:

Any individuals who, by deliberately spreading false or calumnious accusations in public, by offering prices superior to the price asked by the sellers themselves, or by meeting or forming a coalition among the main holders of the same type of goods or foodstuffs, tend not to sell it or to sell it only at a certain price, or who, by any fraudulent means whatsoever, shall raise or lower the price of foodstuffs or goods or public commercial paper above or below the prices that would have been determined by the natural, free competition of trade shall be punished by imprisonment.[10]

We will begin our discussion of this text by putting it in the broader institutional and political context of the post-revolutionary years, and then evoking the meaning judges, ministries and economic actors gave to its main words and expressions. Article 419 was based on so-called speculative movements and inflation during the revolutionary period

---

[9] Hirsch, *Les deux rêves*; Georges Ripert, *Aspects juridiques du capitalisme moderne*. Paris, LGDJ, 1951; Jean Hilaire, *Introduction historique au droit commercial*. Paris, LGDJ, 1986; William Reddy, *The Rise of the Market Culture: The Textile Trade and French Society, 1750–1900*. Cambridge, Cambridge University Press, 1984; Philippe Minard, *La fortune du colbertisme*. Paris, Fayard, 1998.

[10] *"Tous ceux qui, par des faits faux ou calomnieux semés à dessein dans le public, par des sur-offres faites aux prix que demandaient les vendeurs eux-mêmes, par réunion ou coalition entre les principaux détenteurs d'une même marchandise ou denrée, tendant à ne pas la vendre ou à ne la vendre qu'à un certain prix, ou qui, par des voies ou moyens frauduleux quelconques, auront opéré la hausse ou la baisse du prix des denrées ou marchandises ou des papiers et effets publics au-dessus ou au –dessous des prix qu'aurait déterminés la concurrence naturelle et libre du commerce seront punis d'un emprisonnement."*

and later on during the continental embargo.[11] Within this context, ethical and moral arguments played a key role and influenced the attitude of most French political elites who seldom showed unlimited faith in the free market and always sought to combine the market and competition with social order. The new law emphasised market freedom or trade freedom as opposed to guild constraints. According to this approach, the fight against monopolies and speculators had nothing to do with limiting industrial trusts as we know them; it was rooted in the idea that an economy of scarcity threatened the system and that it was therefore necessary to prevent any action aimed at destabilising the markets. Monopolists were, first and foremost, hoarders of essential goods.

It is important to point out that this definition of speculation as hoarding concerned the Criminal Code. This choice by lawmakers did not call market freedom into question; in general, in the nineteenth century, civil judges did not intervene in formulating prices, which was left to the free will of the parties. This general principle was called into question mainly in two situations: When a transaction was regulated at a fixed price, or a ridiculously low price was set by one of the parties, it was possible to terminate the contract. In this case, the intervention remained within the scope of civil law.

However, in other cases, when the market order and public order were more directly involved, the intervention of public authorities was authorised. These were cases provided for by Article 419 of the criminal code. What were they?

During the preparation of the Criminal Code, discussions took place over the meaning to be given to the expressions "deliberately spreading false accusations", "coalitions", "goods and foodstuffs" and "price determined by competition". Prior to this, the definition of speculation was used to delimit the field of application of the norms. In discussions, several speakers pointed out the presence of two forms of speculation: On the one hand, there was good speculation, which ensured the convergence of supply and demand and even eliminated excessive price fluctuations; on the other hand, "bad" speculation was gambling with a view to destabilising markets. More specifically, the

---

[11] Bourguignat, *Les grains*.

notion of "good" or "fair" speculation had gradually emerged during the eighteenth century, when some economists and legal scholars (Pothier, Domat, among others) considered that the traditional opposition to profit making should be overcome. According to this view, not every profit-making act could be categorised as disruptive speculation; "honestly seeking a gain" was legitimate. But how can one identify this form of gain?

The debates on Article 419 of the Criminal Code relied upon the previous debates on the Commercial Code and the institutional definition of a "merchant".[12] As was shown in Chapter 2, after the abolition of guilds, a merchant (or a trader according to the new vocabulary) was someone who paid the trade tax, his (women had a special status) activity had to be carried out on a continuous basis and with a view to making a profit.[13] Licit profit and the legal status of "trader" went hand in hand. It was on this basis that the Criminal Code could separate licit profit from illicit speculation. As one of the authors and first commentators of the code maintained, Article 419 "cannot be applied to open, fair speculation which distinguishes the true tradesman. Such speculation, based on realities, is useful for society. Far from creating excessive declines or rises in prices, it tends to contain them within the limits implied by the nature of the circumstances".[14]

On the other hand, there was speculation that was harmful to competition, which aimed at modifying prices as such and caused prices to deviate from the ones the market would have set. In this case, speculation was synonymous with gambling (*agiotage*); for example, the Dictionary of the French Academy of 1832 defined it as "clandestine maneuvers used either to raise or lower public funds... or to vary, according to one's own particular and secret interest, the price of a given foodstuff or goods on which one speculates".[15] "Bad" speculation was therefore associated with "underground" (clandestine)

---

[12] AN F 12 543 to 546.

[13] Marta Torre-Schaub, *Essai sur la construction juridique de la notion de marché*. Paris, LGDJ, 2002; *Code de commerce annoté*, par T. Compenon. Paris, Plon, 1865.

[14] Jean-Guillaume Locré, *L'esprit du code de commerce*, 10 volumes. Paris, Garnery, 1807–1813. In particular: vol. III: 153 and ff. *Les coalitions de producteurs, les accaparements de stocks et l'article 419 du code pénal*. Nancy, imprimerie Berger-Levrault, 1890.

[15] *Dictionnaire de l'Académie Française*. Sixth edition, Paris, Firmin Didot, 1832–1835; 40 Entry: "agiotage."

maneuvering and mostly concerned state bonds and foodstuffs but also ordinary trade goods.

These two notions of speculation constituted the legacy of the eighteenth century and were intended to reconcile micro-economic control with macro-economic control. The memory of "Law's affair" and the speculation and inflation that occurred during the post-revolutionary years[16] added to the speculation on foodstuffs and raw materials during the Napoleonic wars, and the continental embargo[17] gave these orientations new strength. The distinction between the two forms of speculation stemmed from the idea that it would be possible to separate two possible strategies within the scope of capitalism: One sought to make profit without failing to produce value (or utility, depending on the school), whereas the other was completely parasitical and sought to displace rather than create value. This distinction between the two forms of speculation was to continue during much of the nineteenth century.

The first step consisted of understanding the definition of "rumor", or "deliberately spreading false accusations" as it was described in Article 419. For the economist today, market "rumors" tend to distort the circulation and interpretation of information and hence lead to less than optimal interpretations on the part of the actors, and thus to the continuation or even aggravation of unbalanced situations. This approach is especially widespread in finance, where it seeks to explain the phenomena of snowball effects, speculative bubbles and the explosion, or conversely the control of speculative crises.[18]

However, this notion hardly corresponds to the one that inspired Article 419 of the Criminal Code. The only "rumors" taken into consideration by the code were those concerning foodstuffs and other commodities. The notion was very close to the famine conspiracies of the eighteenth century,[19] which are held to have been the source of the wide gap between the market price and the natural price. Article 419

---

[16] Philip Hoffman, Gilles Postel-Vinay, Jean-Laurent Rosenthal, *Priceless Markets*. Chicago, University of Chicago Press, 2001.
[17] Patrick Verley, *L'échelle du monde*. Paris, Gallimard, 1997.
[18] Drew Fudenberg, David Levine, *Theory of Learning in Games*. Cambridge, Mass. MIT Press, 1998.
[19] Kaplan, *Le complot*.

renewed this tradition insofar as the police, administrative actions and penal procedures were allowed to intervene to regulate speculation.

The question remained as to how a judge dealing with a case of hoarding could decide and distinguish good speculation from bad speculation, that is, the gap between the natural price and the practised price. From the eighteenth century onwards almost until today, economists have discussed this problem (the relationship between value and price, price and utility, natural price and market price) without ever coming up with a truly satisfying solution. It was precisely the relationship between natural price and market price, price and value that was the most problematic for the various economic theories. And with good reason – this relationship leads to questioning the way capitalism works; it is the basis not only for economic but also philosophical and ideological debates on contemporary modern society.

While generations of economists debated this subject, judges were required by the Criminal Code to find a pragmatic answer to the question of the relationship between natural price and practised price, competition and monopoly. Judges were continually asked for decisions by the economic actors themselves (and sometimes by public authorities) who disagreed as to the legitimacy and validity of the market price. This implies that, from the standpoint not of the history of ideas but of economic practises, the correspondence between "natural price" and "market price" (or between price and value, price and utility, depending on the school) could not be ensured without judicial or in any case institutional intermediation. How was this done?

It was rather difficult for a judge to distinguish the price as it appeared in the market at the time of the facts from the "natural" price resulting from the free play of competition, and above all, to attribute the former to the action of a coalition. In nineteenth-century France, judges' decisions were quite divided. For example, a coalition formed in 1832 by virtually all the commission actors of ordinary haulage in Paris was attacked by three foreign commission actors. The Paris court ruled against the coalition, but the Paris Court of Appeal reversed the initial decision and the High Court (Court of Cassation) validated the appeal on the grounds that the link between the coalition and the price increase had not been established.[20]

One widely practised solution consisted of judging the coalition by its goal. If the economic actors formed an alliance to combat a crisis and aggressive tactics on the part of other producers, then this agreement could not be found guilty of a violation. It is important that the Court of Cassation based this reasoning on the commentary made by Locré on the two speculations quoted earlier. According to the Court's view, a "defensive coalition" was supposed to act as a trader seeking to raise a "normal profit", whereas an "offensive coalition" wished to disrupt the market through "pure speculation".

The case concerned some Marseille soda producers that had required their customers to purchase solely through a single intermediary and had also seized control of six closed factories in the Marseille area to keep others from entering this market. These firms had never reopened and therefore, according to the plaintiffs (i.e., the Marseille firms using soda), the price of the product had risen despite the falling price of raw materials. The soda producers argued that they had to preserve their market and independence against the possible "invasion" of other competitors, and thus, their coalition and actions were strictly "defensive". The Marseille court and the Aix-en-Provence Court of Appeal accepted this argument, but the High Court overthrew it using the reasoning quoted earlier.[21]

However, some commentators and justice officials suggested that the aim of the coalition could not be identified "in the abstract", but depended on the specific market concerned (products, essential goods, services).[22] In particular, items such as meat and bread were under particularly severe control, and coalitions formed by butchers or bakers to obtain better terms with customers and municipalities were likely to be repressed on the grounds of Article 419.[23] On this basis, one

[20] AN BB 18 6603, several documents.

[21] Les coalitions de producteurs: 200.

[22] AN BB 18 1677, BB 30, 367 (prosecutors' reports). For magistrates' reactions to the reform projects: AN BB 18 6606, 6607.

[23] Jeanne-Marie Tuffery, Ébauche d'un droit de la consommation. La protection du chaland sur les marchés toulousains au XVIIe et au XVIIIe siècles. Paris, LGDJ, 1998; Raynald Abad, Le grand marché. Paris, Fayard, 2004.

can easily understand why judges tended to support municipalities that accused butchers of "speculation" and "hoarding". For example, in 1841, Avignon butchers were found guilty on the grounds of Article 419 of having formed a coalition for the purpose of obtaining a higher adjudication price from the municipality.[24]

However, if there were no special difficulties in identifying meat, bread and even soda with the "product" mentioned in the text of Article 419, was it possible to prosecute speculation on intangible goods, particularly shares and services?

This apparently purely legal question had strong economic foundations and implications; it responded to the increasing commercialisation of markets, the rise of new sectors and the evolving market structure. In the following pages, I will observe how the notion of hoarding was widened to include other products, then services and finally intangible goods.

REGULATING HOARDING: FROM FOODSTUFFS TO SERVICES

Already in the course of the 1830s, the question arose as to whether one could be accused of the offence of hoarding in a sector such as shipping, that is, a "service" and not a product. The judges adopted varying interpretations: Some maintained that the article in the Criminal Code applied to any type of speculation or concentration, whereas others held that, since it was a criminal law document, an extensive interpretation was not allowed. Even the High Court seemed divided on the subject, although it ended up agreeing to include transportation and services in general among the items regulated by Article 419.[25] This attention was linked to the major development of transportation (in particular canal transportation and maritime trade) during these years.[26] First railways, and the major political debates over this topic

---

[24] Court of Cassation, 3 July 1841.

[25] Cour d'appel de Paris, 29 August 1833; Court of Cassation, 1 February 1834; Court of Cassation 16 May 1845, 3 July 1841, 23 June 1883. Quoted in *La Spéculation devant les tribunaux, recueil de jurisprudence financière*, 1, 1 (11 July 1881); Gaston de Couppey, *Spéculation et les reports devant la loi*. Paris, Guillaumin, 1881.

[26] Verley, *L'échelle*; Lévy-Leboyer, Bourguignon, *L'économie française*.

arose in the early 1830s[27] and influenced judicial litigation and judges' attitudes. Indeed, the debate over private versus state monopoly on railways responded to concerns (raised by other industries – manufacturing and trade – as well as by other transportation companies) about the power of private railways. This movement led to judicial litigation introduced by small competitors and/or transport customers. In sum, the role of the state and monopolies in transportation was the major political and economic stake underlying the technical debate about the interpretation of Article 419.

Since the 1830s but mostly afterwards, the same debate took place with regard to new sectors, such as insurance. French insurance had been placed under the regulatory oversight of various governmental bodies since the industry's beginnings: The Ministry of the Interior (in charge of municipal affairs and national police) under the Ancien Régime, the Ministry of Commerce in the nineteenth century, then the Ministry of Labour until World War II and the Ministry of Finance ever since.[28] In the Commercial Code of 1807, maritime insurance had public recognition; however, under the Restoration, the maritime insurance business was said to belong, along with banks, canals and mines, to those operations that could not take place without government permission (government order of 22 October 1817). Again in 1829, a circular from the Ministry of Trade declared that government control was justified by the fact that insurance companies must not enter into speculative games and therefore threaten public order.[29]

From 1809 to 1829, thirty-five fire insurance companies were created, but between 1817 and 1877, only fifteen life insurance claims were settled, because this branch was viewed with great suspicion – an attitude reinforced by the general limitation the law put on company creation (still subject to government authorisation). From 1830 onwards, a number of permits were signed by heads of state and their

---

[27] Ministère des universités, comité des travaux historiques et scientifiques, *Les transports de 1610 à nos jours, Actes du 104e congrès national des sociétés savantes*. Bordeaux, 1979; François Caron, *Histoire de l'exploitation d'un grand réseau: la compagnie du chemin de fer du Nord, des origines à la nationalisation*. Paris, Mouton, 1973.

[28] Michèle Ruffat, "French Insurance from the *Ancien Régime* to 1946: Shifting Frontiers between State and Market." *Financial History Review*, 10 (2003): 185–200.

[29] Circular of 25 October 1829 quoted in P. J. Richard, *Histoire des institutions d'assurance en France*. Paris, Editions de l'Argus, 1956: 39.

257

ministers of agriculture and trade, and insurance slowly became more commonplace. In particular, the Compagnie du soleil launched a policy of forming alliances, when it did not create other insurance firms itself. Re-insurance was therefore practised within the group. Litigation thus responded to the rapid development of insurance, the process of concentration and alliances.[30] The Court of Cassation and a majority of judges considered that this service came under the notion of "commodity" and therefore, alliances between insurance companies were sanctioned. In turn, this attitude encouraged mutual societies on the one hand and a few large insurance companies on the other (vertical integration was preferred to coalitions).

The cases of transportation and insurance opened the way to legal assimilation of services with goods, at least from the point of view of regulation of speculation. At the same time, the assimilation between foodstuffs, goods and services was encouraged by the fact that, over time, the products themselves were becoming less tangible, at least in contracts, with the rise of futures transactions at the commodities and the stock exchanges. It was therefore in these markets that the issue of the control of competition was to be decided. After foodstuffs and services, judges and economic players were thus led to discuss whether "ordinary" rules on hoarding could also regulate the commodities exchange or whether new rules were required. In fact, the commodities exchange was similar to ordinary wholesale markets and, as such, its operations should be regulated by ordinary trade rules and ordinary criminal rules on markets, including Article 419. But on the other hand, the commodities exchange was similar to the stock exchange, which was under completely different regulation. As in the previous cases, there was interaction and often conflict between various lobbies, officials and judges in the process of seeking a solution.

COMMODITY EXCHANGE AND FUTURES TRADES

I have already discussed the main rules on brokers and product identification at the produce exchange. I am now going to move on to

---

[30] Ibid.

transactions and, in particular, the link between future trades and general rules of competition. Commodity exchanges are interesting organisations to study, for they reveal the connection between product markets, credit markets and the stock exchange. As such, they raise the usual problem of defining what "speculation" was in this context, and whether Article 419 could be enforced.

Generally speaking, futures transactions on commodities modified the aim of the contract and the nature of the exchange; the actors exchanged promises on virtual goods and afterwards, unlike other contracts, bought and sold those promises. In France, numerous rules prohibited or limited futures transactions and commodities exchanges throughout the first half of the nineteenth century. These were not only criminal rules (i.e., Article 419) but also civil rules. In particular, transactions at the stock exchange were put into the same category as gambling. According to Article 1965 of the Civil Code, which was based on canon law, this implied that no sanctions were provided for gambling debts. In turn, the Criminal Code punished bets made on the prices of government securities (Articles 421 and 422). These provisions were dictated by the memory of two phenomena, the Law affair and hyperinflation during the revolutionary period.[31]

Moral economics and the financial and institutional solidity of the State interacted to define the terms of futures contracts. The latter, which were prohibited during the revolutionary period, acquired limited public recognition under the Empire and the Restoration (Decrees of 13 Fructidor an XII, 29 May 1810, 22 June 1814, 23 May 1822). Addressing the State Council, Boscary de Villeplaine, close to Napoleon and to the Haute Banque, declared that futures transactions were not a problem:"When my water supplier knocks at my door and sells two buckets while having only one with him, I know that he will go down to the river and bring back the second one."The same is true with the exchange.[32] This attitude met with the favour of Napoleon who at that time supported the Haute Banque as well as the speculation carried out by the Banque of France itself.[33]

---

[31] Hoffman, Postel-Vinay, Rosenthal, *Priceless*.

[32] Boscary de Villeplaine, *Mémoire des actors de change au ministre des Finances*. Paris, 1810, Second edition, 1843: 44.

[33] Leon Say, *Les interventions du Trésor à la bourse depuis cent ans*. Paris, Alcan, 1886: 8–10.

However, already in 1822–1823, under pressure of critical public opinion towards "speculators", some case law voided futures transactions.[34] This occurred in a context in which the fall of values at the stock exchange added to a similar collapse of prices at the commodity exchange. Critics of the Royalist groups in power at the time attributed the crisis to the military support France gave to the reactionary King Ferdinand of the Two Sicilies. At the same time, those critics agreed with the Royal elites that, in this specific case, the crisis was linked to undue speculation at the exchange on the part of some brokers at the exchange, who were thus identified as the sources of instability. Control over the exchange became synonymous with social, political and economic stability. This was strengthened by the return to a Catholic moral order of the market and society as a whole, which developed in the 1820s.[35]

This attitude changed under the July Monarchy when several case law decisions ruled against the buyer and in favour of the seller, voiding an uncovered transaction carried out by the latter, whereas the other futures transactions were recognised as valid.[36] Increasing investment by the public (as evidenced in estate practises), the Haute Banque and some capitalist groups in stock exchange securities also encouraged this evolution. Upward trends in values facilitated this shift and led to the so-called fever of gambling and partnership companies in the early 1830s. However, a further, sudden fall in values and prices in 1836 appeared to stop this trend; as public opinion and newspapers denounced "immoral speculation", a new law forbidding games and gambling was adopted.

This halt was only temporary, for beginning in the early 1840s, as we have seen, public debate and economic policies focused on the massive building of railways. Railways quickly became the symbol of the strength and future power of France; public and private funds were

---

[34] Court of Paris, 18 February 1823, 10 April 1823 and 11 August 1824. Prosecutors' reports in AN BB 18 6606.
[35] Syriès de Marinhac, "Report of the Chamber of Deputies on the bill relating to the accounts of 1823". *Moniteur officiel*, 9 March (1823); Abbé Buyon, *Réfutation des systèmes de M. l'abbé Baronnat et de Mgr De la Luzerne sur la question de l'usure*. Clermont-Ferrand, imprimerie Thibaud-Landriot, 1824.
[36] Paris, 29 March 1832, 9 June 1836, 17 February 1842 in AN BB 18 6606.

required and thus a more conciliatory attitude towards gambling and stocks. The shift was confirmed in 1849, particularly under the Second Empire, when, with the rapid development of banks and industries and their interests in the stock exchange,[37] all futures transactions were recognised by judges' decisions, with the notable exception of gambling.[38] Reforms followed in close succession during the second half of the century: 1866, abolition of the brokers' monopoly; 1867, a new law on companies and the end of governmental authorisation of limited liability companies; 1885, the law on futures transactions; and 1886, freedom of interest rates. These reforms were linked to each other; for example, once the free creation of limited liability companies was allowed, it became difficult to limit issuing and circulating their securities, especially as the abolition of the brokers' monopoly opened the door to multilateral negotiations involving substantial amounts of capital and sizeable transactions. The ensuing question is that of understanding the link between these reforms, their implementation, political debates and broader economic and social tendencies under the Third Republic.

FROM LIBERALISATION OF FUTURES MARKETS TO "ANTI-SPECULATIVE" PROTECTIONISM (1885–1900)

Futures transactions were legalised in 1885, when Article 1965 of the Civil Code was amended. This rule stated that the law provided no sanctions and protections for gambling. Under gambling were included transactions of state obligations, operations at the stock and market exchanges and futures. This measure was spurred by the impact of the speculative crises in the early 1880s,[39] particularly the

---

[37] Paul-Jacques Lehmann, *Histoire de la bourse de Paris*. Paris, PUF, 1997; Georges Gallais-Hamonno, Pierre-Cyrille Hautcoeur (eds.), *Le marché financier français au XIXe siècle*. Paris, Presses Universitaires de la Sorbonne, 2007.

[38] Louis Bergeron, *Banquiers, négociants et manufacturiers parisiens du Directoire à l'Empire*. Paris, Mouton, 1978; Jean Bouvier, *Un siècle de banque française*, Paris, Hachette, 1973; Bertrand Gille, *La banque et le crédit en France de 1815 à 1848*. Paris, PUF, 1959; Michel Lévy-Leboyer, *Les banques européennes et l'industrialisation dans la première moitié du XIXe siècle*. Paris, PUF, 1964.

[39] Paul Leroy Beaulieu, "Les syndicats, les accaparements de stocks et la hausse des métaux et des valeurs des mines." *L'économiste français*, December 24 and 31 (1887): 773 and 805. Debates on the law of 1885 in AN BB 18 6603.

collapse of Union Générale. This fact was all the more important as the bank had been founded in 1878 and managed by Paul-Eugène Bontoux, a Catholic and militant Royalist who announced the new bank as a weapon against Jewish and Protestant banks. Socialists, radicals and representatives of peasants and craftsmen spoke out in favour of returning to regulation and a more strict application of Article 419 of the Criminal Code. In stark contrast, others (including the Haute Banque and wholesale traders) emphasised that speculation was being encouraged by the obstacles still standing in the way of futures transactions. They maintained that market liberalisation rather than regulation could put an end to speculation and crises.[40] The arrival of Léon Say, Jean-Baptiste's grandson, at the Ministry of Finance gave strong support to the latter interpretation, which prevailed even though it was a compromise solution. Article 1965 of the Civil Code was thus changed, and the "gambling exception" was excluded for futures transactions.

The extension and interpretation of this reform were immediately thrust to the forefront. Whereas the National Assembly adopted a bill that liberalised futures transactions altogether, the Senate, where the forces hostile to the stock and commodities exchanges were stronger (farm lobbies, Catholic groups, Christian-Socialists, etc.) modified it by dividing futures transactions into two categories: real market transactions and fictitious market transactions. The first concerned future goods with a real probability of acquisition at the time of contract stipulation (e.g., the commission agent indeed had contacts with the producers). According to some, this distinction was made to exclude the "gambling exception" only for "real" futures transactions. However, the wording of the law was not clear and in practise it became impossible to distinguish between these two cases, and the judges that heard disputes in these areas often ended up dismissing the proceedings. Several judges considered that the "gambling exception" was inadmissible for "fictitious contracts" and gambling, but also for "real" futures contracts, whereas several others adopted the opposite position. As the years went by, the High Court, initially favourable to the former orientation, finally modified its initial interpretations and accepted all

[40] Jean Bouvier, *Études sur le krach de l'Union générale*. Paris, PUF, 1960.

forms of futures transactions ("real" and "fictitious"), and the "gambling exception" was supposed to be definitively abandoned.[41]

Of course, the debates about the "gambling exception" in the Civil Code intersected with those pertaining to Article 419 of the Criminal Code. The question was whether the new civil rules should lead to a change in the interpretation of the Criminal Code, and if so, whether the latter had to be reformed. A decision handed down by the Paris Court of Appeal on 5 August 1890 considered that the new law of 1885 had not implicitly eliminated Article 419. Professional associations and elected representatives appealed either to change the Civil Code or, conversely, to adapt the Criminal Code to the new Article 1965. These debates occurred in a context in which price instability, fluctuating share prices and the repeated outbreak of national and international crises helped to sharpen the debate. In the National Assembly and the Senate, the number of bills multiplied between 1890 and 1914, most of them aimed at returning to the prohibition of futures transactions both on the stock exchange and the commodities exchange (allowed under the "new" Article 1965 of the Civil Code) while modifying Article 419 of the Criminal Code.[42] Reforming the rules to facilitate the judges' task met with favour from all those (elected republicans, socialists, members of cooperatives, farmers, certain circles of manufacturers and traders) who considered themselves victims of "free speculation". However, within this broad trend, I must distinguish two main periods, one running from the late 1880s through the early 1900s and the second reaching the outbreak of the First World War. During the former period, futures transactions at the commodities exchange were frequently put in the same category as stock market transactions; both were criticised for intensifying the "depression", particularly in agriculture; this was said to be part and parcel of the new (immoral) finance society. Speculation on raw materials and foodstuffs was associated with the rise of Russian and U.S. agriculture, and therefore control over the commodities exchange went with protectionism.[43]

[41] AN BB 18 6603. Court of Cassation Civile. 22 July 1898, *Dalloz* 1899,1,5.

[42] AN F 12 2174.

[43] AN F 12 2174; *Chambre des députés*, n. 1937, session of 16 June 1896 ("Bill to modify the law of 28 March 1885 and Art. 419 cp by M. Rose, member of parliament") in AN BB 18 6603.

The lobbies behind this movement were clearly positioned: cattle breeders and farmers, along with certain socialist groups seeking to defend the peasants, even if it meant going against lower prices for foodstuffs and hence a rise in real wages. All of these groups stigmatised "the lure of money" and the "speculation" of the large merchants. Against this view, wholesale traders and manufacturers mobilised.[44] According to the Chamber of Commerce of Paris, the code should not be changed; the gambling exception could not be reintroduced and brokers' freedom of trade and the names of the actors involved should remain confidential; otherwise, French traders would be at an extreme disadvantage in relation to foreign competitors. On the other hand, the Chamber of Commerce did not oppose a modification of Article 419 in the sense of separating speculation from the formation of a coalition. As the chancellery of the Ministry of Justice noted in commenting on the memorandum of the Chamber of Commerce, it was obviously important from the point of view of the major traders and financiers of Paris to maintain absolute contract freedom in the Civil Code, whereas a limited reform of the Criminal Code did not seem to worry them.[45] This confirms how poorly the law was understood by these actors (consumer associations, socialists and radical parliamentary groups) who thought that strengthening criminal law would be instrumental in reaching a given objective, whereas most professionals and legal experts knew perfectly well that the chances of criminal law achieving this outcome were slim compared with civil law. This explains their united front against any reform of the latter.

This association of speculation with hoarding and forward transactions diminished in the coming years, notably with the business recovery at the turn of the century. More and more Frenchmen invested in the stock exchange; although criticism continued to be voiced, the stock exchange no longer raised the fears of the preceding years.[46] At the same time, it was precisely the rising price of commodities and foodstuffs that set off further debate over the issue of commodities speculation and hoarding, but this time in a different context.

---

[44] AN F 12 2174; AN BB 18 6603.
[45] AN BB 18 6603.
[46] Hamonno, Hautcoeur, *Le marché financier.*

It was no longer a question of protecting national production from international speculators, but of protecting French consumers from the schemes of both French and foreign wholesale traders.[47]

A NEW USE OF THE LAW? SPECULATION AND THE COST OF LIVING (CA. 1900–1914)

The struggle against the high cost of living brought together members of cooperatives, socialists, consumer leagues, peasants and craftsmen.[48] Indeed, the rise in prices affected mainly foodstuffs and rents, whereas the cost of services rose more slowly and the price of manufactured goods even tended to stagnate.[49] The stabilisation of market prices predicted by the partisans of absolute freedom of future transactions did not occur, and waves of speculation repeatedly affected the various marketplaces in France and other countries from the late 1890s to the outbreak of the First World War.[50] Numerous bills were introduced to prohibit one product or another from futures transactions (sugar, flour, combed wool, coal, etc.).[51] Significantly, on every occasion, the associations complained less of "globalisation" than of the actions of a clearly identified and often mythical speculator. Lawsuits pertaining to speculation on sugar, probably the most widespread at the time, provide a sufficiently comprehensive view of these cases. Between 1885 and 1910, the consumption of sugar increased by 45–55 per cent in France (during this same period, the consumption of wheat increased by just 5 per cent).[52] To this, one has to add the massive recourse to sugar in the wine industry still recovering from phylloxera. However, this sharp increase occurred after some decades (between the 1860s and the 1880s), when falling final prices linked to fast transportation,

---

[47] AN BB 18 6603, *Chambre des députés*, n. 2234, session of 29 March 1901: "Report of the commission in charge of examining the bill introduced by Claude Rajon"; "Report by parliamentary representative Honoré Leygue."

[48] Jean-Marie Flonneau, "Crise de vie chère et mouvement syndical, 1910–1914." *Le mouvement social*, 72 (July 1970): 49–81; Tyler Stovall, Colette Friedlander, "Du vieux au neuf: économie morale et militantisme ouvrier dans les luttes contre la vie chère à Paris." *Le mouvement social*, 170 (1995): 84–113.

[49] Flonneau, "Crise de vie chère."

[50] AN BB 18 6603, 6604, 6605, 6606, 6607.

[51] AN BB 18 6603.

[52] Bourguignon, Levy-Leboyer, *L'économie française*: 39.

and then to the "long depression", contributed to a concentration of production in both the colonies and in France for refining. Thus, the price of sugar was an extremely sensitive topic in the public sphere.

On 28 July 1900, a certain Mr. Brabant, a sugar trader and exporter in Paris, filed a complaint with the public prosecutor's office. He claimed that since 1898, his trade had been impeded by hoarding operations by person or persons unknown. He explained how the sugar market at the Paris commodities exchange worked and tried to show that, by the way the transactions were carried out, speculators could hoard the product and prevent exporters such as himself from meeting their obligations. In other words, he emphasised that the contracts he had signed were very "real" (in the legal sense of the term), and that if he was unable to deliver the sugar at the agreed time, it was only because speculators had taken possession of it. During the court investigation, the investigating judge pushed him to specify the names of the "speculators"; Brabant mentioned the name of Jazulot, a deputy of Nièvre and managing director of the Say sugar refinery, one of the largest at that time. He also listed other brokers said to have contributed to the operations. The latter then signed a joint petition which they sent to the prosecutor and the Minister of Justice, asserting that Brebant's accusations were baseless and that he was simply trying to avoid the commitments he had made to them which he could honor. The judge and the public prosecutor were perplexed: They thought that the market had probably been altered by the expansion of the Say refinery. However, to prove that the company was guilty of hoarding, it would be necessary to examine its books and those of the implicated brokers and then prove that the transactions were interrelated and that they had indeed significantly affected prices. Such investigations would require searching their offices. The public prosecutor expressed doubt that the case warranted such measures.

During the following weeks, however, the situation changed. Jazulot spontaneously appeared before the investigating judge; he admitted that his books were cooked. Furthermore, the judge observed that the Paris commissioners who were Brabant's creditors were also right in the sense that Brabant had denounced them only after realising that he would be unable to meet his obligations. A report from the Paris Court of First Instance to the investigating judge of the Paris court shows that Brabant was even awaiting bankruptcy proceedings. The report reveals two things: On the one hand, Brabant's problems in 1901 arose without any hoarding on the part of the other brokers at the Paris exchange. But on the other hand, the problems had begun in 1899 and at that time, there had indeed been an unusual rise in prices. According to the testimony of the brokers at the Paris exchange, the rise was due to the activities of Jazulot and his company, Say.

The Public Prosecutor of Paris did not altogether accept the opinion of the Court of First Instance; he thought the rise in prices could not be attributed to Jazulot's activities. Thereupon, whereas the chancellery and the minister remained uncertain, the union of sugar refineries turned to the Ministry of Agriculture, emphasising that a delay in the ruling and suspicions against Say could destabilise the market and encourage speculation. The Minister of Agriculture then wrote to the Minister of Justice requesting a prompt decision in favour of the accused (letter dated 11 October 1901).

The chancellery shared the opinion of the Solicitor-General of the Court of Cassation against the orientation of the Paris court: Hoarding in itself was not an offense; it could not be distinguished a priori from supply. Based on this reasoning, the case should be dismissed.[53] The report also suggested that there had been no coalition or "rumors"' or "slanderous accusations" as required under the Criminal Code. Moreover, the report concluded, the investigation showed that no fraudulent maneuvers had accompanied the hoarding. Finally, the price of sugar had indeed changed in 1899, but "it was difficult to prove that the rise was caused by these operations." The decision was then made to dismiss the investigation,[54] arousing the opposition of several newspapers, including certain socialist papers that protested against the speculators, the republican lobbies and the judges linked to them.[55]

After the elections of 1905, the new parliament was immediately faced with a new "sugar affair". Mr. Jazulot who, in addition to running the Say sugar refinery, was also managing "Printemps" department stores,

[53] Paris Court of Appeal, 28 February 1888, *Dalloz*, 1893, 2, 89.
[54] AN BB 18 6603, 6604, "Cases of sugar speculation".
[55] "Above the law", unsigned article, *La Lanterne*, 16 March (1902); Henri Tuzot, "Des cas abandonnés". *La petite république socialiste*, 16 March (1902).

filed for bankruptcy. Cronier, chairman of the board of Say, committed suicide. Letters of denunciation and complaints against "speculators" accumulated at the Ministry of Justice. Confronted with the outcry caused by these events in Parliament and public opinion, in 1906, the Minister of Trade decided to set up a commission to study the operation of the commodities exchange.[56] The commission submitted the results of its work in 1908. It suggested imposing more control over brokers but refrained from proposing any modification of the norms in force. Then, in September 1909, the price of sugar suddenly rose again. Consumer associations and the ministries of Agriculture and Trade voiced their objections to the Ministry of Justice, denouncing the fact that farmers, "honest tradesmen" and consumers were victims of speculation. Parliamentary questions followed. Like the newspapers, several members of Parliament accused a certain Santa-Maria, a Chilean, of destabilising the Paris exchange.[57] The Minister of Justice then decided to open an investigation.[58] Warehouses were searched, but the investigation was unable to prove the responsibility of Santa-Maria or of any other broker.[59]

During the weeks and months that followed, Santa-Maria was accused of every sort of "speculation" and of changing the prices of alcohol, sugar and wheat. In these cases as well, the farm lobbies, the socialists and the consumer associations launched public opinion campaigns against international speculators. When an investigation took place, it was often on the initiative of the minister himself or following complaints filed by tradesmen. However, no convictions followed in any of the cases. The arguments evoked by the judges were the same as those used in the case of sugar. On the one hand, no cause-and-effect relationship had been established between hoarding and price modifications; the "globalisation" of prices denounced by public opinion was specifically mentioned to demonstrate that a speculator could not be the source of these price fluctuations.[60]

[56] AN BB 18 6603.
[57] AN BB 18 6603.
[58] AN BB 18 6604. "Letter from the Public Prosecutor of Paris to the Minister, 13 March, 1908."
[59] AN BB 18 6604. "Report of the Public Prosecutor to the Minister, 8 August 1908."
[60] AN BB 18 6603, 6604.

In the face of these rulings, the groups already mentioned – farmers, socialists, consumers – mobilised. At the National Assembly, several deputies evoked the difficult conditions of agriculture and the damage the sector had suffered as a result of speculation. A new extraparliamentary commission was set up in September 1910 to study the organisation of the commodities exchange and a possible reform of Article 419. An initial proposal was put forth on behalf of several deputies by Claude Rajon, Deputy of Isère, suggesting the following modification of Article 419: The passage "by meeting or coalition between the main holders of the same type of goods or foodstuffs" was to be replaced by "isolated or collective *maneuvers of hoarding or agiotage*".

The proposal also called for requiring the transactions to go through authorised brokers. Some members of the commission made the usual proposal to prohibit fictitious markets and therefore partially reintroduce the gambling exception in the Civil Code.[61]

However, several chambers of commerce, including the Paris Chamber, protested: It was necessary to reform and regulate fictitious markets rather than prohibit them, for these futures transactions ensured worldwide distribution of resources. Without futures contracts, explained the president of this chamber of commerce during his hearing, there would be sudden fluctuations in the prices of these commodities.

The Minister of Trade drafted a counter-proposal that made no mention of using authorised brokers but did introduce some changes in commodities exchange operations. The chambers of commerce, the commercial courts and the Consultative Committee of Crafts and Manufactures (under the Ministry of Trade) worked together to determine the nomenclature and define the main goods to be traded and set "general conditions for the creation, organisation and operation of these markets". The bill also provided for mandatory bookkeeping on the part of brokers.

There remained the question of Article 419. The Minister of Trade proposed a new version of this provision which, in contrast to the law in force, no longer required fraudulent means or the presence

---

[61] AN F 12 2174.

of a coalition and clearly distinguished the titles of the goods. The Chancellery of the Ministry of Justice accepted these suggestions, and the proposal thus received the ministry's support.[62] The commission approved it and asked the government to introduce a bill in Parliament, which occurred in November 1911.[63]

While awaiting the debate in Parliament, the professional associations mobilised and, as usual, those in agricultural regions defended the new bill, whereas those in the large cities and ports opposed it. In the meantime, new cases of speculation were reported in newspapers, in Parliament and before the Ministry of Justice concerning wheat, sugar, alcohol, phosphates and coffee. Sometimes, the public prosecutor's office opened an investigation.[64] However, in virtually all cases, the courts were unable to prosecute because they could not prove any link between the observed rise in prices and the schemes of one or another wholesale trader or group of traders. Indeed, the expertise that judges requested from trade representatives, brokers, and others always detected the source of the increased price of the products concerned in overall market trends.[65] These issues arose so frequently that they encouraged critics of new market trends to reform the law; at the same time, stability in legal disputes over "speculation" stabilised economic expectations in a highly unstable economic world.

To sum up, in France, during the "long" nineteenth century (from 1789 to 1914), speculation was associated with hoarding. Control of the markets was not only a question of economic logic but also of public order. The "rumor" of famine as a variable of economic action and public policy was in large part carried over from the Ancien Régime to industrial society, from commodities exchanges to service exchanges, all the way to the stock exchange. This led to an instrumental use of the justice system: Public debates and political pressure forced the Ministry of Justice to incorporate actions initiated by individuals or groups in autonomous referrals to the courts by the

---

[62] AN BB 18 6603. "Chancellery Memorandum. 28 February 1911."
[63] *Chambre des députés*, n. 1228, session of 7 November 1911. "Bill proposed by Armand Fallières, President of the Republic, Jean Cruppi, Minister of Justice and M. Ch. Couyba, Minister of Trade and Industry."
[64] AN BB 18 6603, 6604.
[65] AN BB 18 6603, 6604, 6606, 6607.

ministry itself. However, the judicial issue did not lead to any major decision in the sense of condemning "speculators". The ideal of the competitive market was a benchmark not only in terms of economic theory, but also for economic policy making and court decisions (the practised price had to be compared to the theoretical price resulting from pure, perfect competition).

This leads us to our last section: Once the application of Article 419 was extended from foodstuffs to commodities, then to services and stock markets, what about the other enormous new phenomenon of capitalism involving futures trading at the turn of the nineteenth century, namely trusts and cartels? Were these organisations a form of speculation and hoarding as well? This question is all the more important because, as I have shown, a "coalition" was explicitly required by Article 419, but over time, judges were increasingly uncertain that it should be considered a necessary (though insufficient) condition to justify prosecution for hoarding and speculation.

SPECULATION AND INDUSTRIAL CONCENTRATION

Historiography can easily identify the presence of trusts and cartels in Germany even before 1914, and, from a different angle, in Great Britain and the United States as well. In contrast, doubts are constantly raised about the French case, which would seem to have been distinguished by a rather marginal presence of such organisations, at least prior to 1914.[66] However, some sector studies have revealed the importance of concentrations, above all in mining and metallurgical industries.[67] Yet the rate of cartel formation and its role in an economic system

---

[66] Patrick Fridenson, "France: The Relatively Slow Development of Big Business in the Twentieth Century." In Alfred Chandler, Franco Amatori, Takashi Hikino (eds.), *Big Business and the Wealth of Nations*. Cambridge, Cambridge University Press, 1997: 207–45.

[67] Marcel Gillet, *Les charbonnages du Nord de la France au 19e siècle*. Paris, Mouton, 1973; Michael Smith, "Putting France in the Chandlerian Framework: France's 100 Largest Firms in 1913." *Business History Review*, 72, 1 (1998): 46–85; Jean-Pierre Daviet, "Some Features of Concentration in France (End of the Nineteenth/Twentieth Century)." In Hans Pohl (ed.), *The Concentration Process in the Entrepreneurial Economy since the Late Nineteenth Century*. Stuttgart, Franz Steiner Verlag, 1988: 67–89, reproduced in François Crouzet (ed.), *The Economic Development of France since 1870*. Aldershot, Edward Elgar, 1993, vol. II: 501–23.

depended not only on economic practises, specific sector features and national and international trends in the area concerned, but also on institutional variables. The way in which a "cartel" was defined by law had repercussions on the organisation of firms; conversely, the dynamics of the latter called for institutional and legal changes. We must therefore take these elements into account to understand how trusts and cartels emerged and evolved, and from there, how the control of competition in France and in the other "Western" countries developed.

As late as 1879, the Court of Cassation, upholding an 1877 decision of the Court of Rennes, declared a union of producers of iodine to be in violation of Article 419. This decision conformed to previous jurisprudence and mentioned previously cited convictions of butchers and bakers for "hoarding".[68] Legal files at the turn of the century reveal that, according to the judges, forming coalitions was no longer an offense, insofar as they were permitted by the law of 1884 on trade unions and trade associations; moreover, all the interested parties had to do was set up a company to eliminate the possibility of an accusation of hoarding.[69] Indeed, from the late 1880s onwards, with the development of companies and the stock exchange and the liberalisation of futures transactions, judges were asked to rule on whether a merger of companies could be considered a form of speculative hoarding. For example, in 1888, the Paris court applied Article 419 to a Parisian mineral water syndicate which imposed fixed prices on their suppliers, requiring that they sell to non-syndicate members at a higher price. But in other cases, the judges refused this assimilation, relying on jurisprudence established by the Court of Cassation in 1838, which excluded the partners and therefore the establishment of a company from being put into the same category as speculation.[70] A similar decision intervened in 1902, when the Paris court decided that the fixing of minimum prices by an agreement between syndicates of book publishers and booksellers did not violate Article 419.

---

[68] Quoted in Freedeman, "Cartels and the Law": 475.
[69] AN BB 18 6603. "Memorandum of the Criminal Affairs Department, 20 September 1910."
[70] AN BB 18 6603. "Memorandum of the Criminal Affairs Department, 20 September 1910."

An analogous problem arose for the trade unions and employer federations that multiplied beginning in the 1880s. This phenomenon found institutional legitimacy in the law of 1884 on freedom of association and its economic justification in the decline of prices and the depression during the last quarter of the century. The creation of these associations and their activity were often brought before judges by the members of competing associations, or even by individual actors (winegrowers, wholesale traders, manufacturers). The latter considered imposed prices, the control of outlets and recourse to contractual forms and clauses illegal.[71] How can one explain such differences in courts' decisions?

Available sources − archive files, commentaries − would seem to indicate that judges made a distinction between "good" and "bad" *ententes*. The former were "in harmony with the natural operation of supply and demand" whereas the latter were not.[72] In the same vein, the Commercial Court of Périgueux argued in 1895 that an *entente* of lime producers violated Article 419 in that it resulted in abnormal profits.[73] This was the same distinction we had found between the two meanings of the speculation in the parliamentary debates and in judges' decisions. Even if some convictions were recorded, as a whole, *ententes* did not seem to suffer from Article 419.[74]

Of course, several members of Parliament and some political forces, as well as representatives of cooperatives, the rural world and small tradesmen, criticised these interpretations and proposed a bill in 1895 to eliminate the immunity of companies and trading posts (*comptoirs*) from the offense of hoarding. To a certain degree, this was the French equivalent of an attempt to pass the Sherman Antitrust Act that the United States had just adopted. The bill failed, however.[75] This was a French specificity compared with other countries: In France, no

---

[71] Pierre Vernus, "Regulating the Activity of a Business Community: Employers' Organizations in the Lyon Silk Industry, 1860s-1939." *Business and Economic History Online*, vol. 2 (2004) at: http://www.thebhc.org/BEH/O4/vernus.pdf.

[72] "Bonneton v. Societé des tuileries." *Dalloz*, 1895, 2, 221.

[73] *Dalloz*, 1893, 1, 49.

[74] Alessandro Stanziani, *Histoire de la qualité alimentaire*. Paris, Seuil, 2005.

[75] Court of Cassation, 26 January 1838; AN BB 18 6603; *Chamber of Deputies*, n. 1505, session of 11 July 1895, "Report of the parliamentary commission in charge of examining the bill introduced by Henri Blanc. By Marcel Habert, Deputy."

special rules governing industrial concentrations were adopted at the turn of the nineteenth century, when the phenomenon was growing. The economic and legal problems posed by these concentrations continued to be settled using existing legal rules, particularly those regarding hoarding, as they were inherited from the Ancien Régime and were gradually transformed in the course of the nineteenth century. Over the very long term, this solution expressed an attempt on the part of French elites to combine economic power (through industrial concentrations) with social equilibrium (through the control of hoarding), or in other words, the private order and the public order of the market. The discussions that took place at the time, in the mainstream press, in economic journals and among legal specialists, confirm this tension. All of them wondered how the demand for large firms or associations of firms capable of competing internationally could be reconciled with the need to ensure domestic competition in such a way as to protect both small firms and consumers.

Their answers varied. Several manufacturers (particularly in the chemicals industry), supported by the Ministry of Trade and political officials such as Méline, spoke in favour of the development of French trusts and cartels. These associations were considered necessary to enable competition with foreign firms and trusts – American, English and partricularly German. To critics who maintained that trusts and cartels were harmful to competition and especially to employment, these actors retorted that the opposite was true. They justified this conclusion using the argument just mentioned, linked to international trade, and added that ultimately it was free, unbridled competition that caused the drop in prices and thereby the downturn for firms and the rise in unemployment. Several newspapers and economists shared this point of view. These arguments were also supported by economists who, under the influence of new approaches to the theory of competition (particularly Marshall's theory), emphasised the importance of economies of scale and of external factors, and hence of trusts and cartels for economic development.

The first measure suggested by the partisans of trusts was a modification of Article 419 of the Criminal Code to prevent judges from applying it to these associations. According to the actors mentioned, to avoid any misunderstanding, it was necessary to affirm unequivocally that the activities of trusts and cartels did not come under the heading of hoarding and speculation. Even if lawsuits based on Article 419 seldom resulted in a negative outcome for them, they argued that their business could not withstand the uncertainty of jurisprudence and the judges' will.[76]

Criticism of trusts and cartels, on the other hand, came first of all from manufacturers and business circles that felt threatened by foreign competition. This was the position of French shipping companies and the Compagnie Transatlantique when German, English and American companies created the "Ocean Trust" at the very beginning of the twentieth century.[77] Similar reactions came from associations linked to the metallurgy industry (the Société Anonyme des Hauts-Fourneaux de Pont-à-Mousson, Meurthe-et-Moselle, the Union of Pipe Manufacturers in Nancy, the Central Committee of French Miners, the Committee of Smiths, etc.), which felt threatened by German trusts and cartels.[78]

Criticism of the trusts and cartels also arose from certain economists in defence of free competition. Towards the end of the century, these arguments found support in several currents of thought which emphasised the benefits of perfect competition and the distortions of monopoly. The new "economy of well-being", originating in neo-classical thought which developed precisely at the turn of the century, backed these arguments by demonstrating that the negative externalities of trusts on productivity and prices exceeded the advantages in terms of economies of scale.

These arguments were shared by certain socialist ideas that attacked monopolies and trusts, accusing them of raising prices, lowering employees' standard of living and increasing unemployment. In view of these

[76] AN BB 18 6603. Ministry of Trade: in favor of allowing freedom to trusts, due to international competition. *Report of 12 November 1902, from the 3rd bureau of the Ministry of Trade (Post Office Department) entitled: Memorandum for the Question of Mr. Etienne (Vice-President of the Chamber of Deputies*, dated 10 June 1902; AN F 12 8848, "Speech by Méline in the Chamber of Deputies in 1902." On businessmen's attitudes, see AN BB 18 6603, "Oskar Eykens, chemical products."

[77] AN F 12 8848, "Trusts and cartels"; AN F 12 8849; AN F 12 6603 dossier "Trust de l'Océan". Also: Gaston Cadoux, *Le trust de l'océan et les intérêts français*. Paris, Librairie Ch. Delagrave, 1902; Paul de Rousiers, "Le trust de l'océan." *Revue de Paris*, 15 June (1902): 828–48.

[78] AN F 12 8850.

considerations, the critics proposed to strengthen the enforcement of Article 419, even if it meant adopting genuine anti-trust measures like those in the United States. However, no such measures were adopted before the First World War.

Concretely, this means, as the correspondence between the Ministry of Trade, the Ministry of Justice and economic actors shows, entrepreneurs and groups who were interested in establishing alliances anticipated the eventual reaction of their competitors and the judges' interpretation and thought that the outcome of a lawsuit on the grounds of Article 419 was likely to be unfavourable to them or at least harmful to their public image. This accounts for the contractual forms adopted by the actors when they set up such associations. They preferred to sign contracts rather than merge with other companies. This prevented them from being accused of criminal behaviour, but in their eyes it also diminished their power in the international market.

To sum up, Article 419 created discontent among both the partisans and the opponents of trusts and cartels, the former because they saw themselves as being under undue threat from the law and the latter because they thought the law did not protect free competition. Neither side was able to raise a majority in the Parliament to change the law in the direction it wished. Before coming to a conclusion, we need to consider the question of whether or not *ententes* could have been regulated by the Civil Code. Indeed, Articles 1131 and 1133 nullified illegal *entente* and stressed "freedom of trade", whereas Article 1382 regulated unfair competition and mentioned the obligation to compensate for damages caused by personal wrongdoing. However, it is quite interesting to note that people who made use of the law to denounce *ententes* and cartels usually addressed the criminal courts and not the civil system. Without full documentation on their "real motives", we can only speculate on the basis of the available sources. In the few cases that were referred to civil courts, the plaintiffs lost because judges had problems linking the wording of the law ("freedom of trade") to *ententes*. Judges looked for both prejudice and wrongdoing. The defense of property was the ultimate aim of these norms.[79] However, in most cases under litigation,

[79] Michel Pelletier, *Droit industriel*. Paris, Baudry, 1895: 283.

the defendants argued that they had formed coalitions not to avoid competition (from the plaintiff) but to enhance it in the face of new international groups. This argument was quite often accepted by judges.

Thus, the control of trusts and cartels in France was not based on special norms as it was in the United States, but on recourse to the old notions of speculation and hoarding. Rather than control of the market, it was indeed the compliance of cross-sector playing rules with institutional forms that seemed to worry business associations and public opinion the most.

This outcome was partly related to the structure of the French market, which was dominated by small firms; these forms of organisation were concerned primarily with issues of succession, transfer of trademarks, patents and trade names as well as the training of workers (apprentices) and their circulation. On these topics, Article 1382 was intensively enforced, whereas for *ententes*, it was enforced even less that the Criminal Code. The solution adopted (to keep the old Criminal Code regarding hoarding and apply it to cartels) encouraged the establishment of temporary companies focused mainly on trade-oriented bilateral contracts. Of course, these legal aspects were added to the strictly economic considerations of firms often at the local level, in which families were usually in charge of management and it was difficult to reach cooperative agreements with other firms, whether in France or abroad.

In France, the absence of rules of competition was not really related to the protection of existing codes, but rather to the long-term legacy of an approach to monopolies through speculation and hoarding. Somehow, the strength of this legacy rendered any new ruling superfluous; the various parties concerned insisted instead on small corrections and reinterpretation of existing rules. At the same time, the early success of the case law idea of unfair competition and the flexibility of such a notion ultimately provided an effective response from French institutions to economic and institutional demands at the turn of the century.

The fact that there was no genuine antitrust case law or legislation in France only partially explains the fact that there were fewer cartels than in the United States or Germany, whereas vertical

concentration was more widespread.[80] Such absence of legal initiatives could also be explained by the overall attitude of public
opinion towards monopolies. For example, the fact that in France,
rules of competition linked to various forms of hoarding foodstuffs
encouraged special surveillance of the food markets, whereas banking coalitions and some industrial groupings were less of a concern. Competition was regulated by the Criminal Code (hoarding
or coalition offences) and unfair competition was regulated by civil
law (action causing injury to a third party), whereas consumer protection remained on the sidelines of this movement. This attitude
and the general difficulty in enforcement of rules on monopoly put
France in a particular situation: Except in extreme cases (mostly
concerning foodstuffs), rules on monopoly were not often enforced.
The control of trusts and cartels in France was not based on special rules, as it was in the United States, but on recourse to the old
notions of speculation and hoarding. This should be kept in mind
when emphasis is placed on the relative weakness of large French
trusts and cartels compared with their American, German or even
Belgian competitors during the same period.

At the same time, just as no specific norms were imposed on trusts
and cartels and their development was regulated by standards inherited from the Ancien Régime, unfair competition was given a major
boost by case law. Rather than control of the market, it was indeed
compliance of cross-sector rules to institutional forms that seemed to
worry business circles and public opinion the most.

UNFAIR COMPETITION

The notion of unfair competition perfectly expresses the fact that, far
from producing a just, well-balanced outcome, competition requires
correction. "Too much competition is harmful to competition" is
the generic common dictum for justifying this. From this point of
view, this notion is part of the economic approach that has taken the

[80] Tony Freyer, "Legal Restraints on Economic Coordination: Antitrust in Great Britain
and the Americas, 1880–1920." In Naomi Lamoreux, D. Raff (eds.), *Coordination and
Information: Historical Perspectives on the Organization of Enterprise*. Chicago, University of
Chicago Press, 1995: 183–206.

imperfections of competition into consideration since the end of the nineteenth century, not to bring about a radical reform of the market and of capitalism, but on the contrary, to come up with legal, fiscal and economic adjustment mechanisms. Since then, economic theory has developed numerous models that show how particular contractual clauses act as barriers to entry into a given market and hence distort the principle of competition.[81] At the same time, it is significant that, from the point of view of mainstream economic theory, it is possible to include in the same mould unfair competition in the areas of entry into the market, trademarks and goodwill and the imposition of unfair prices.[82]

However, from the standpoint of both law and historical practises in economics, this is not the only way of looking at things; the issue of fair prices was often distinguished from clauses governing market entry, penalties and transfers of trademarks and goodwill. It is necessary to understand the reasons for these various orientations and their impact on market organisation and dynamics.

In France, the notion of unfair competition was based on Article 1382 of the Civil Code (the obligation to compensate for injury caused by personal wrongdoing). In this case, the judges looked for both prejudice and wrongdoing. The defence of property was the ultimate aim of these norms.

Starting in the 1840s and especially during the second half of the nineteenth century, the notion of unfair competition was accompanied by the possibility of ordering these sanctions independently of any violation of a property right, but it had to be based on the exercise of freedom (in this case, free trade). In other words, free trade was called into question; the great case law invention of the turn of the nineteenth century consisted of including in the same group formerly distinct elements, such as counterfeiting a trademark or a patent, fraud,

[81] J. Brodley, Ching-to Albert Ma, "Contract Penalties, Monopolizing Strategies, and Antitrust Policy." *Stanford Law Review*, 45, 5 (1993): 1161–213; Philip Aghion, Michael Bolton, "Contracts as a Barrier to Entry." *American Economic Review*, 77, 3 (1987): 388–401; Michael Spence, "Entry, Capacity, Investment and Oligopolistic Princing." *Bell Journal of Economics*, 8, (1977): 534–44; Oliver Williamson, *Markets and Hierarchies: Analysis and Antitrust Implications.* New York, Free Press, 1975.

[82] Joel Dirlam, Alfred Kahn, "Price Discrimination in Law and Economics." *American Journal of Economics and Sociology*, 11, 3 (1952): 281–313.

migration of clientele, and so on. These distinct elements were united under the principle according to which they all were violations of the principle of "fair competition". As has been developed in previous chapters, the increasing transmission of businesses and the more widespread diffusion of labels and trademarks were at the origin of this accentuated judicial activity in this field. A widespread attitude among political elites, business milieus and general opinion raised doubts about unlimited competition. A general notion of fair trade and competition therefore emerged. As a manual of industrial law stated at the time: "'unfair competition' means any action carried out to capture customers of an industrial or similar commercial establishment for the benefit of the author".[83]

The plaintiff accused the seller of the business of retaining these elements in order to engage in "unfair competition". During the second half of the nineteenth century, this expression was increasingly employed by judges and the parties in all cases where, aside from the issues linked to the sale of patents or the business name, the seller of the firm or business would recover part of his former clientele for his new establishment.

This notion was rather broadly conceived: Reputation was not only an asset of businesses and firms; unlawful use of the title of former employee, former apprentice or former partner constituted unfair competition. Such use could be declared unlawful because it was untrue (e.g., a worker who had never worked in a workshop where he claimed to have been employed; a worker who claimed to be a former apprentice or worker when that was not the case),[84] as well as for other reasons.

This same confusion could be a violation if it concerned the quality definition of the object rather than the actor. The usurpation of the distinctive shape of the product or of its colour, packaging or other attributes could therefore be considered unfair competition.

---

[83] Pelletier, *Droit industriel*: 283.

[84] Court of Paris, 24 April 1834, *Dalloz*, 1834, 2, 129; Court of Bordeaux, 9 February 1886, *Journal arr. Bordeaux*, 18 86, 1, 197, quoted in Ambroise Rendu, *Des marques de fabrique et de commerce et de la concurrence déloyale*. Paris, Imprimerie et librairie générale de jurisprudence, Cosse et Marchal imprimeurs, 1857: 295.

For example, today the Perrier bottle belongs to the distinguishing features and qualities of its mineral water.

Of course, the notion of unfair competition could be evoked whenever a product did not have the qualities it was claimed to possess. This variant of unfair competition took two main forms: adulteration and falsification, which we mentioned earlier, and misleading advertising. The latter, in turn, encompassed not only the cases in which a product did not have the qualities and virtues claimed by the seller, but also cases of advertising that denigrated a competitor.[85] In all these cases, the principle was the same: Economic behaviour aimed at maximising profit within the scope of free competition should be regulated by law. This was justified by the fact that the market was relatively opaque and, due to its opacity and the imperfect circulation of information, gains could be made through unfair practices. This restriction on free competition was made in the name of competition itself. In other words, although business often continued to be protected by Criminal Code provisions ultimately aimed at the defence of property in the early nineteenth century, during the second half of the century, especially in the last quarter, a major change took place. Business came increasingly under civil law; contracts and control of competition were the pillars of this new legal spirit of capitalism. Of course, criminal proceedings were still an option, but civil provisions, which allowed for simplified disputes and reduced expense and evidence, were a far more advantageous instrument for the world of business.

This legal development corresponded to a parallel one in economic thought which, also beginning in the middle of the century, took the problems resulting from the imperfections of the competitive market increasingly into consideration. Protection of trademarks, reputation and clientele was accepted in order to limit the negative effects of competition, against the opinion of ultra-liberal thought, which saw them as a form of monopoly. Finally, the shift in law and economic thought reflected the change occurring in the real economy. During the second half of the nineteenth century, the definition of product qualities and intellectual property as well as their transfer played an ever-increasing role in market dynamics. Hence, the evolution of case law was partly

[85] Tribunal commercial de la Seine, 1 June 1860, quoted in Pelletier, *Droit industriel*: 319.

in response to the wishes of the economic actors who were constantly in a quandary and quarrelled over how they should compete with each other, oscillating between the right to a virtual monopoly on clientele and the unrestricted right to open a new establishment. The notion of "unfair competition" encompassed two phenomena: the increased circulation of industrial and commercial establishments and technological progress. At the time, both of these phenomena were perceived as the cause of "progress" and of the collapse of the old competitive world (which never really existed, as we know).

It would be difficult to account for the second industrial revolution without the new rules of competition, which were at once the result and the cause of these upheavals. Unfair competition thus made it possible to protect intangible property (industrial and intellectual). This same action guaranteed the dissemination of new instruments of promotion, primarily marketing, insofar as misleading and libellous advertising was condemned on these grounds.[86] Unfair competition was therefore one of the chief supports for the methods of capitalist expansion in the twentieth century. Concretely, this meant, for example, that businesses were perfectly able to withstand the rise of department stores, and trademarks became an important component in strategies to enhance French firms, especially as libellous and comparative advertising was prohibited. This was an important point of divergence from the United States and Great Britain, where comparative advertising was permitted and, in general, unfair competition became an issue relatively late and was identified with trademark protection.

This outcome was partly related to the structure of the French market, which was dominated by small firms; these forms of organisation were concerned above all with issues of succession, transfer of trademarks, patents and trade names. The priority given in France to fair trade rather than to concentration can thus be explained by the relationship between the overall control of competition and unfair competition. The concentration of firms was governed by norms pertaining to exchanges and to hoarding, whereas technical progress,

---

[86] Laurent Pfister, "La naissance de l'action en concurrence déloyale et le droit commun de la responsabilité délictuelle." *Cahiers du centre lyonnais d'histoire du droit et de la pensée politique*, 2 (2004): 119–67.

advertising and company transfers were controlled by fair competition rather than the power of firms in the market. The institutional construction of an equilibrium therefore meant emphasising relationships between firms rather than between firms and end consumers, which was the case in the United States. It is time to compare the control of competition in France with that of other countries (mainly Great Britain, Germany and the United States).

II

THE LAW OF COMPETITION AND UNFAIR COMPETITION IN OTHER "WESTERN" COUNTRIES

As we have seen in the case of France, those on different sides of the competition-control debate tended to assume either that monopolies diminished social well-being and efficiency or that concentration and monopoly reduced overall costs, increased efficiency and were not necessarily opposed to the general interest, in the sense that they supported national companies against international competition. This argument was criticised by those who believed that efficiency played only a minor role in the matter, and that it was the relative force of pressure groups that was responsible for the rules of competition, as well as for their application.

A third argument consists of asserting that the boundary between acceptable competition and prohibited monopolies varies, depending on place and time, according to political and economic interests, and according to legal rules and their judicial interpretation. How the line is drawn is certainly not the same in Great Britain in 1870 or the United States in 1932. Even in the same place at the same time, judges have interpreted rules and precedents in different ways. We must therefore seek to trace the origins of this shifting boundary line between free and illegal competition, the manner in which rules are implemented and finally the impact of these elements on economic dynamics. I will start with the control of forward transactions and then will examine the relation between concentration and unfair competition. I do not intend to provide a full development of competition policies in all the mentioned countries, but only

Original draft translated by Susan Taponier.

to summarise their main insights in order to fully understand the French case.

THE CONTROL OF FORWARD TRANSACTIONS

It would be a mistake to assume that hostility towards forward transactions was specific to France. On the contrary, in the years between the mid 1870s and the First World War, this attitude prevailed in most Western countries. As in France, legal restrictions on establishing limited liability companies were rooted in more general attitudes towards the stock market and speculation. Throughout the nineteenth century in the United States, in the absence of real antitrust rules (the Sherman Act was not passed until 1890), freedom of trade and alliances was promoted, albeit with one exception: foodstuffs defined as essential. Hoarding these products was regularly prosecuted, and this attitude hardened in the 1880s, exactly as it did in France, Great Britain and Germany.[1]

In the last quarter of the nineteenth century, market speculation on the one hand and movement of virtual produce (produce exchange) on the other led to public and academic debates and to tension between professionals in most European countries, and even in the United States and Great Britain. In all these countries, farmers expressed the same concern: Forward transactions and the globalisation of markets were held responsible not only for the decline in agricultural prices, but also for their instability and volatility, putting agricultural producers in an increasingly difficult situation.[2] In the 1890s, and even more so at the beginning of the twentieth century, investigative commissions, petitions and other measures came into being in Germany, the United States and Italy. The associations of agricultural producers were not the only ones involved. They were sometimes supported by consumer associations (for example, for wheat and sugar), as well as by industrial lobbies (regarding speculation in cotton).

[1] Herbert Hovenkamp, *Enterprise and American Law, 1836–1937*. Cambridge, Mass., Harvard University Press, 1991: 291–3.
[2] Henry Crosby Emery, *Speculation on the Stock and Produce Exchanges of the United States*. New York, Columbia University Studies, 1896; Lester Telser, "Future Trading and the Storage of Cotton and Wheat." *The Journal of Political Economy*, 66, 3 (1958): 233–55; Hoolbrook Working, "The Theory of Price of Storage." *American Economic Review*, 39 (1949): 1254–62.

In France and in the other countries mentioned, the solution adopted by wholesalers consisted of reducing the risk through reciprocal offsets and new contractual clauses. These solutions, often presented as a protection against speculation, in reality allowed wholesale traders actively to participate in speculations. They played such an extensive role that observers agreed that henceforth, forward transactions set current market prices rather than the opposite.

In Germany, as in France, strong reactions against speculation and market deregulation were recorded.[3] In 1896, Germany even succeeded in prohibiting certain types of speculative future trades on agricultural products and raw materials. These measures reinforced the protests of those who, in France and elsewhere, wished to see such measures adopted. Ethical considerations were joined to considerations of a purely economic nature.[4]

In other words, at the turn of the nineteenth century, voices were raised throughout the capitalist world against speculation and globalisation of markets. These phenomena were perceived as a confirmation of the fact that capitalism was now established on a worldwide scale and hence that intangible, immaterial values (shares, the stock market) were taking precedence over material values, to the great displeasure of small manufacturers, farmers and workers. This focus was a response partly to the circulation and borrowing of ideas and partly to common economic and political phenomena. No doubt law conferences as well as political and business conferences on customs practices contributed to the spread of ideas in this area. At the same time, this anti-speculation movement was a response to changes in the markets,

---

[3] Martin Geyer, "Defining the Common Good and Social Justice: Popular and Legal Concepts of Wucher in Germany from the 1860s to the 1920s." In Willibald Steinmetz (ed.), *Private Law and Social Inequality in the Industrial Age: Comparing Legal Cultures in Britain, France, Germany and the United States.* Oxford, Oxford University Press, 2000: 457–86.

[4] Barry Gordon, *Political Economy in Parliament, 1819–1823.* London, Macmillan, 1976; Barry Gordon, *Economic Doctrine and Tory Liberalism, 1824–1830.* London, Macmillan, 1979; Norman Gash, *Aristocracy and People: Britain, 1815–1865.* London, Arnold, 1979; Peter Mandler, *Aristocratic Government in the Age of Reform, Whigs and Liberals, 1830–1852.* Oxford, Clarendon Press, 1990; Peter W. J. Bartrip, "State Intervention in Mid-nineteenth Century Britain: Fact or Fiction?" *Journal of British Studies,* 23, 1 (1983): 63–83. Henry Butler, "General Incorporation in Nineteenth Century England: Interaction of Common Law and Legislative Process." *International Review of Law and Economics,* 6 (1986): 169–88.

linked in particular to concentration and to technological progress and to the "crisis" affecting small businesses and the agricultural sector.

Hostility to concentration and speculation was translated into rules with similar aims but different formulations, depending upon the legal traditions of the countries concerned. A fundamental difference was that in some countries, special rules were adopted to control competition, whereas in other countries, business was regulated by case law within the framework of existing rules. Contrary to widespread arguments, this opposition was not between countries ruled by civil law and countries ruled by common law, in the sense that the former imposed rules of competition whereas the latter allowed the free play of competition with the possible aid of legal sanctions. On the contrary, special laws to regulate competition and fair trade were adopted in the United States (1890 and 1914), Germany (1909), Greece (1914), Austria (1923), Switzerland (1943) and Turkey (1958). France, Belgium, Spain and Great Britain relied on case law decisions, based on the Civil Code for the first three of these countries and on common law in the case of Great Britain. In other words, some common law countries adopted rules for competition and others did not, and this same distinction applied in much the same way in the case of civil law countries. These observations contradict the idea that common law spontaneously regulates competition, whereas civil law leads to state and legislative intervention in this area. If not by the kind of law or by the real rate of concentration, then how are we to explain the different types of competition control and their impact on the economy?

GREAT BRITAIN OR UNREGULATED COMPETITION

Great Britain is usually presented as the perfect example of laissez-faire economics. However, we have already found numerous rules regulating the market in foodstuffs and trademarks in the nineteenth century; similar considerations have been put forth in studies on the regulation of labour and companies.[5] Thus, economic regulation

---

[5] Some references within a huge bibliography: Ron Harris, *Industrializing the English Law*. Cambridge, Cambridge University Press, 2000; Brian Cheffins, "History and the Global Corporate Governance Revolution: The UK Perspective." *Business History*, 43, 4 (2001): 87–118.

was widespread in nineteenth-century Great Britain. This context must be kept in mind in examining rules to protect competition. In fact, case law precedents regarding unfair competition were primarily concerned with labour relations (Lumley v. Guy in 1853, and again, in 1881, Bowen and Hall) and were subsequently widened to include other services.[6] Without an ad hoc system of law (as in France), the general attitude of the judges was to refuse to sanction unfair competition as long as it was "reasonable", in the sense that it did require protecting the justified interests of the parties and was not contrary to public policy. For example, four firms engaged in selling bricks entered an agreement whereby A should make the most favourable bid to a company which had requested offers, and A, at the same time, obligated himself to purchase a certain quantity of bricks from the other parties of the agreement, B, C and D. The latter, on their part, agreed not to sell any bricks to the company in question for a certain number of years. B breached the contract, and A was successful in an action brought to prohibit delivery to the company. This was so because the judges considered that the contract was reasonable.[7]

The predominant approach was to tolerate or even encourage the operation of cartels except in rare cases of abuse. In the late 1880s, the Court of Appeal ruled in an important decision that cartel agreements would not be enjoyed except in cases of manifold abuse, but that the courts would also intervene to enforce such agreements.[8]

A contract was hardly a matter of public order. Contractual clauses were free and the prices determined between professionals were legally valid.[9] Thus, boycott was considered a legal means of combating competition.

---

[6] Vincent Palmer, "A Comparative Study (from a Common Law Perspective) of the French Action for Wrongful Interference with Contract." *The American Journal of Comparative Law*, 40, 2 (1992): 297–342.

[7] Quoted in Fritz Koch, "Methods or Regulating Unfair Competition in Germany, England and the United States." *University of Pennsylvania Law Review and American Law Register*, 78, 7 (1930): 854–79.

[8] John Perry Miller (ed.), *Competition Cartels and Their Regulation*. Amsterdam, North-Holland, 1962: 59.

[9] Ewald T. Grether, "Resale Price Maintenance in Great Britain." *Quarterly Journal of Economics*, 48, 4 (1934): 620–44.

In 1898 and 1901, the House of Lords discussed the following case: The national federation of Retail Newsagents, Booksellers and Stationers demanded that a wholesaler boycott a designated outsider, and upon refusal of the demand, a boycott was instituted by the federation against the wholesaler. Among the retail dealers who, because of this boycott, had ceased business relations with the wholesaler was the plaintiff. The House of Lords dismissed the complaint on the ground that "if the purpose of the cooperation of two or more persons is not to injure a third part[y], but to promote or protect the business of the parties to the contract, no illegal act is committed in so far no illegal means such as threats, duress, inducement to breach the contract etc. are employed".[10]

A still more demonstrative case occurred when a number of steamship companies agreed with one another as to the number of ships to be sent to a certain port, the freight to be charged and other matters. The companies informed their customers that a certain rebate would be granted in the case of exclusive use of their lines, and they forbade their agents, under penalty of dismissal, to engage in any activity for other lines. When the plaintiff, an outsider, sent ships to this port, the members of the ring reduced their freight rates and increased the number of ships. They forbade their agents to be of service to the plaintiff who was therefore forced to run his ship at a loss. This case contained a number of measures for regulating competition: boycott, deferred rebates, and price cutting. All of them were declared by the court to be fair.

In short, up to the First World War, no antitrust rules or rules to protect fair competition were adopted either in France or in Great Britain. The reasons for this were sometimes analogous and sometimes different. In Great Britain, the confidence expressed in case law solutions, however conflicting they may have been, was accompanied by ambivalent feelings about the effect of monopolies on the economy. Fears expressed within conservative and business circles over widening such rules to include the labour market contributed significantly to this outcome. In other words, the lack of antitrust rules and judicial decisions in Britain was not so much linked to a widespread belief

[10] Koch, "Methods or Regulating".

in competition, but quite the contrary, to the aim of limiting free competition on the labour market while enhancing concentration in business. This evolution was considered necessary to face the growing competition from the United States and Germany.

The fact that in France, competition rules were linked to various forms of hoarding foodstuffs encouraged special surveillance of the food markets, whereas banking coalitions and some industrial groupings were less inconvenienced. In these industries, competition was often presented as profitable to "national interests". In Great Britain, on the contrary, labour rather than food constituted the litmus test for antitrust rules. Paradoxically, precisely the organisation of the food industry (as I have shown in the chapters devoted to shops and food regulation) made it one of the most concentrated in Britain.[11]

Let us now examine the countries that adopted specific rules to control competition and unfair competition. Here again we are looking at both a common law country (the United States) and a civil law country (Germany). What were these rules and why were they adopted?

THE UNITED STATES AND THE FIGHT AGAINST MONOPOLIES

The origins of antitrust rules in the United States can be found in the interplay of legal-economic culture and historical dynamics. Until almost the end of the nineteenth century, American judges and economists used the word "competition" to refer both to labour and to the market in general. From this viewpoint, "competition" applied primarily to contracts and hierarchies (e.g., between employer and employee), whereas "horizontal" competition between firms in the same sector was hardly taken into consideration.[12] However, from the end of the nineteenth century onwards, two distinct notions emerged. With regard to the market in general, several of the main economists (Fisher and Taussig, among others) considered that concentration had a

---

[11] Michael Smith, "Putting France in the Chandlerian Framework: France's 100 largest firms in 1913." *Business History Review*, 72, 1 (1998): 46–85.

[12] Francis Walker, *Political Economy*, 3rd edition. New York and London, Macmillan and Co., 1888.

beneficial effect on efficiency whereas coalitions in the labour market were pernicious.[13] At the same time, the age-old connection between economics and ethics remained unbroken; economic efficiency would not become the dominant criterion in economic thought until after the First World War, when economic theory was defined as economics rather than political economy.[14]

It is from this perspective that we must approach the famous Sherman Act. Adopted in 1890, the Sherman Act was a genuine anti-trust law; however, it was modified several times in the following years and influenced the adoption of the first law (the Clayton Act of 1914) pertaining to unfair competition. In particular, the first version of the Clayton Act was modified to make it compatible with the Sherman Act. Practises considered legitimate under the Sherman Act could not be prohibited as unfair competition. Negative advertising and boycotting through competition (without an underlying coalition) were accepted, as were price reductions made in good faith.[15] In contrast to the situation in France, where competition was regulated by the Criminal Code (hoarding or coalition offences) and unfair competition was regulated by civil law (action causing injury to a third party), the direct relation between rules of competition and unfair competition in the United States stemmed from the fact that American case law traditions drew no distinction between the two phenomena. Throughout the nineteenth century, contracts and agreements restricting trade and business were ruled out in the United States. From this standpoint, the Sherman Act was limited to applying criminal sanctions and sought instead to standardise at the federal level the antitrust laws that had already been adopted in fourteen states of the Union.[16]

---

[13] Irving Fisher, *Elementary Principles of Economics*. New York, Macmillan, 1911: 304–5; Frank William Taussig, *Principles of Economics*. San Diego, Simon Publication, 1911. 2nd edition, 1919: 49–66.

[14] Hovenkamp, *Enterprise*.

[15] Koch, "Methods or Regulating."

[16] James William Coleman, "Law and Power: The Sherman Antitrust Act and Its Enforcement in the Petroleum Industry." *Social Problems*, 32, 3 (1985): 264–74; Hans Torelli, *The Federal Antitrust Policy: Origination of an American Tradition*. Baltimore, John Hopkins University, 1955.

At the same time, the Sherman Act was part of the slow evolution of an American tradition in case law and economics. For much of the nineteenth century, there was a much closer connection between economic and legal thinking in the United States than in Europe. For a long time, American judges and economists remained faithful to classical English economics emphasising distribution, as well as to Scottish moral economics of the eighteenth century. As a result, they were hardly in a position to intervene to restore contractual balance, and above all, to resort to concepts of liability or extra-contractual sanctions. On the contrary, most case law decisions sought to preserve contractual freedom. It was on this basis that practises restricting entry into a particular market were prohibited.[17] In this context, one case alone stands out as an exception to the rule: that of so-called essential foodstuffs, as was already mentioned earlier. In this case, the United States adopted specific rules both at state and federal levels.

From the 1870s, these attitudes were reoriented towards a different approach. Firstly, so-called essential foodstuffs were no longer treated as a special case; secondly, market freedom implied that certain contracts should henceforth be prohibited and extra-contractual liability identified precisely in order to preserve competition. This evolution in case law was accompanied by a change in economic thinking which became increasingly sensitive to neo-classical theories of "market imperfections" and external factors (monopolies, harmful influences, etc.) and thus suggested measures to be adopted to correct such problems without questioning the principle of the market itself.

No doubt, farmers were unhappy about the drop in agricultural prices, their growing bank debts and also with the practices of the railway companies, which were accused both of charging high prices and of supporting speculators, wholesalers and bankers that were able to mobilise huge resources to control the markets. Such arguments mirrored those of European farmers behind the movement and adoption of rules against speculation and hoarding. In the United States, the movement achieved wide political consensus, and the two main political parties, along with the growing radical party,

---

[17] Hovenkamp, *Enterprise.*

sought the farm vote by supporting measures to curb speculation and regulate railway prices.[18]

A different interest group was behind the Sherman Act: the banks and high finance. This group also criticised the major firms – railway companies in particular – which, since the 1870s, had replaced a strategy of cooperation and the formation of cartelisation (price agreement) with hostile strategies to stifle competition and to bring suppliers and distributors to the edge of bankruptcy so that they might be bought out at low prices. This solution greatly reduced bank assets, because the banks had loaned heavily to firms that were taken over or struggling, leading to a call from the banks for measures prohibiting such practises.[19]

However, due to protests by the farmers, both judges and politicians had an eye on takeovers and cooperative agreements to form cartels. Cooperative agreements had dominated the strategies of large American firms, above all the railway companies, and had been openly supported by the authorities for a good part of the nineteenth century as a measure that reconciled domestic growth with international protection.[20] In the 1870s and 1880s, however, case law decisions were quite critical of such practices. With the changing political climate due primarily to the economic problems of farmers, these case law decisions led to the adoption of the Interstate Commerce Act of 1887, specifically prohibiting speculation and the formation of cartels. Such prohibitions also extended to the practises of wholesaler traders who, as in France and Germany, reacted to growing price instability by imposing fixed prices and rigorous contractual clauses both on farmers and retail tradesmen.[21]

---

[18] Coleman, "Law and Power"; Frank Dobbin, Timothy Dowd, "The Market that Antitrust Built: Public Policy, Private Coercion and Railroad Acquisitions, 1825 to 1922." *American Sociological Review*, 65, 5 (2000): 631–57.

[19] William Roy, *Socializing Capital: The Rise of the Large Industrial Corporation in America*. Princeton, NJ, Princeton University Press, 1997.

[20] Dobbin, Dowd, "The Market"; Thomas Mc Craw, *Prophets of Regulation*. Cambridge, Mass., Harvard University Press, 1984; James Wilson, *The Politics of Regulation*. New York, Basic Books, 1980.

[21] William Becker, "American Wholesale Hardware Trade Associations, 1870–1900." *The Business History Review*, 45, 2 (1971): 179–200.

Consumer protection remained on the sidelines of this movement. No doubt consumers' leagues spoke out at the time, complaining of price increases, fraud and monopolies. Such topics were initially brought up on several occasions in congressional debates. However, as time went by (Sherman filed the first bill for his proposals in 1888, and it took two years for it to be approved), these issues drew less and less attention as consumers were now said to be automatically protected by fair competition between manufacturers.[22] The same argument lay behind the French law of 1905 concerning fraud and the falsification of foodstuffs. Taken together, these debates indicate that, contrary to the strictly economic argument, neither concern for efficiency nor consumer protection lay at the root of antitrust laws, but rather the short-term convergence of varying interests (in particular between farmers and bankers). At the same time, supporters of the Sherman Act never reasoned in terms of economic efficiency in the current sense of the term, but instead connected it to ethical considerations.[23]

Starting from these premises, we will now turn to the application of the Sherman Act and its impact on the economy. Opinions were divided. As early as 1900, some complained that the Act was rarely applied, either because it was poorly formulated[24] or because economic lobbies and possibly corrupt judges weakened its implementation.[25] Others, on the contrary, accused the Sherman Act of being too widely applied and thereby slowing American economic growth.[26] A further argument maintained that the unpredictability of case law decisions increased the uncertainties of business and thus led to a decrease in investment. Still others suggested that by discouraging cooperation and cartels, the Sherman Act had ultimately encouraged mergers.[27]

[22] Christopher Grandy, "Original Intent and the Sherman Antitrust Act: A Re-examination of the Consumer-Welfare Hypothesis." *The Journal of Economic History*, 53, 2 (1993): 359–76; Earl Kintner (ed.), *The Legislative History of the Federal Antitrust Law and Related Statutes*. New York and London, Chelsea House, 1978; Herbert Hovenkamp, "Antitrust's Protected Classes." *Michigan Law Review*, 88, 1 (1989): 1–48.
[23] Wilson, *The Politics*.
[24] J. H. Benton, "The Sherman or Antitrust act." *The Yale Law Journal*, 18, 5 (1909): 311–27.
[25] Coleman, "Law and Power."
[26] George Bittlingmayer, "Antitrust and Business Activity: The First Quarter Century." *The Business History Review*, 70, 3 (1996): 363–401.
[27] Roy, *Socializing*.

In reality, during the years between the adoption of the Sherman Act and the First World War, there was considerable uncertainty regarding the control of competition, which was due less to the decisions made by judges than to the multiplication of bills in Congress either to modify or to eliminate the Sherman Act. Many of these proposals came from business circles and large groups such as the railway companies which were still attempting to persuade the government to change course and give up all antitrust control. Most of these proposals were rejected, which confirms the strength of the coalition of farmers, small and middle-sized businesses and consumer organisations.[28]

However, this institutional and political outcome was not necessarily the economic outcome the promoters of the Sherman Act had hoped for. The impact of the Sherman Act can be summarised as follows: The prohibition on agreements to form cartels, the adoption of fixed prices and control over market shares ensured that contracts between firms were often extremely short-lived and that, within the same sector, periods of competition alternated with periods of cooperative agreement.[29]

In general, cartels and price agreements, which had predominated during the first three quarters of the nineteenth century, and the aggressive strategies of the 1870s gave way to mergers and co-existence strategies between companies of varying size. The new antitrust rules also encouraged full-scale investment by banks in the capital of major firms.[30]

In contrast to the situation in France, the notion of unfair competition took longer to become established, whereas antitrust policies were developed rather early. American judges generally considered unfair competition as a wider form of trademark protection.[31] The first

---

[28] Bittlingmayer, 'Antitrust''; Hovenkamp, *Enterprise*.

[29] Theodore Marburg, "Government and Business in Germany: Public Policy Toward Cartels." *The Business History Review*, 38, 1 (1964): 78–101; Theodore Marburg, *Small Business in Brass Fabricating: The Smith and Griggs Manufacturing Company of Waterbury*. New York, New York University Press, 1956; Neil Fligstein, *The Architecture of Markets*. Princeton, NJ, Princeton University Press, 2001.

[30] Neil Fligstein, *The Transformation of Corporate Control*. Cambridge, Mass., Harvard University Press, 1991.

[31] Derenberg, "The Influence of the French Code Civil".

doctrinal case law to examine unfair competition dates from 1909,[32] but it was not until 1916 that the expression appeared in a Supreme Court decision.[33] This ruling declared that common law in the area of trademarks constituted only a part of the more general law on unfair competition. However, this approach did not become widespread until after the First World War. As a result, in the United States, competition law was identified primarily with industrial concentrations and seldom with fair competition practices. Hence, commercial and economic strategies with regard, for example, to advertising or boycotting which were prohibited in France became accepted in the United States. The importance of marketing in the United States is not entirely unrelated to these rules' approaches.

INDUSTRIAL CARTELS AND FAIR TRADE IN GERMANY

Germany is usually presented as a special case, where the State was said to encourage cartels and industrial concentrations. According to this interpretation, such support was expressed in the development of cartels, the adoption of protectionist tariffs and of dumping (selling German products abroad below cost, offset by a concerted rise in prices within Germany). These policies are said to have fuelled the economic and technological growth of Germany at the turn of the nineteenth century. We will question these conclusions.

In the area of cartels, the German reference document was a law on the regulation of trade (21 June 1869), adopted by the Reich on 16 April 1871. A passage in this law declared that "trade is free and open to all, unless statutes define exceptions limiting this general rule".[34] This caveat, validating statutory exception, was a particular feature of German law and was regularly evoked by cartels under attack from competitors and accepted by the courts in the case of disputes.

---

[32] Harry Nims, *The Law of Unfair Competition and Trade-marks*, New York, Vooris 1909 (new edition 1947).
[33] Hovenkamp, *Enterprise*.
[34] Marburg, "Governement": 81.

Extra-legal justifications by judges should also be noted. For example, in an 1897 decision, the Supreme Court of the Reich ruled that the Saxon Association of Timber Manufacturers was not in violation of the law according to the article mentioned earlier, and added that this association was even beneficial to the interests of society since, by avoiding competition and price decreases, it had no adverse effect on employment or German interests. In other words, public interests should be defended against the individual interests of a few firms that claimed to be harmed by the cartel's activities. In the opinion of the judges, this consideration was especially important in times of "crisis", which was the case in the last years of the nineteenth century.[35]

At the same time, due precisely to such considerations, a strong connection was made in Germany, in contrast to France, between the control of competition and unfair competition. In both cases, contractual and Civil Code arguments were used, even though they were ultimately justified by considerations of public order. What was specific to Germany at the time was the fact that the public order of the markets came largely under Civil Code provisions; they were designed to serve the public order of the markets, which was, in turn, identified with the power of large groups. A second major difference from France was that unfair competition was regulated by a law and not only by case law. This law, adopted on 27 May 1896 (the *Gesetz zur Bekämpfung des unlauteren Wettbewerb*), condemned dishonest advertising, denigration and slander in business, fraud committed in the use of trade names and business names and violations of commercial or trade secrets.

The new Civil Code came into force in 1900, allowing judges to apply certain provisions relative to civic liability in commercial transactions. The definition of unfair competition was widened, but problems arose as a result with regard to the compatibility of the Civil Code and its interpretations with the law of 1896. These discussions led to the adoption of a new law on 7 June 1909, which remained in force until the unification of Europe. Its general principle consisted of condemning all transactions contrary to good practice. However, trusts and cartels were rarely considered to be in violation of this principle.

---

[35] Ibid.; Ivo Schwartz, "Antitrust Legislation and Policy in Germany: A Comparative Study." *University of Pennsylvania Law Review*, 105 (March 1957): 626–35.

Consequently, boycott agreements, exclusivity requirements, and the like were considered legitimate, and as such, were not subject to litigation before the courts by members outside the cartel. Litigation arose only in those instances in which members of the cartel considered they had been injured.[36] The positions adopted by the courts relied not only on legislation but also on public opinion, which on the whole was favourable to trusts and cartels, in the sense that they were seen as organisations that protected employment and the country's wealth. Even long-time socialists like Karl Bücher or Lujo Brentano rallied to their defence.

Naturally, this favourable attitude towards cartels did not prevent conflicts, which occurred either within the cartel (members considered themselves injured parties), or between a cartel and its contractors or finally between a cartel and other companies in the same sector of activity. Even though the courts usually ruled in favour of the cartel, these conflicts created extreme tensions between members of the same trade associations.[37]

From these elements, we can attempt to assess the interaction between economic rules and practises relating to the formation of cartels. Thus, the stated aims of contracts for the formation of cartels in Germany mentioned at least three objectives: to protect company profits, influence the government and act in accordance with official rules.[38] All these elements combined testify to the sometimes cooperative but usually conflictual relations between cartels, national representative institutions and local trade associations. The protectionist tariffs demanded and obtained by these associations demonstrate how effective their actions were, even when they did involve more than just "pressure" or even "corruption" of politicians. Although numerous

---

[36] Eric Golaz, *L'imitation servile des produits et de leur présentation.* Droz, Genève, 1992; Basil Markesinis, *The German Law of Tort.* Oxford, Clarendon Press, 1986; Norbert Horn, Hein Kötz, Hans Leser, *German Private and Commercial Law: An Introduction.* Oxford, Clarendon Press, 1982; Marburg, "Government"; Heinrich Kronstein, "Cartels Under the New German Cartel Statute." *Vanderbilt Law Review*, 1 (1958): 271–301; Heinrich Kronstein, "The Dynamics of German Cartels and Patents." *The University of Chicago Law Review*, 9, 4 (1942): 643–71.

[37] Robert Liefmann, *Kartelle und trusts.* Stuttgart, Moritz, 1905; Robert Liefmann, *Cartels, Concerns and Trusts.* New York, Dutton, 1932.

[38] Kronstein, "The Dynamics."

elected representatives were in fact linked to the interests of one group or another, favourable attitudes towards cartels went beyond these narrow interests and responded to more general policies of the elites and of the German civil society at the time, which were on the whole in favour of large industrial groups as an expression of German power. These policies won out over attempts by other parties (small tradesmen, craftsmen, farmers) to impose the adoption of antitrust laws.

Of course, agreements and cartels already existed in the states of the future Reich during the first half of the nineteenth century, notably in the salt and coal sectors. These organisations multiplied in the 1860s in the sectors of nitrates and rail manufacture.[39] However, the rapid growth of cartels actually occurred from the 1870s onwards, above all in the sectors of railways, metallurgy and later in chemicals and the pharmaceutical industry. By 1901, 450 cartels had been identified in various sectors: chemicals, the pharmaceutical industry, metals, textiles and even banking.[40]

These cartels helped to ensure the profitability of the member companies in three ways. They obtained higher prices in domestic markets, protectionist tariffs and the possibility of selling below cost in international markets. The profits were often used, in turn, to support a transition from cartel formation to genuine vertical integration, and thus to benefit from economies of scale. This process naturally depended on the structure of the specific branch of activity. In particular, firms that resorted to inputs from cartels were more encouraged to practise upstream concentration, and this trend was more pronounced in heavy industry than in light industry.[41]

The question that remains open is whether this concentration brought not only bigger profits, but also favoured a rise in productivity and quality. This debate, which began precisely in the last years

[39] Marburg, "Governement"; Liefmann, *Cartels*; John H. Clapham, *The Economic Development of France and Germany, 1815–1914*, 4th edition. Cambridge, Cambridge University Press, 1936.

[40] Steven Webb, "Tariffs, Cartels, Technology and Growth in the German Steel Industry, 1879 to 1914." *The Journal of Economic History*, 40, 2 (1980): 309–30; Jacob Riesser, *The German Great Banks and Their Concentration in Connection with the Economic Development of Germany*. New York, Arno Press, 1977; Ivo Lambi, *Free Trade and Protection in Germany, 1868–1879*. Wiesbaden, Franz Steiner Verlag, 1963.

[41] Webb, "Tariff."

of the nineteenth century, is still unresolved, not only because of its current political implications (which type of competition should be adopted in Europe?), but also because the numerous assessments made since then produced varying results, depending on the sector of activity, prices, contract terms and other factors. In general, it would appear that at least in some sectors (metallurgy, for example), German productivity was higher than that in Great Britain. At the same time, a close analysis of employment and production conditions shows that these differences were not significant, and that because of this, German success on the international markets, notably at the expense of Great Britain, was related less to productivity than, on the one hand, to pricing policies and dumping[42] and, on the other hand, to novel commercial strategies, notably to the role of flyers, advertising and travelling salesmen.[43]

CONCLUSION OF PART IV: THE INVENTION OF COMPETITION IN THE CAPITALIST WORLD

The notions of competition and competition law as we know them today are the result of a radical transformation which took place at the turn of the nineteenth century. Until then, the notion of competition referred as much to labour as to relations between businesses; in general, priority was given to controlling the market of essential foodstuffs, and the issue of concentrations and industrial alliances was not really raised. For the idea of competition as we know it, a restructuring of the supply of essential foodstuffs and the emergence of a legal notion of fairness in business were necessary.

---

[42] Donald McCloskey, *Economic Maturity and Entrepreneurial Decline: British Iron and Steel, 1870–1913.* Cambridge, Mass., Harvard Economic Series, 1973; Charles Kindlerberger, "Germany's Overtaking England, 1806–1914." *Weltwirtschaft Liches Archiv,* 111 (1975): 477–504.

[43] Ross J. Hoffman, *Great Britain and the German Trade Rivalry, 1875–1914.* Philadelphia, University of Pennsylvania Press, 1933. For France: AN F 12 9183; AN F 12 6353, 9183; Alessandro Stanziani, "Economic Information on International Markets: French Strategies in the Italian Mirror (Nineteenth–Early Twentieth Centuries)." *Enterprise and Society,* 11, 1 (2010): 26–64.

Within this overall scope, it would be difficult to pinpoint a difference between common law and civil law on the subject of competition, at least in the sense of civil law controlling competition through legislation and common law resorting to market self-regulation with the help of disputes that arose. In both cases, written rules and case law intervened. Both were based on economic, legal, ethical and political considerations. The boundary between legal and illegal competition was a flexible one, both historically and geographically. Furthermore, at the same time and in the same countries, different parties and rules defined this boundary in different ways.

From this point of view, the control of competition did not begin with the European Union, nor was it an invention of the regulating states at the time of the Ancien Régime (France and Prussia). This long and relatively shared history of the control of competition shows evolutions, at times with breaks and differences between periods and countries. These differences cannot be reduced to oppositions between civil law and community law, nor to the opposition between "liberal" states and interventionist states, and even less to an evolution which could be described as bridled competition up to the end of the eighteenth century, followed by a liberal period that was in turn replaced by new forms of regulation in the twentieth century, which are only disappearing now, through competition law. These oppositions and chronologies miss the main point, which is that competition has always been structured with a view to reconciling stability and innovation and individual gain with public well-being (this last being in turn identified with quality of life, economic growth or with the rise of a given sector, etc.).

This ambition is true of capitalism in general. Subsequently, within this common framework, certain differences emerged; these differences were related to the relationship between unfair competition, supply and overall control of competition. In particular, it is important to know whether the control of competition was separated from foodstuffs at the onset of industrialisation or even before the development of genuine industrialisation, or whether this separation occurred later on. Indeed, the birth of competition law as we understand it today took place in most countries at the turn of the nineteenth century.

Yet, at that moment, the state of the economy and the rate of industrialisation was not the same in Great Britain, France, Germany and the United States. Great Britain had already experienced more than a century of industrial growth, the United States was rapidly developing, as was Germany, wagering above all on the second industrial revolution, whereas France pursued its long transformation, associating small and large firms, craftsmen and manufacturers, employees, tradesmen and peasants. In these distinct yet related contexts, the separation between competition and fair trade, industrial concentration and hoarding responded to different logics.

In particular, in France, competition law remained rooted in case law decisions, which focused on fairness without taking concentrations and alliances into account. The latter phenomenon was controlled by criminal law related to the hoarding of foodstuffs and products. This also means that competition between firms was seen primarily as a question of fairness. This approach was partly related to the fact that competition took place between small and medium-sized firms. This relation was reciprocal, in the sense that competition law, as it was conceived and applied in the nineteenth century, was intended for and supported this type of firm. Thus, the legal notion of loyal competition gave guarantees and considerable economic value to intangible capital (patents, goodwill, etc.) and to its circulation, which reduced the weight of stock market and bank financing and supported self-financing and relations between companies, between shopkeepers, between shopkeepers and wholesale traders, etc. The network effect was thus considerable; however, it was all the more significant in that the competition law ensured that this "confidence" was institutionally protected.

In Great Britain, on the contrary, free trade became the rule very early on, and the control of competition and fairness was based on case law decisions. The English industrial revolution relied on competition controlled by rules introduced at the very beginning of the trade and proto-industrialisation process in the seventeenth century. This system was to have difficulty meeting the demands of the second industrial revolution, if only through the problem of giving the economic actors reliable expectations founded on case law. Case law was not outdated but rather faced with increasing heterogeneous decisions, which only grew with the gradual economic integration of the commonwealth countries and management of the British Empire. The turmoil undergone by the English model during the inter-war period was the result of those tensions.

In the United States, unlike Great Britain, France and Germany, antitrust law came into being very early, under the impetus of the American legalist economic tradition, which was closely related to classic English thought, especially Scottish theory, together with the importance of the agricultural frontier. There was less focus on fairness because it tended to be reduced to patent law, both by judges and economic actors. It was the patent market, rather than that of businesses, as in France, which prompted the emergence of certain institutions such as competition law, just as antitrust focused for a long time on cartels rather than mergers and vertical integration. These elements in turn supported the development and power of capitalist big businesses rooted in family dynasties. The secondary position given to fair competition enabled the rise of advertising (including comparative advertising).

Finally, in Germany, capitalism was primarily the capitalism of the second industrial revolution and cartels. With the help of bank penetration in industry, these aspects did not oppose but rather supported the growth of a movement against speculation and the stock market. These elements were opposed only in economic and political theory; in reality, they complemented each other perfectly.

However, beyond these different paths and institutional structures of market economies, some general features of capitalism and its history can be summarised.

GENERAL CONCLUSION:
MARKETS, EXCHANGE AND THE IDEAL
OF NON-COMPETITION

The opposition between rules and markets is an ideological and historiographic construction which does not correspond to the real workings of capitalism, particularly industrial capitalism. The latter resorts to a wide range of rules which cannot be reduced to administrative law either in the variant of the Ancien Régime or the variant of Keynes and the welfare state. On the contrary, in the eighteenth as in the nineteenth and twentieth centuries, the rules of law sought by various pressure groups and applied by numerous private and public institutions regulated essential market operations. What changed over time were the forms of this regulation. The economic categories as we know them today emerged in law less through legislation than through case law, and this took place rather late, at the turn of the nineteenth century, and for some even in the late twentieth century. From the point of view of economic history, this conclusion implies that the (first) industrial revolution was achieved using the economic forms and actors of the Ancien Régime: family-based firms and rules of competition inspired by hoarders of essential foodstuffs. Control over the markets, the relation between production and trade, agriculture and industry as they were practised in the nineteenth century represent less a break from than continuity with the economic and institutional forms of the preceding century. The specialisation of the sectors and labour remained limited, as did the amount of capital invested and the size of firms.

If there was a break in the economy and in economic law, it was not related to the first industrial revolution, but rather occurred at the turn of the nineteenth century, in relation to the second industrial revolution and the emergence of the welfare state. The birth of the consumer and of mass consumption, the rise of limited liability companies, of new sectors, of the crucial role of industrial property and of intangible property, the transformation of mortgage loans and of estate capitalism into credit rooted in entrepreneurial projects and financial capitalism – all these elements implied a real break in relation to previous periods. The second industrial revolution, urbanisation and the rise of limited liability companies, standardisation and mass production were all interrelated. Urbanisation created a market for intensive agricultural production and for new industrial products, at the same time as the growth in the size of firms relied on ever-greater amounts of capital and on new types of companies. This transformation would have been impossible without fiscal advantages and legal transformations such as the evolution of contract law (questioning the notion of free will to contract), of family law (decline in the authority of the head of the household), of credit law (rise of the warrant, hypothecation and of banking instruments) and of consumption (heightened protection of the consumer as distinct from the generic buyer).

Thus, the rise of food industries, the industrialisation of agriculture, the development of semi-luxury products or even the standardisation of agricultural products and of industrial products relied on rules defining the aims of the contract, which provided institutional definitions of products and a framework for negotiating innovations. In this context, the legal definition of the consumer, accompanied by a growing desire for labelling, supported the process of product standardisation and, together with it, established hierarchies within the various sectors concerned, usually associated with a concentration of production and a process of vertical integration.

The new definitions of product qualities interacted with the new forms of firm organisation. In the nineteenth century, access to credit was of prime importance for small firms and was obtained primarily through the family. Financing through marriage transactions and family law were therefore crucial; the control of dowries and of successions, as well as the status of the head of the household and the exclusion of wives from tradesman status, ensured stability and flexibility (emptied of inter- and intra-family hierarchies, of course) within this system. The flexibility of family organisations was derived primarily from family law and from corresponding credit regulations. If small businesses were able to withstand the changes, it was not only because of demand or because the French consumer preferred personal contact. Although these aspects were important, they were surrounded by rules specifying a price and a legal value both to products (labels) and customer contact (goodwill). The resistance of small businesses was thus related above all to the possibility of playing several hands at once: family law and credit law, hypothecation and commercial credit, all of them under the umbrella of favourable (to them) fiscal policies.

The crisis of small businesses is fairly recent, dating from the second half of the twentieth century. Taking all this into account, we may conclude that most historical interpretations of capitalism are anachronistic and oversimplified – anachronistic, because they attribute certain phenomena to the nineteenth century (standardisation, capital companies), which in fact belong to the following century; oversimplified, in the sense that these interpretations look for pure systems (large firms, mass consumption, etc.), whereas the growth of one or other forms of economic and institutional organisation is never complete or definitive, as the continuing if not increasing importance of small firms in recent times confirms.

At the same time, these common elements have been accompanied by considerable differences historically and geographically. In particular, the legal status of the actors remained far more important in continental Europe than in common law countries, as the legal definitions of the tradesman and the consumer demonstrate. Current differences between business law and consumer law in European countries and at the international level testify to the tenacity of these diverging orientations. Thus, in France, the control of forward transactions was situated at the intersection of the old norms regarding monopoly and the new concerns of wage earners and farmers faced with "globalisation". In the United States and Germany, on the contrary, new controls on forward transactions were defined in relation to farmers on the one hand and industry concentration on the other. These differences had equally far-reaching consequences. In France, the recognition of know-how and reputation as forms of capital helped small shops, whereas elsewhere, these items were immediately included in the valuation of all forms of enterprise. In common law countries, the reputation of the actor and of the products and services he offered came together in the trademark, the trade name and goodwill. In France, on the contrary, this convergence proved to be more problematic, and the solution was found in rooting reputation more strongly in a territory (*Appelation d'Origine Contrôlée* – AOC).

Finally, these differences also reflected those between fair competition, free trade and overall control of competition. In France, the notion of fair competition gradually emerged in case law during the second half of the nineteenth century, whereas no antitrust laws had been adopted and industry concentration was regulated by long-standing norms pertaining to goodwill.

In the United States, on the contrary, even though antitrust norms developed rather early on, the notion of unfair competition was less pertinent than in Germany or France because it tended to be reduced (by the judges as well as by the economic actors) to patent law. In the United States, these aspects in turn supported the development and strength of major family-based company capitalism, just as the secondary place assigned to fair competition was to enable the rise of advertising (including comparative advertising). In other words, if the United States enjoyed a successful second industrial revolution, it was because forward transactions were quickly regulated, fairness was identified with patent ownership, and advertising and alliances between groups were allowed, whereas sector control was prohibited.

Conversely, if France's performance over the very long term (from the eighteenth century to today) ultimately proved to be more stable than that of its Anglo-Saxon rivals, it is because it afforded no protection to the consumer during the nineteenth century, fairness preserved vertical integration as a rampart for the ideal of competition and finally the private order of the market was never altogether disconnected from the public order.

Beyond these differences, some general trends in the legal and economic history of capitalism emerge. Innovation, in the broad sense of the term (new techniques, new organisations, new business practises, etc.), is both the mirage and fear of any economic actor. Everyone wants to be the first and, above all, to benefit from a monopoly on his innovation; at the same time, in this case and in the event that others introduce novelties, everyone wants rules to set the limits on

this innovation and an institutional framework to negotiate its implementation. Patent and trademark law, the laws governing fraud and
falsification and bankruptcy and company law – all these rules seek to
define an institutional framework that will regulate the introduction
and management of innovations. Rather than protection of private
property, the various parties require clear and stable rules that enable
them to manage innovations. This is also the reason why businessmen
do not like innovative, creative Schumpeterian capitalists and, in fact,
the rules of law seek precisely to limit this kind of activity, which is
never undertaken outside a specific institutional context.

The guiding principle uniting these rules designed to ensure
stability and innovation is competition law. The notion of fair competition gradually emerged during the second half of the nineteenth
century in response to these upheavals. Through trial and error, often
prompted by violent political, institutional, legal and economic conflicts, the various parties and pressure groups finally came to an agreement on the need to regulate fair competition. From then on, fairness
lay less in certain informal characteristics and trust than in formal rules
governing the transfer of property, sales criteria, customer relationships, product promotion and service offers and so on.

In turn, fair competition was incorporated into an even wider category: the control of competition. At a time when financial speculation has been deregulated, certain social and institutional groups were
attacking speculation at produce exchanges, and from there in real
estate, financials and other markets. This tension between economics and ethics was therefore not specific to the Ancien Régime, but
has been found throughout the history of capitalism. The control of
competition offers a possible response to these concerns: It identifies
justice and fairness with the institutional construction of a kind of
competition that comes as close as possible to "pure and perfect competition", which is believed to be the most effective solution, both
legally and in terms of efficiency. The history of the French economy
and of the economies of the main European and Western countries
in the nineteenth century testifies to the impossibility of juxtaposing
liberalism to interventionism, given that different forms of regulation
coexisted throughout this period. The opposition between regulation
and freedom was purely ideological; in reality, a mixture of different

forms and aims of intervention was in operation. From this point of view, the attempt to build free competition from scratch is not an invention of the technocrats in Brussels, but rather one of capitalism's long-term ambitions. This ambition is perfectly in keeping with another which consists of curbing the markets in the name of competition. This is not a contradiction of capitalism, but on the contrary, its actual way of being. The ideal of non-competition serves to reconcile growth with stability, innovation and social hierarchies.

In short, market control and operations in the nineteenth century were closer to those of the previous century than to those of the twentieth century. It was the twentieth century that brought about the second industrial revolution and the welfare state. The standardisation of production, concentration, the enhancement of intangible capital, the new control of consumption, innovation and companies, not to mention employment, sprang from the intersection of these tensions. Unlike nineteenth-century rules, the rules introduced at the turn of the nineteenth century sought to bring renewed stability to markets and give greater support to the weaker ones. Current trends in law and in international and European economic policies aim at calling these rules into question in the name of liberalism and equal opportunity. These principles claim to be inspired by the nineteenth century. In reality, as we have seen, the liberal economy of the nineteenth century was not only highly regulated, but it knew virtually nothing of the capitalism which was to prevail in the twentieth century and which continues to this day: the capitalism of large corporations, mass consumption and powerful technological advances. In fact, equal opportunity and competition did not take hold until the twentieth century, whereas they were in the background in the nineteenth century. To return today to an ideal of competition that never existed in the past would be equivalent to believing that deregulation and the ensuing market instability are the sources of stability. Past experience proves that they are not.

INDEX